Dedication

For my husband, Wes, who has been the best husband and father the girls and I could ever ask for.

For Alexa, who has been the best big sister and daughter, a bright light in our darkness, and the kindest soul.

For my family, friends, hospital care team, and community who supported us and held us up in the deepest valley.

For Kendall, my beautiful blue-eyed princess whom I can't wait to hold again in Heaven someday.

Table of Contents

Part One: Kendall's Cancer Journey
Chapter 1: When Life Was Seemingly Perfect 1
Chapter 2: When Life Turned Upside Down 10
Chapter 3: Pumping in the Poison 29
Chapter 4: Finding Our Smiles Again 36
Chapter 5: Home at Last 50
Chapter 6: The Ups and Downs of Chemo................................ 59
Chapter 7: Welcome to New York 74
Chapter 8: The World's Longest Surgery...(or so it seemed)..... 88
Chapter 9: A Christmas Miracle Gone 102
Chapter 10: The Pure Evil That Is Transplant 108
Chapter 11: The Never-Ending Transplant 117
Chapter 12: Radiation Days 131
Chapter 13: Back Down the Roller Coaster We Go 139
Chapter 14: Kendall's Fourth Birthday 143
Chapter 15: It Wasn't Supposed to Be This Way 149
Chapter 16: The Last Chemo Round 159
Chapter 17: Homebound 172
Chapter 18: Hospice Days.. 179
Chapter 19: A Celebration of Life 196

Part Two: Life After Loss
Chapter 20: What Do I Do Now? 215
Chapter 21: Making Sense of Suffering 223
Chapter 22: Finding My New Purpose 233
Chapter 23: Honoring Kendall in Everything We Do 240
Chapter 24: Signs and Dreams of Kendall 252
Chapter 25: The Difficulties of Being a Bereaved Mother...... 261
Chapter 26: Continuing on in Life... 270
Chapter 27: Kendall's Legacy... 276
Accepting the Gift of Christ 285
How to Help a Family That Has Lost a Child 289

~Part One~

Kendall's Cancer Journey

Chapter 1
When Life Was Seemingly Perfect

There have been moments in my life when I would look around me and think to myself, *Wow, life sure feels pretty perfect*. Moments when life was going my way and according to my plan. Moments when I felt like I had it all and my dreams were coming true. Moments like the time I found my Prince Charming at the university where I was attending college.

Wes was different from most guys I had encountered up to that point. He was definitely charming with his nice smile, thoughtful gestures, and how he serenaded me while playing his guitar. He came from a close-knit family with strong religious roots like mine. They lived in a small town out in the country, surrounded by farmland. So small actually that Wes often joked, "Don't blink or you'll miss it" while driving through. He wasn't kidding, as there was only one traffic light in the entire town and he graduated with a class of twenty-five people. It wasn't long before we decided to start dating and three years later, he proposed to me on North Myrtle Beach, another moment in life that felt perfect.

About another year after the proposal, we were married and well on our way to happily ever after. We had landed jobs right out of college, purchased our first home, and got a little dog whom we named Rylee. We did a lot of traveling and had some great times with friends and family before we decided to settle down and start a family of our own. We both had never really seen ourselves as parents, but it seemed to be that time in our lives when our friends started having children. My sister also had already had her first child, and spending time with my niece had made me think that maybe I did want to be a mom after all. I will never forget the excitement inside of me the day I found out I was going to be a mom. I was dancing around my house, thanking God for this blessing of life, while anxiously waiting for Wes to return home from work so we could celebrate.

Before I knew it, our daughter Alexa was born into this world the year of 2011. She was cozy inside my tummy and did not want to be disturbed, making it a long 19 hours in labor before she was placed on my chest. The moment we looked into each other's eyes I knew my life had forever changed. I wasn't living for just myself anymore, but now also for a life God entrusted to me to care for and raise.

While we had so much joy in our precious gift, we also were fighting feelings of doubt and insecurities as new parents. Alexa had a bad case of colic and nothing we seemed to do would soothe her. She would cry every evening from 6 p.m. to midnight like clockwork. It continued to increase from there and we worked tirelessly trying to position her and rock her to a place of comfort. Wes and I took turns bouncing her in our worn-out arms as we walked our home, desperately trying to calm her. I cried and cried, as she cried and cried. I ended up being diagnosed with postpartum depression and feared I really wasn't cut out to be a mom after all. It was a helpless, worthless feeling as a mother who couldn't comfort her own baby. I remember staring out the window sobbing, wondering how I was going to do this. I was able to get some help for my depression from my doctor and once Alexa was two months old, I was able to get her some help too. Her pediatrician prescribed some acid reflux medicine to help soothe her, but it wasn't until she was about four months old that the colic finally started to taper off.

At this point in motherhood, I had already decided to not return to my job. I had never imagined myself as a mother, let alone a stay-at-home mom. But, with Alexa being inconsolable most of the day, I felt it was best. I had a retail management job that required crazy hours and a lot from me physically. It just wasn't conducive anymore with having a family.

Wes had moved on to his second job since college and his salary was plenty to keep us afloat. Choosing to leave my job was one of the scariest, yet best decisions I made in my life. It allowed me to focus on my new role as a mother and be there for Alexa the best I could. I had every intention of finding a new job with better hours one day. I always saw myself as a businesswoman in a fancy suit, working in a sky-rise office building in the city. But I put my dreams on hold and embraced motherhood.

***

From the age of five months on, things seemed to be a breeze caring for Alexa. She no longer had colic and she had become a happy baby. I started making friends with other moms and having play dates. My depression was starting to lift, and I was becoming more confident as a mother. I learned so much from spending time with other moms and enjoyed their company on the longer days. Before long though, I was anxious to get back to work. When Alexa was around nine months old, I took a part-time position. It worked out great because I could make my own schedule, as long as I got the work done within the week. Once again, life felt perfect. *"How did I get so lucky to find this job!?"* I thought.

My job allowed me to still contribute some to our income, while giving me the freedom to continue play dates and fun outings with other moms. I joined the Early Childhood PTA in my community and came to know even more moms and went on field trips with them and our kids. I felt so thankful and blessed for the life God had given to us. I found myself falling more in love with my husband as he fathered Alexa and I was proud of how far we had come as parents.

When Alexa turned two, we then felt it was time to try for just one more child. God blessed us with a second daughter, Kendall, who was born in 2014. This made the girls just shy of three years apart, which was how we had planned it. I worked up until she was born, and then decided to stay home again as the client I was working with decided to pull out of the program, causing my job to change in unfavorable ways.

So now there I was a stay-at-home mom to two precious little girls. I had prayed daily and for specific growth factors weekly as Kendall grew inside of me. I prayed over and over that she would be a calm, easy, healthy baby without colic. I didn't know how I would handle the stress of caring for a toddler and a newborn with colic, so I prayed hard for an angel baby. God answered my prayers with Kendall. I had an easy delivery and though of course there were times of fussiness, it was nowhere near the amount of discomfort Alexa had. Kendall grew to be the happy, joyful, cuddly angel baby I had hoped and prayed for. Alexa was so good with her and loved to make her laugh and help feed her. My home was filled with so much joy and I was so thankful for these adorable girls that made me a mom.

Although I did not have postpartum depression with Kendall, I still faced many challenges mentally as the girls grew. I struggled with feelings of not being good enough for them. I had so much anxiety over the many pressures and expectations young moms were facing at that time. Things such as breastfed or bottle-fed, sleep and feeding schedules, organic baby food versus nonorganic, vaccinate or anti-vax, how much screen time to allow, and the list went on. I constantly felt like I just didn't measure up to other moms and that the girls deserved a better mom than me. The days were long and thankless in their little years. I felt like all I did most of the day was change diapers and clean the same mess up 20 times. I was drowning in motherhood and cried a lot. I would often find myself saying, "This is so hard!"

One morning at a moms' group at church, all the bottled emotions I was holding came pouring out of my eyes at the table I was sitting at. It felt good to admit I was struggling and to have some other moms come alongside me to help carry me. Some moms could even relate to what I was feeling so that helped to know that I wasn't alone. Through a book one mom later sent me, I was reminded that though my job felt thankless, God still saw me. He is the God who sees.

That was a turning point for me in my motherhood. I realized that though I was doing work in the home, taking care of the house and kids, that God still saw everything I was doing. He was with me and leading me on the beautiful journey of motherhood. I started reading Christian books on motherhood and shifted my focus to what God thought of me, instead of what the world thought of me. There was so much freedom in that! I realized that he had entrusted the girls to me for a reason. He was confident in me and would equip me to be a good mother to them. He knew that they would need me just as much as I needed them. I was chosen by God for the girls. I was enough.

***

Once Kendall turned one, she was getting into everything. With Alexa we never had to worry much, but Kendall was the toddler that climbed the shelves of the refrigerator! If you turned your back on her, the next time you saw her she would be unraveling the entire toilet paper roll and putting toothbrushes in the toilet! One time she even emptied out the entire tube of diaper cream and painted the top of her Pack N Play with it! It was forever stained! She kept us on our toes and the girls loved getting into mischief together. They thought it was so funny to dump out the laundry basket full of folded clothes, and they loved to hide from their dad when he pulled in from work. When he walked into the house, they would jump out and scare him.

The house was loud and crazy with the girls laughing, singing, and arguing…as siblings do. As the girls continued to grow, and I became more and more confident in my mothering abilities, I adapted a phrase into my motherhood. It was to "Live each day to the fullest for you never know what tomorrow may bring." I had come to the realization that while I was so blessed, and life seemed so perfect, that yet it could all be taken away so suddenly. Once you have other people to care for, your eyes become more open to all the suffering around us in this world. As a mom, I feared school shootings, car accidents, drownings, the girls crossing the street, and so much more. I would fear something happening to Wes or me as well, so that is why I adapted the phrase to make sure we were making the most out of our days. I realized how fragile life could be and how quickly it could change.

***

When Kendall turned two, her wild toddler days seemed to diminish. She became calmer and had a gentle spirit. She had the biggest blue eyes, glowing porcelain skin, and bright, blonde flowing hair. Some would even tell us she looked like an angel and that there was just something different about her. She loved her baby dolls, and you could see the compassion she had inside of her in the way she cared for them. She always seemed to feel other people's pain so deeply for only being two.

Kendall looked up to her big sister and wanted to do everything she did, of course. She seemed to grow up quicker because of that and she had a sense of maturity about her for her age. People would often comment on how well-behaved she was and how much patience she had. While she could turn a room into a tornado during playtime, she also could sit and play with Barbies for hours. She was always very determined to do things herself. She would sit and try to button her shirts for as long as it took.

The girls loved to put their costumes and dress-up shoes on and perform shows for us. The movie *Frozen* was a favorite in our home so "Let it Go" was often the song of choice to dance and sing to. Kendall called Elsa "Go-Go," which was the cutest.

Kendall was a little behind with her speech so we had her evaluated. She started a speech program that included in-home visits with a therapist and before long, words started to form. I loved hearing her call me "Momma" and all the short sentences she was forming. I loved her sweet little voice and how she talked. It was just the cutest hearing her attempts at three-syllable words like "strawberry." For some words like "white" she would leave the beginning sound out so she would say it as "ite." "Blue" was also a tough word for her, but it was so adorable when her lips would finally come together to push out the beginning sound of "blue." She would be so proud of herself and I was so happy that she was learning more words.

Though the girls were little princesses, they both also loved the potty talk and if I told them to stop, they just did it more. They couldn't seem to control themselves and thought it was downright hilarious. A lot of times they did get me to laugh with them and they loved to get a reaction out of me. Much of our conversation in the home revolved around potty humor in those early years. Yep, that's my girls! (You'll see why I'm sharing this tidbit later.)

As the girls grew older, it was easier to leave the house with them. This helped me get through the long days so much better. We usually had some kind of activity scheduled every morning around 10 a.m. That got us out of the house for a couple of hours before we were back home for lunch and an attempt at naps. We went to many places with our PTA such as farms, trampoline parks, library story time, playgrounds, museums, zoos, and splash pads.

We had made many friends over the years between great neighbors, church, and the PTA so we had a lot of playdates and backyard fun. Kendall loved to swing so I would push her for what seemed like hours most days on our swing set. We took the girls to indoor waterparks for mini vacations and down south to the beach to see their great-grandmother "G.G." yearly. The summers were even more packed full of fun. We would have a morning activity like strawberry picking, head to our neighborhood pool in the afternoon, and then hang out with the neighbors in the evenings as the kids ran around our circle together.

The girls enjoyed swimming at their nana and papa's pool, fishing with Grandpa and Grandma, and exploring the various beaches around us. They loved their Sunday school classes at church and I so enjoyed getting them all dressed up in their Sunday best. I was enjoying all the memories we were making each day and finally felt like I had a good grasp on motherhood, as well as a great "mom tribe" in place to do life with. I had such immense love for my daughters and wondered if it was possible to love someone too much. I couldn't get enough of holding them and kissing their sweet cheeks. My heart and my arms were full. Motherhood had forever changed me for the better. Life was so wonderful, and we were living it to the fullest. I can only look back and think that God was preparing me for what was to come.

Chapter 2

When Life Turned Upside Down

It was near the end of May 2017, just a couple of months shy of Kendall's third birthday when she came down with a weeklong fever. The worried mother that I am took her into the doctor to see what could be wrong. I was told a virus was going around lasting around 7-10 days, and to give it more time. We went home and carried on with life as usual. Kendall seemed to get better and was being her playful, silly self. As the weeks continued, Kendall still felt hot to the touch at times. Her temperature would always be around 99 degrees and she was still being herself, so I tried not to worry too much. There were times though when I noticed that her back felt so warm, but her forehead felt normal. At those times the thermometer would read a normal temperature, so I was very perplexed and drove myself crazy with worry.

Despite my concern, we continued with the start of our summer activities. We took the girls to an outdoor concert where they had a blast singing, dancing, and eating yummy fair food. We took trips to nature centers, open gyms, and playgrounds. In between all the fun and living our life, Kendall seemed to be acting a bit off. She was giving us a hard time eating and often would run into the living room at dinner time and plop herself on the couch while saying in a sad voice, "My belly hurts." She seemed to be getting more irritable as well, which wasn't like our calm little angel. The littlest things were upsetting her.

While our daughter Alexa was attending Safety Town one day, Kendall and I went to her evaluation for an IEP. We were hoping Kendall would qualify to receive some extra help with her speech as she was set to start preschool in the coming fall. Kendall was not herself that day and even her speech therapist who attended with us was seeing a side of her that she had never seen. She was inconsolable and did not cooperate whatsoever. She cried and cried and just wanted me. She couldn't separate herself from me, which was so odd. Luckily, they had another evaluation of her the week prior which she did a little better at, so they were able to use that to measure her by. Kendall qualified for the IEP, and while I felt relief, I was also sad because it confirmed that my sweet girl needed extra help.

While her speech wasn't too poor, I still felt worried and concerned as her mom that she was a bit behind. I do tend to overreact, like the time I cried for days when Alexa got glasses. It just is never easy as a mom to hear that anything is wrong with your child. I left the school in tears that day wondering what was going on with Kendall.

When we arrived back to Safety Town to pick up Alexa, Kendall would not walk. She wanted me to carry her. This was another thing that continued with her in the next week or two. She was wanting to be held a lot or pushed in her stroller instead of having to walk. The next concern that was odd was that Kendall began to take naps again. Both of my girls were always a struggle to put down for naps. They both quit napping around two years old. Hey, I tried! All the other symptoms I've mentioned were still occurring as well in addition to her tiredness. I would talk over my concerns with Wes, but he assured me it was just typical two-year-old behavior and to try not to worry.

***

One night, we went to watch fireworks over the lake. Kendall was so impressed and was standing up with her arms stretched wide over her head, shouting "Wow, Wow!" Then the next minute, while the fireworks show was still going on, she lay down and fell asleep. We really didn't think anything of it that night other than that she must have worn herself out. As we moved into that next week, Kendall was looking a little pale and frail. She was struggling to keep her pants pulled up and was taking more and more naps. One day she took three!

We headed out with our PTA to a farm one warm summer day. Kendall once again was staying close to me and not interacting much with her friends or the animals. She stayed in her stroller for most of our time there and I shared my concerns with my mom friends. They all agreed that I should take Kendall back to the doctor. Mono was even mentioned as a possible diagnosis. I went home even more worried and made her an appointment for the next day.

That night, when I went to get Kendall ready for a bath, her abdomen was distended. I could see all her ribs and her veins were so blue and visible. I yelled for Wes to come and look. I took pictures and started texting my friends and family with concern. I started to panic at that point. Wes believed her distended abdomen was due to her lack of appetite, which could have been possible. I knew something was not right though and my momma instinct was telling me something was terribly wrong.

***

It was mid-morning Wednesday when we arrived at the pediatrician's office. We saw the nurse practitioner that day. She began to examine Kendall, who immediately started screaming and crying. She clung tight to me and hid her face in my chest. She turned bright red from all the crying. The worry in me was growing as I knew my girl was just not herself. Kendall had never acted like this at the doctors. The nurse practitioner looked into her ears and said she had an ear infection. I felt relief. *Just an ear infection? Okay, we can handle that*, I thought. But then I lifted her shirt and asked her to look at her belly. The nurse practitioner said to hold on and that she wanted to get the doctor to come and take a look. Worry set in again.

Kendall calmed down as we waited. The doctor arrived and examined her abdomen. She said Kendall needed to get bloodwork and an ultrasound done right away. The office got her scheduled at a nearby hospital that afternoon. Before we left, the nurse practitioner checked her ear again. This time it was not red. She said she didn't have an ear infection after all and that it probably flared up from her inconsolable crying. We headed out with no answers.

I called Wes as we left the office and asked him to come with me to the appointment. He was able to leave work, and we got someone to watch Alexa. I was so worried about what they might find. I was thinking that maybe Kendall ate something she shouldn't have, like a Lego. I asked her if she did, and she said no. The anxiety was already starting to get heavy on my chest and I just wanted some answers.

First up was getting Kendall's blood drawn. As you can imagine, she screamed. It was so hard to watch, and I felt horrible for her. She was showing her strength as she fought so hard to resist getting poked. We had to help with holding her down for the blood draw, and then also for the ultrasound. She writhed her body all over that table and never laid still through the entire procedure. We left exhausted and still confused as to what was going on with Kendall.

We got a call with the results shortly after returning home. We were told that her ultrasound was normal and that they did not see anything suspicious. Her blood though was questionable, and an appointment was made for that Friday downtown at the

Cleveland Clinic Children's hospital to see a hematologist who could evaluate her further. There was talk about possible anemia.

I tried hard not to worry and proceeded with the evening plans Alexa and I had with some friends. It felt good to go have some fun and get my mind fixed on something else for a couple of hours. Upon returning home, Kendall was in good spirits and being her silly, usual self.

***

Thursday of that week, our dog Rylee had an appointment at the vet. I loaded the girls into the car and headed out. Upon arrival at the vet, we were placed in an exam room. Rylee was taken to the back, and then my phone rang. It was Kendall's nurse practitioner again. This time the directions had changed. She told me we needed to pack our bags and head downtown to the Cleveland Clinic ER. Confused, I asked, "Why?" She replied that more bloodwork came back, and something was off with Kendall's red blood cells. She said that the ER staff knew we were coming and that they would be waiting for us so we could get this figured out.

My heart began to beat so fast, and I could feel the adrenaline rushing through my body. I went into panic mode and started crying. Forget holding it together in front of the girls. I couldn't. I swung open the door of the room we were in and stepped out into the hallway. I went to the desk and told the tech that I needed my dog right away. I said, "We need to leave. There's something wrong with my daughter and we have to go to the hospital right now." She could see the sheer horror on my face and grabbed Rylee for us and said to not worry about the payment; they would get it the next time from us. So back to the car we went.

Alexa was asking so many questions and I just kept saying, "I don't know yet honey, the doctors will figure it out." I called Wes and said to come home right away. I made arrangements with my mom to drop off Alexa with her for the night. We went home and packed our bags just as we were told and headed downtown with Kendall. Wes had calmed me down some and was helping me to stay positive. He is always so good at not jumping to conclusions.

It was early evening by the time we arrived at the hospital. The Cleveland Clinic's main campus can be very overwhelming and we had not spent much time there at all. It is like its own college campus. We parked a little further than we needed to but eventually found our way to the ER. They took us right back to a room upon check-in just as we had expected. Many different nurses and doctors kept coming into the room and asking us the same questions. We told them all the symptoms Kendall was having and how long this had been going on for. Again, they wanted more blood and then another ultrasound (since Kendall didn't stay still for the first one). I was becoming annoyed because we had just done this and now my baby was about to get poked again. We had to hold her down again so they could draw her blood, and she screamed again as well. It was awful. Playing on the TV in the room was a St. Jude Children's Research Hospital commercial. Wes said to me, "Can you imagine what parents of kids with cancer go through?"

Next up was the ultrasound. Again, Kendall would not lie still so the tech asked me to hold her on top of me. I got on the table and Wes laid Kendall face up on top of my body. This worked better and Kendall stayed still long enough for them to get the ultrasound done. The radiologist came into the room and was conversing with the tech. Wes overheard him say to call up to the oncology floor, which he shared with me after we were sent back to our ER room. I wasn't sure he had heard right though, as an intern had come in to tell us her ultrasound looked good. We were confused and said to her that it seemed the radiologist had found something. She looked perplexed and fumbled on what to say in response. She said she would be right back and exited the room. At this point, I was hangry and just wanted to go home. I felt like we were getting the run-around. And if I had to tell the same story to another intern, resident, nurse, or doctor one more time I was going to lose it!

In came the intern again. This time she came to tell us that we were being admitted. Frustrated, I asked, "Why? You just said they found nothing." She replied that her blood was still off, and they wanted to run more tests and get to the bottom of it now. Looking back, I believe they were trying to protect us from knowing the truth until we got settled in a room and could talk to the doctors who could help Kendall. I was so mad though and I am sure they knew it by my attitude.

We grabbed all our bags and Kendall was wheeled up to the fourth floor of the M building. Upon entering our room, I realized we were not alone. We had a roommate and only a curtain separated us. My blood began to boil a little more. *Just great*, I thought. A sweet nurse came in and began telling us about all they could offer us during our stay at the Cleveland Clinic. She mentioned something about art and music therapy, and I looked at her and said hastily, "Oh we won't be here long. We are not staying here." That poor nurse! I am not proud of my attitude, but I was tired, frustrated, and still hangry. It was around 11 p.m. at this point and we all had had enough.

Before long, a doctor, her intern, and a resident came to our room. The doctor said to come out into the hall when Kendall was asleep so we could talk. Again, I gave a little attitude and said "Okay." They left the room and we waited for Kendall to get comfortable. She fell asleep by midnight. I wasn't too keen on leaving her in the room while there was another family on the other side of the curtain, but the nurse said she would look after her. I did not like the way I was feeling inside, and I feared what news would meet us in the hallway. I was terrified, really.

When we made it to the hallway, the doctor and her team led us into the floor's playroom. They had some chairs already set up and asked Wes and me to have a seat. My body began trembling with fear. The doctor sat directly across from us, and the other team members sat at her sides. There was one intern to the left of me. All I wanted was to be back home and not in that room being stared at by everyone.

Then the popular question of the night came out of the doctor's mouth. "Can you tell me what symptoms Kendall has been having?" My first thought was, *you have got to be kidding me! Doesn't anyone communicate around here? Can't they read the chart!?* So, of course, more frustration spewed out of my mouth in reply.

The doctor was so gracious and didn't take long to reveal to us what they had found. Before I knew it, our world came crashing down. It was June 23, 2017, when we received the most shocking, devastating news.

"We found a large mass inside Kendall's abdomen," the doctor said in the calmest, quietest voice.

"Excuse me, what?" I asked as fear took over me further.

The doctor went on to say that she believed it was neuroblastoma, but more tests and scans would need to be run to confirm, along with a biopsy and bone marrow aspiration. I could barely make out what she was saying. I felt disembodied. Tears began to pour from my eyes. I was already so tired and starving, so I began to think maybe I was dreaming. This couldn't be real life.

I remember the doctor continuing to speak as I still was fixated on the word "mass." *What does that mean? Wait, is this a cancerous mass?* I started to tremble. I felt a deep ache in the pit of my stomach. It was gut-wrenching pain like someone had just taken all my breath out of me. I began to rock in my chair back and forth while running my hands over my arms, and then down my legs as if to see if I was really there in that room.

I asked out loud, "Am I dreaming? This is just a bad dream, right?"

The intern next to me placed her hands over my hands and I could see tears streaming down her face, as she looked into my eyes and mouthed, "I'm so sorry."

I was trying to stay composed when everything inside of me just wanted to scream and collapse onto the floor. Then I heard it. The emotions from my dear husband had risen to the surface and were now pouring out of him. I had never heard my husband cry until that moment. It wasn't just tears falling, but loud, gasping sobs were coming from him. I put my hand on his leg and cried even harder as I heard him. Wes is always so strong and positive so to see him in such anguish made it all even more real to me and verified that this was really bad. This was in fact not a dream, but a real, living nightmare.

I finally got the courage in between sobs to speak up. "So, you think she has cancer?" I asked. I could barely mouth the dreadful "C" word. The doctor reiterated that she believed it was a type of pediatric cancer called neuroblastoma and we would find the staging out later in the next week. She said there was a tumor around the size of a small football inside her abdomen. I suddenly had many more questions like, "Will her hair fall out? Does she have to get chemo? How long has this tumor been inside her? Do we have to stay in the hospital for treatment? What about my other daughter?"

The doctor, who would become Kendall's main oncologist, was so kind, gentle, and sensitive and she answered all my questions. She told me this wasn't going to be a sprint, but a marathon. She said that kids are so resilient and that they had medications to help with nausea from chemo. She was trying her best to ease my fear and worries, but all I wanted was to wake up from this nightmare. *How could this be happening? This only happens in movies. God, why??? Not my baby. Did I do something wrong to deserve this?*

Then it was time for us to say goodnight to the team and head back to our room. I asked the team, "How are we supposed to go back in that room? We need our own room so we can be alone and try to process this news." They were already working on getting us a room on the fifth floor on M50, the pediatric oncology unit. We didn't have to wait long before we were all transported to our new private room.

Wes and I held each other in the pull-out chair all night as we wept. We were now the parents of a child with cancer. Hours before in the ER it wasn't on our radar. We never saw it coming. Seeing Kendall lie there in the hospital bed and knowing what she was going to wake up to the next day broke me. I was completely shattered. How do you tell your two-year-old they have cancer? It was so hard for me to even say the awful "C" word, let alone explain to my daughter just how sick she was.

We both had never even heard of neuroblastoma until then and we had so many questions. We wondered if it had anything to do with her brain. Of course, I went to Google to see just how bad this was. I didn't like what I saw in the search results or the rate of survival. This was every bit as bad as it sounded. I did learn though that while neuroblastoma can spread to many parts of the body, it typically starts in nerve cells, and the main tumor usually is found in the abdomen on an adrenal gland. The doctor had probably already explained that to us but we were too paralyzed to hear.

It was around 1 a.m. at this point and as much as I wanted to call people, Wes suggested that we let everyone sleep and call them in the morning. The news wouldn't change between now and then. All I wanted was to call my mom, but I knew she had to work the next day and I didn't want to cause her to be up all night. That was agonizing in itself though to lay there with this news kept to ourselves. I thought the morning would never come. Looking back, it didn't matter what time I told my mom because either way, she wasn't going to be able to do her job after hearing such tragic news.

They let Kendall rest up that night and then morning came. It was around time for my mom to get up for work. I texted her and told her she needed to call me as soon as she could. She replied, "Is it bad?" I texted back to, "Just call me." She called right away, and I went into the bathroom in our room to talk so Kendall wouldn't hear me. I stood in the shower and broke the news to my parents while sobbing and shaking. "My daughter has cancer" are words no parents should ever have to speak. One minute I was getting ready to leave for a girls' trip with my friends that coming weekend, and the next my life as I knew it was over. Life would forever be separated into "before cancer" and "after cancer" and there was nothing I could do about it.

***

As the morning progressed, we became overwhelmed as more information was given to us and tests were scheduled. Our room started to flood with Kendall's care team. Kendall continued to rest as we met nurses, doctors, palliative care nurses, social workers, the psychologist, and child life specialists. It was a whirlwind of information. Kendall was scheduled to head down for her biopsy, bone marrow aspiration, and a CT scan. The nice child life specialist took us under his wing and braced us for her surgery and procedures. He helped us explain to Kendall what was going to happen step by step. We told Kendall she had a boo-boo in her belly, and that she was going to have to get some medicine at the hospital to make it better. Everything was happening so fast. We were forced into a world we didn't want to be in. The roller coaster ride had begun, and we had no idea when we would be able to get off of it. Kendall was being wheeled to her procedures before we even had time to fully process what was happening to our baby.

The child life specialist helped Wes get scrubbed up to go to the operating room (OR) with Kendall. Only one of us could go with her and I couldn't handle going at that moment. This was just the beginning of numerous times that Kendall would be sedated. The bone marrow aspiration involved taking a sample of the bone marrow to see if the cancer had spread there. She would have two small holes on her lower back where they took the sample from. The biopsy required taking a sample of the main tumor to determine what type of cancer she had.

Kendall went into the OR and Wes returned to the waiting room after the procedure began where we had time to call more family members. I continued down the list calling my father and his wife, my siblings, my grandparents, and my friends. Wes called his parents, sisters, and his boss while sobbing during each call. Our hearts broke, as their hearts did as they received the shocking news.

As we waited to meet Kendall in recovery, we went to the cafeteria and grabbed some lunch to bring back to the waiting room. The Cleveland Clinic was a whole new world for us. Our first impression of the food and gift shop wing was that it closely resembled the airport. There were many different franchised food options like Subway, Aladdin's, and Moe's. There were a couple of gift shops and cafeterias. They even had multiple Starbucks! We were grateful to have so many options for dining.

While we were in the waiting room, we wondered where exactly we were in the hospital in relation to where we had parked the night prior. We had a lot to learn about the best ways to navigate the hospital. One thing for sure was that we were going to get our steps in as the hospital was so large. While we pondered where we were, we figured we better check in on Alexa and on our dog who was at the neighbor's. We had left home in such an uproar and had no idea we would be gone this long. Little did we know we were about to embark on a 28-day stay before Kendall would see home again.

***

As the news about Kendall got around to our family and friends, our phones began to blow up with texts and calls. It became overwhelming very quickly. There was no way I was going to be able to respond to every text or call as they came in. People wanted to know what they could do to help and offered their prayers. Some asked if they could come to see Kendall and we had to turn many away as it was just too overwhelming for all of us as we were trying to process and learn a whole new way of living. We were touched by the outpouring of support and concern from everyone, but I was still in a deep fog, and it was hard to know what to tell people we needed early on besides their prayers. Our immediate family had already planned to come later that day and bring some of the belongings we were missing. That was as far ahead as I could think through at that moment.

Before long, we were reunited with Kendall in recovery. She was still asleep when we got to her room. I sat down next to her bed and let her know I was there. The nurses were so kind and gentle with us and Kendall. We were quickly learning with every worker we encountered at the Cleveland Clinic just how nice they all were. There was even helpful staff that asked if we needed help finding our way any time we gazed up and down a hallway, appearing lost.

Kendall eventually woke up and was quite uncomfortable with the bandages over her incisions on her back. We returned to our room on M50 and let her rest some more. Wes and I continued to be overwhelmed with information on what the week would look like for Kendall and learning all the medical terminology in the cancer world. Kendall's hemoglobin was low so first up was a blood transfusion. I cringed when they brought the bag of blood to her room. I didn't like the thought of someone else's blood going into her body at first. But like this and many other things, I just had to get comfortable with it really quickly. I always had control of my daughter's care but now the doctors were caring for her and knew what was best. I wondered how I was ever going to succeed in my new title as a cancer mom. I was completely inundated.

***

Kendall slept a lot and was weak and uncomfortable the first few days. She didn't want to play, she rarely talked and never smiled. Her belly was still distended and growing by the day from the tumor pressing against her organs, making it hard for her to breathe or eat. I would sit there and admire her beautiful hair and long eyelashes, knowing that she was going to lose them very soon. The doctor had told me that by the second round of chemo, most children with neuroblastoma have lost all of their hair.

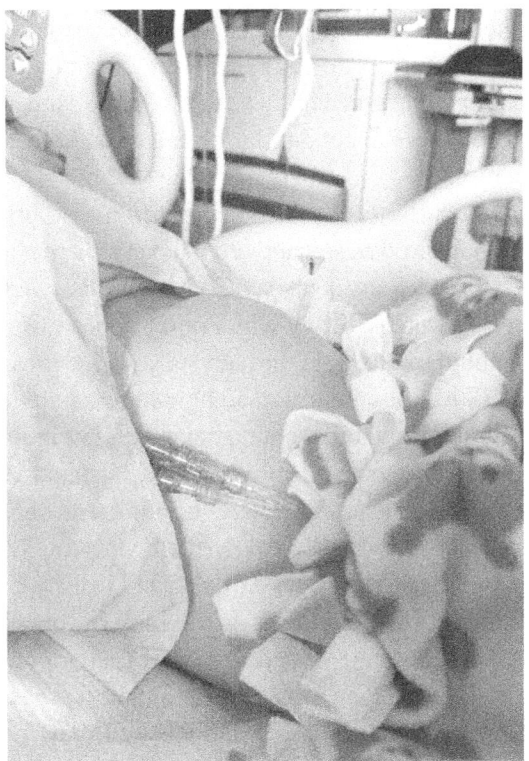

Kendall's stomach at diagnosis

The room we were in was not the most comfortable and didn't have much space to store our items. There was some noise too with being close to the elevator and entrance door to the floor. We had the nicest nurse, and I expressed my concern about the room to her. I also asked her if this was where we would be staying or if there were bigger rooms for patients with extended stays. Someone had already mentioned the Ronald McDonald House (RMH) to me. I didn't know much about it but asked her if it was possible to stay there. I learned that Kendall wasn't going to be able to go anywhere and while we were welcome to stay at the RMH, we then would not be in the room with Kendall through the night.

So, the next best thing happened. The nice nurse moved us to a room a little further down the hall away from the noise. It had a nice view of some greenery instead of the roof and a lot more storage cabinets. We got our things moved and unpacked into our new room.

Family had started to arrive to comfort us and bring us food and other items. I was so happy to have my parents and siblings there. I felt so sick inside and could barely lift my legs to walk because they were so heavy with grief. My head was spinning and all I could say to them through sobs was, "How am I going to do this? I just don't understand how I am supposed to live this life." They offered their encouragement and we brainstormed what we could do to help survive this. My sisters were already looking into making a schedule for cleaning and shopping for groceries and toiletries. We talked about who would care for Alexa over the next few days as Wes and I were not about to leave Kendall. We also didn't want to miss her oncologist stopping by her room. We had so many questions and were anxious to hear any updates.

As the week continued, Kendall received more blood transfusions, an MIBG scan, an X-ray, an ultrasound, and an EKG. The MIBG scan would help locate where all her cancer was in her body and would help determine along with the biopsy if she indeed had neuroblastoma. She was poked multiple times a day for blood draws until her port was placed later that week (another surgery). It was so horrible having to hold her down so the anesthesiologist could get the needle in her arm. As soon as their team walked into the room she started to cry because she knew the pain she was about to endure. I cried with her as I told her I was so sorry, and that they would be done soon. Big teardrops fell from her beautiful blue eyes as she would reply, "Otay, otay," which is how she said "Okay." Kendall didn't have any time to recover between all these procedures and she went through more in one week than some go through their entire lives.

As if all of this wasn't enough, Kendall also had to get an NG (Nasogastric) tube placed to start feeding her. The doctors told us that Kendall's main source of nutrition would be from the formula fed to her through this tube. The nurses began to train us and let us work the pump so that we would be ready to feed her once we were home. I felt so bad for her that she had this tube up her nose, down her throat, and taped to her face. I wished I could just kiss her boo-boo and make it all better so she didn't have to go through all of this.

The waiting was the hardest. In our waiting, we prayed. I cried out to God to please let this not be neuroblastoma. I started praying for a miracle right away and asking God to please remove this tumor and let the scans be clear so we could go back to our seemingly perfect lives. We had our congregational care pastor and one other pastor from our church come to pray over Kendall and anoint her with oil. In scripture, James says, "Are any of you sick? You should call for the elders of the church to come and pray over you, anointing you with oil in the name of the Lord" (James 5:14, NLT). Kendall was so cute and lifted her little hand to our pastor's hand to hold it while he prayed. She did not make one peep while we prayed over her.

In my own prayers, I begged God to just let me trade places with her. To let me be the one to suffer. She was just an innocent child. She had done nothing wrong to deserve this. I asked God if it was something I did to bring this on. Was I being punished? Did I complain too much about how hard motherhood was? I am a Christian and I serve you and follow you Lord so can't you please fix this? This was exactly the place the enemy wanted me. Feeding me lies that somehow, I was responsible for this and convincing me that I was a terrible mother who would never be able to take care of a child with cancer.

***

Once Kendall got her port placed, we began to learn even more about how to care for Kendall. We were given a thick 3-inch yellow binder full of information on her care and treatment plan. I didn't even know where to start with it. We were given an hours-long lesson on all the medications she was going to get, including her chemo. I remember being so tired as the nurse and pharmacist went over everything with us. I kept nodding off and could barely pay attention or retain any of the information. It was all over my head and I didn't know how I was ever going to get a grasp on this new life in the cancer world.

Kendall's port was a direct line into her heart so we had to be trained on how to care for it and keep it clean to avoid any infections. She was going to be getting a lot of different meds so the doctors felt a double-lumen Broviac catheter would be best for her. I didn't like that this foreign object had to be placed inside of our daughter, but I knew that it was needed.

We practiced cleaning her catheter on a dummy a few times with the vascular access team. We also had to learn how to change her dressing that went over her catheter. It was a sterile process, and I was terrified that I would infect her line. We had to wear masks, including Kendall and had sterile gloves to be worn. There was a whole kit just for her dressing change with a step-by-step process with nearly 20 steps! I took notes the best I could and was thankful to have Wes by my side. I was hopeful that if I missed something, he would remember and vice versa. We were in this together. Luckily, cleaning her catheter was easy to get the hang of and I rarely had to change her dressing. The vascular access team came to change it during her inpatient stays or outpatient visits so we wouldn't have to worry about it much.

Wes, Kendall, and I had a lot to get used to with the revolving door of staff in our room, the hospital noises, weight and vital checks, and early morning blood draws. None of us had had much sleep and Kendall continued to have fevers throughout the week because of the tumor and developed a cough from lying in bed so much. She wanted to go back home so badly and was already tired of being disturbed so often. She wasn't fond of any of her care team and she would tell her nurses, "Me not like you." I couldn't blame her as she was so little and didn't understand why she kept getting poked and bothered. Then, the moment we had been waiting for all week came.

Kendall's oncologist came into our room and asked if it was a good time to talk. I had my parents and neighbor visiting at the time and I told the doctor she could tell us the news in front of them. The doctor revealed that tests confirmed it was indeed neuroblastoma. We then learned that it was stage IV and had spread to her hips, underarm, above her knee, and around her heart (the bone marrow aspiration came back later and the cancer had not spread there). I couldn't believe what I was hearing. This was the worst-case scenario. My prayers were not answered, and I was crushed all over again.

"What is her prognosis?" I asked.

The doctor replied, "She has a 65% chance of beating this."

Tears began to form in my eyes again.

"65%? That doesn't sound very good. Did I cause this to happen to her? Was it something I ate when I breastfed her? Could her iPad have given her cancer?" I asked as I tried to make sense of this.

She assured me that nothing that I did caused Kendall to get cancer. She further explained it was possible that she was born with these cancer cells and that they could have just recently formed into a tumor in the last month when her symptoms began. She assured me childhood cancers are not typically caused by lifestyle choices, rather they are mostly due to genetic mutations.

The doctor then shared what her treatment plan would be to try to cure her and explained that she would need to stay inpatient for every treatment. She told me to focus on one part of her treatment at a time and day by day we would get through this. She wasn't kidding that this would be a marathon, not a sprint. She would receive 18 months of treatment on the Children's Oncology Group (COG) plan. It was an aggressive treatment plan that would start with six rounds of chemo followed by a tumor resection surgery, two stem cell transplants,

20 rounds of radiation, and then immunotherapy. She shared that chemo would start the next day. I had hit rock bottom. I didn't know how much more bad news I could handle. I was horrified by what my daughter was about to go through. I just wanted a way out, but some wise words shared by Kendall's psychologist on our team were that – "The only way out was through."

Chapter 3

Pumping in the Poison

Everything was happening so fast and I couldn't believe Kendall had to start chemo already. I barely had any time to process and prepare as our lives were turned upside down and we went from one horrible thing to the next. I would have loved nothing more than to run away and escape our reality, but I couldn't. Kendall needed me to be strong for her as she began her treatments.

I hadn't slept well in days and anxiety consumed me. I knew Kendall needed to get chemo in her right away and that it could save her life, but I also feared how she would react to it and the long-lasting effects it would have on her life. I also absolutely dreaded her losing her beautiful hair and had already started looking for cute chemo hats and turbans.

The nurses and patient care assistants on M50 were so good to us. We felt so blessed to have such gentle, compassionate people taking care of our daughter. The first bag of chemo arrived and was hung on the pole. The nurse hooked it up to her port and the chemo began pumping into her. The nurse cheered her on and gave us hope that we were one step closer to getting this cancer out of her body. I tried to be positive, but I was cringing on the inside over seeing the chemo bag and was absolutely terrified.

Kendall had to get diaper changes every two hours while she was receiving chemo so it didn't irritate her skin. I had to wear gloves when I changed her so that I didn't expose my skin to the chemo. The chemo ran over five days and made her counts drop eventually (her white blood cells, red blood cells, platelets, hemoglobin, and neutrophils are what made up her counts that I am referring to). She needed blood and platelet transfusions until her counts recovered.

There was also something called neutropenic fevers we learned about. When her counts were low, if she spiked a fever over 100.4, we would have to bring her back into the hospital because she was at high risk for infection. She would have to stay a minimum of 48 hours each time. Little did we know then how often she would be admitted due to these fevers. Common germs that were usually harmless now had an opportunity to cause infection in her immune-compromised body. We had to be very careful with anyone she was around. We were told that even if they had a little sniffle they needed to stay away.

The first round of chemo was pretty uneventful. It is hard to remember every detail, but I don't remember her throwing up during her first round. She did however get a greenish sediment in her line. Because of fear of infection, she, unfortunately, had to go under anesthesia again to get it replaced. They scheduled the procedure quickly and after it was replaced with a new catheter she was in a lot of discomfort. She would tilt her head to the side it was placed on to help alleviate some of the discomfort. She did this so much that over time she gave herself torticollis. She had to have physical therapy in the weeks ahead to help straighten and stretch her neck back out.

I was beginning to find my way around the hospital and getting into a routine. My friends had come and decorated Kendall's room with a *Frozen* theme, which was still her favorite movie at the time. It made the room brighter and we had life-size cardboard cutouts of Anna and Elsa in the corner of her room.

There was always someone around to watch Kendall so I could run down to get food or a shower, whether that was a visitor or a friendly hospital volunteer. I had started bonding with her care team and was comforted by all their support. So many gifts, plush animals, food, and flowers were sent to us. Our room filled up so quickly (minus the flowers as Kendall was not allowed to have those in her room due to the germs they carried) and I was so thankful for the extra storage cabinets we had in our room. Child Life also brought Kendall new toys almost daily, so we had quite the collection going. Kendall still hadn't wanted to play much, talk, or even smile in those first couple of weeks. Art and music therapists would come by, but she wouldn't give them the time of day. We were lucky if she would even let the music therapist sing to her.

We received many texts from friends and family daily asking for updates. After meeting with the social worker, she suggested that we set up a CaringBridge page so we could update everyone all at the same time. I was silent on social media the whole first week after Kendall was diagnosed. I had so much going on at the hospital that I didn't have time for that, nor did I feel like talking to anyone. Plus, I was waiting for the type and staging of her cancer before I made a post. I was so overwhelmed with text messages that I couldn't find time to reply to them all, so I decided to try CaringBridge. That allowed all my family members and friends who did not have a Facebook account to read my updates as well. It was not easy to make my first post and I remember shaking while writing it. Breaking the sad news to everyone made it even more real.

My neighbor also set up a private Facebook group called "Kendall Kicking Cancer" so I could post updates there as well. The page quickly grew as family and friends joined and added their friends and family as well. It never grew to thousands of people like some sick children's pages do since I had hers set to a closed group. I had to approve who requested to join her page and that was the only way I felt comfortable sharing her story on social media. I wanted to protect Kendall and our family the best I could.

***

Back home, my neighbors and community began rallying around our family. Our lawn was cared for, flowers were planted, my house was cleaned, laundry was done, and the food kept on coming. A PTA friend set up a meal train for us and it was full all the time! Since it was hard to know what to tell people we needed, it was good to have people in our lives who just saw a need and got it done for us. I loved when people would text us and asked if we needed anything from the store. More times than not we needed something.

After the first round of chemo was run, I went home for the weekend to take a break from the hospital and to be with Alexa. I noticed a change in her right away. She was angry and upset with me. She didn't want to see me or spend time with me. She just wanted to be with her friends. That was a hard weekend to get through and I did all that I could to show her that I loved her and was sorry I was spending so much time away from home. She was only five years old, and it was hard for her to understand what was happening to her sister. Her life had been turned upside down too and she felt abandoned. She was going from house to house those first couple weeks as we stayed with Kendall. We were not around much to care for her so Alexa had every right to feel what she was feeling. She let out a lot of tears that weekend and expressed her frustration that everyone only cared about Kendall. My heart broke again, and I wondered how our family was ever going to survive this.

It was nice to be back home and able to shower and sleep in my own bed. I refreshed my clothing in my bags for the hospital and grabbed some other useful items. I took Alexa to the botanical gardens which were close to the hospital on our last day together. She was not happy about going and not her silly usual self. I asked her to come to the hospital with me afterward to see Kendall. I had to switch places with Wes as he was going to be returning to work that week. She resisted and I had to use some bribery to get her to come in.

I imagine it was hard and scary for her to see her sister in a hospital bed hooked up to all kinds of tubes and machines. We had explained to the girls what was happening to Kendall the best we could without instilling fear. The child life specialist provided many books and reading materials to help us out, along with a plush chemo duck complete with a port. We had told Alexa the same thing we told Kendall: that she had a big boo-boo in her tummy and the doctors would give her medicine to help get it out. We told Alexa there was nothing she did to cause this to happen to her sister and that this was not contagious. She could still play with her, hug her, love on her, and help take care of her. Though at this point in Kendall's journey, Alexa was still hesitant, especially since her sister wasn't back to her smiling, goofy self yet.

Alexa wouldn't come too close to Kendall in the beginning. She would sit back and observe or occasionally look at one of Kendall's new toys and say something to her about it. On Alexa's visit that evening, she climbed up on the windowsill and decorated Kendall's windows for her with window markers and clings. I was thankful for small victories and knew Alexa would eventually come around in her timing.

***

I was preparing to face my first week at the hospital without Wes. This would be our new normal in the months to come. Wes went to work Monday through Friday and was home with Alexa in the evenings Monday through Thursday. Then Wes and I traded off on Friday evenings so I could have a break from the hospital on the weekends and see Alexa. It was never easy though to be away from the hospital for either Wes or me. And the girls both just wanted both of us, which made it even harder. It was impossible to not be thinking about our dear daughter suffering in the hospital when we were home, and hard when we were at the hospital with Kendall but missing out on time with Alexa.

Alexa was an especially picky eater so before the weekend ended, I had to run to the grocery store to get some of her favorite foods she liked. I tried to avoid going to the store as much as I could in those early weeks after Kendall's diagnosis. I was in no shape to walk through a store and risk running into someone but sometimes, I had to do it.

The first time that I had to make the trip, it took all my strength to pick up my legs and walk through that store. My legs felt so heavy and like I could collapse at any moment. I was in such a fog and could barely see straight as the weight of it all consumed me. The world around me was carrying on, while my world had collapsed. I would think to myself how no one in the store knew the depth of the pain I was carrying. That brought the popular phrase "Be kind to everyone you meet for you never know what someone is going through" to a whole new light for me.

After getting everything set for the week ahead for our family and walking Wes and Alexa to the hospital elevator to say goodbye that evening, I headed back to settle into my hospital stay with Kendall. I made my way down the long, stark, white hallway that led to M50. It was so hard to walk that hallway those first few times. I didn't want to go back and face our new reality. I wanted to go home and back to the way things were.

I had brought more items from home to help make us more comfortable during our stays. Items like thicker blankets to be used for padding on the uncomfortable hospital bed, and our own bed pillows and bath towels. I brought Kendall some comfortable pajamas so she didn't have to stay in her hospital gown all the time, as well as some of her favorite toys.

Slowly we were learning and finding our way in the childhood cancer world. Day by day, hour by hour, we were starting to put the broken pieces of our life back together.

Chapter 4

Finding Our Smiles Again

Do you ever look back on your life and see how God has worked in it so clearly? I found myself so incredibly grateful that I had felt a prompting to quit my job when Kendall was born. God knew that I was going to need to make all of those memories with her and then be by her side as she fought her battle with the beast that is neuroblastoma.

I was thankful that Wes had a kind, caring boss that allowed him the time off he needed, and that we were not going to be losing any income since I already did not work. This is not the case for many families. Some parents cannot even be there with their child because they must go to work to provide for their families and have health insurance so their child can get treatment. I would see this scenario right on the floor we were staying on. I was starting to see what I could still be thankful for even in our deepest valley.

As the weeks progressed and we waited to see how Kendall responded to the chemo, we met even more of her care team. There was a different pediatric oncologist inpatient each week and they all were so wonderful. I loved that they gave us their cell phone numbers when they met us. It told me they cared about my daughter, and that they would be there for her and our family. They seemed to love these children like they were their own.

One day while I was discussing Kendall's treatment plan with the doctor and others on our team, an insurance issue came up. Again, I am not great at remembering the details, but it referred to her transplant, and our insurance would only pay for it if it was done at another hospital. The doctor mentioned that we possibly would need to travel to a hospital a few hours away in the future while she received her stem cell transplant.

This did not end up being the case, but at that moment that was enough said to me to throw me over the edge. It seemed impossible to travel for her treatments. I broke down in front of the whole team. Mind you, it was always so awkward having this team of around 6-10 people coming into your room for rounds first thing in the morning. Most of the time I was still asleep, had bedhead, and was in my pajamas. I was always so embarrassed by my appearance on those mornings.

I remember starting to have a panic attack and crying over the possibility of traveling. I kept saying, "I can't do this. I just don't think I can do this. How am I supposed to do this?" Then I said it and immediately regretted it. "I just wish someone would shoot me so this nightmare could be over." Well, that was not the right thing to say, and it got me a meeting with the psychologist. Wes had to come back up to the hospital that evening because I was not doing well.

When he arrived, we both spoke with the psychologist together. She took us to a room across the hall from Kendall and I remember that I still kept repeating "I just can't do this" over and over. I slid down the wall that was supporting me into a puddle of tears on the hospital floor. I remember her asking Wes if he knew how I got through hard things in the past. He replied, "She just needs more time. Just give her some time and space and she will pull herself together." The psychologist asked me if she had to worry about me harming myself. I said, "No, I wouldn't do that." We talked through some more things, and she helped me work through my thoughts and feelings. She felt she could leave me with Wes and said she would check on me again the next day.

That was the lowest of lows for me. I thought I had already hit rock bottom, but alas I had hit even further. I was not proud of myself for how I was responding to all of these disappointments. It wasn't good for anyone and especially not for Kendall. She needed me to be strong for her. Since I was not feeling very strong in those days, I knew I was going to have to press into my faith and ask God to pull me up off that hospital floor and give me the strength and courage I needed to embrace our new life.

I share all of this to show you that this journey was far from easy, and darkness enveloped me. I was so focused on all that I had lost. If I didn't have my faith to turn to, I am not sure where I would have mustered up the strength to keep going. My own strength was not going to sustain me.

Once I accepted that I was not in control and surrendered the situation to God, he began to help me see clearly and to be more open to trusting him. I realized that God chose me for this mission for a reason and it was time now to dry my tears and be the mother Kendall and Alexa needed me to be for a time such as this. I couldn't focus on what once was or what could lie ahead in the future. I had to focus on the present. I said to myself, "Okay if this is where God has us and we will be living in this hospital for most of the next 18 months, then we are going to make the best of it and spread God's love here."

A friend put it so well when she wrote to me and said, "God strengthened your faith, prepared your heart, and set your tribe in place." And that he did! I was so thankful that he had equipped me for this journey. I trusted that he would continue to provide and give us what we needed to walk through this.

***

One of the first Bible verses that came to my mind was "I can do all things through him who strengthens me" (Philippians 4:13, ESV). I would pace Kendall's hospital room and recite it over and over, especially on days I didn't feel so strong. I guess I felt like the more I said it, the more I would start to believe that I could do this. I continued finding Bible verses that would encourage and strengthen me for this battle. I wrote them on a big piece of poster board to hang on the wall in our hospital room. That way I could see them daily and be reminded of God's truths. I turned on worship music and praised God, even though I was hurting. But, when I did that, I suddenly felt so much better. The lyrics were always just what I needed to hear and were so encouraging. They lifted me up.

Worship music had always been one of the strongest ways I could feel God's presence so he knew that he could speak to me through song. He had my attention finally and I was listening. I was ready to learn from him and give him all the glory in this journey. One of the first songs that spoke to me was Jeremy Camp's, "Same Power." The lyrics were perfect and timely. They explained and reminded me that God's power was still available for me to tap into today. With God, it was possible for me to walk through the darkness and overcome my fears. Worship music would become one of the biggest ways God communicated to me and empowered me as the months went on.

***

As our first hospital stay continued day after day, Kendall had some challenges. She was still spiking fevers, had high heart rates, and woke up to some bad nose bleeds from having low platelets. She had a slew of drugs she had to take. They encouraged her to take them by mouth, but we could only get her to take the "pink one," as she referred to it because the rest tasted bad to her.

She also went under anesthesia another time to have a G tube placed, which was a more permanent feeding tube that went directly into her stomach. This allowed a better quality of life for her and was also another way to get her medications into her, which we had been using the NG tube for up to that point. Having the G tube meant we wouldn't have to worry about her throwing up her NG tube and having to get a new one placed every time. They told me the child NG tubes were not as thick and irritating to the throat as adult ones were, but I had to get an adult NG tube placed at one point in my life and it was downright awful! I was so thankful to get the NG tube removed from Kendall's nose and be able to see her pretty face again.

Physical therapy came to work with Kendall often and her child life specialist made her a reward chart to motivate her to get out of bed. If she filled up her chart, she would earn a *Frozen* singing Elsa doll! Day by day, Kendall got a little stronger and spent more and more time out of bed. She eventually filled the chart and earned her doll. I was so proud of her. After enduring some very depressing and sad days, Kendall found her smile again, and I did too. Wow, did it feel good!

Seeing Kendall out of her bed and trying to play, eat, and make jokes helped me to feel so much better. She started giving the art and music therapists the time of day, as well as her nurses. She quickly made so many "friends" at the hospital and she was learning the ropes. She knew to hold her arm up as soon as the patient care assistants walked in so they could take her vitals. She was becoming a favorite patient on the floor as she showed her true, funny, sweet personality to everyone. She was full of joy!

She was discovering that there was a lot of fun to be had in the hospital. She had a blast the first time she played with the art therapist. They sat down on the playmat in the room together and Kendall got to pick from her paints and make her own masterpiece. Kendall loved to mix a bunch of different paints together to make this blueish-purple color. Her paintings always came out that same color. She enjoyed her time with her art therapist so much and always asked for her to come as the days went on. She missed her very much on days when she wasn't there or when she was working with other children and couldn't stop by. It helped that she was so much fun and would bring other things to do with Kendall as well, like the Melissa and Doug sticker playsets Kendall loved.

After spending more time with the art therapist, Kendall became pretty comfortable around her. So comfortable that she learned of Kendall's potty humor early on. Kendall loved to squirt all the paint out of her bottles until they made a tooting noise. She thought it was hilarious and she made us all laugh.

The music therapist was just as much fun. Both the art and music therapists were bringing so much joy to our room. Smiles and laughs were aplenty and Kendall loved having new people to play with her. The music therapist sang so well and knew all of Kendall's favorite songs. "Let it Go" from *Frozen*, "How Far I'll Go" from *Moana*, and "Can't Stop the Feeling" from *Trolls* were often requested by Kendall.

One day when Alexa was visiting, Kendall was being silly and threw the music therapist for a loop. When she was with her sister she always had more confidence to be herself and when they were together you could guarantee that there would be potty humor. The girls had discovered some potty-training jingles on YouTube. I was so humiliated when Kendall asked the music therapist to play "The Poop Song." There was my sweet, beautiful princess cracking herself up over this song.

The music therapist had such a lively personality and she was silly right back. "The Poop Song?" she questioned. "I don't know that one." Well, Kendall got out her iPad and made sure to show her the video. Kendall sang along to it while she banged on the keyboard. I even have a video of all of this going down! It's hilarious! I tried to teach Kendall when it was okay to have fun and when we had to act appropriately, but she was hard to control! Before long everyone on her team knew about her love for the poop emoji and toots. I couldn't conceal it any longer, and hey it made her happy to make others laugh.

***

All the fun and laughter we were suddenly having helped to boost my mood. I felt like the fog was finally lifting and God was giving me the strength I desperately needed for each day. I remember learning of the phrase "Choose Joy" shortly before Kendall got sick. I ordered myself a Choose Joy t-shirt not long after Kendall's diagnosis. I liked the phrase because it was a reminder to me that there was always joy to be found in each day if you just opened your eyes and looked hard enough. From the joy of a home-cooked meal brought to us, to the joy found in a sunset, it was all around us and we could choose to find it. Little did I know that I still had so much to learn about what choosing joy meant.

I soon discovered a book by Kay Warren titled *Choose Joy Devotional: Finding Joy No Matter What You're Going Through*. I ordered it right away and had it read in no time. She explained joy so well and gave me a biblical perspective on it. I was so excited I had found this book! It was my reminder that God was with us in this storm, he had not abandoned us, he loved us, and we could praise him, even though we hurt. I held on to the promise of Heaven and that one day, there would be no more pain and suffering. Between Kendall's response to her suffering, and finding this book, I had finally found a motto for Kendall's journey…"Choose Joy!" No matter how hard life got, we ALWAYS had our joy in Jesus, and nothing could steal that away from us.

Now make no mistake, choosing joy did not mean that we were happy all the time or happy about our circumstances. Before I studied joy, I too had always thought joy and happiness were the same things. But after studying joy, I learned that happiness is dependent upon what is happening around you and how you feel about it, while joy is gladness that is not circumstantial. It can't be based on circumstance because the joy

I am speaking of can only be found in our Father above. It was an unwavering joy that came from my relationship with Jesus. Psalm 16:11 says "You make known to me the path of life; in your presence there is fullness of joy; at your right hand are pleasures forevermore" (ESV).

I found a deep sense of joy in Christ that filled me and overflowed from me. It was a joy that couldn't be found in the pleasures of this world. It was deeply rooted in the love of Christ and who he is. So, while the sorrow remained and I didn't like what was happening to my daughter, I rested in the hands of Jesus, my true source of joy. I had joy because of his presence in my life, and all that he had promised to us. I was thankful for all that he was providing in this trial which led to a joyful heart.

If I had to come up with my own definition of what choosing joy meant to us, it would be that we would look for the beauty all around us, try to stay positive and cultivate a grateful heart, and remember all that we have in Jesus.

The phrase "Choose Joy" caught on fast with our friends and family. Once I shared about our choice to choose joy, it quickly became a popular hashtag on Kendall's Facebook page and people's personal Facebook pages. Every time I would go to a store, it seemed I would find some item that had that phrase on it. Before long, my house filled up with mugs, plaques, wall art, magnets, journals, pillows, etc. that people had bought for me. I loved the message behind "Choose Joy" and that it was reaching and inspiring so many people. Our family's response to the unfairness Kendall was experiencing started prompting others to change their perspectives on their own lives and the trials they faced.

***

Day after day, Kendall remained in the hospital. We were into July and her birthday was nearing. We had a week to get her well enough to be home by her birthday and I wondered if we would make it in time. In the meantime, Child Life had arranged for Dec My Room to come in. This is a wonderful organization that decorates hospital rooms for kids who are there for an extended stay. I was excited for them to come, but also sad because I figured it meant the team didn't think she was going home anytime soon.

Dec My Room did an amazing job with Kendall's *Frozen*-themed request. They brought in an Anna and Elsa comforter and a large *Frozen* rug Kendall could get out of bed and play on. They brought tons of *Frozen*-themed toys, a hooded bath towel, and princess wall decals. They covered the chairs in our room with comfy blankets and gave me a cozy body pillow, along with towels and rugs for the bathroom. They brought in a large tote that had Kendall's name on top of it with a princess crown. We used it to store many of Kendall's toys. They also brought in a Little Tikes pink basketball hoop which we thought was just the coolest. Our room filled up even more with stuff, but Dec My Room brought so much joy and life to our room and made it feel so inviting.

The amount of support we were receiving was so comforting. Not only did we have an army of friends and family surrounding us, but people we didn't even know were coming into our lives offering support and kindness. Wes and I had put off taking my sister up on her offer to start a Go Fund Me page. We felt bad taking money from others and knew we couldn't repay them. It's a hard place to be in. We knew people wanted to help, but Wes and I just didn't feel right about it. We had always taken care of ourselves and were able to provide for our family, so it just felt funny. But so many people kept asking how they could donate to our family.

We finally let go of our pride after my mom had a conversation with us. She said that giving money was a way that many felt they could help, and we couldn't rob them of that. We got the Go Fund Me page up and running with my sister's help. Many people donated right away, and I wondered how I could ever thank all of them. We were blown away by how many donations rolled in, not only from friends and family but complete strangers too. In a journey like this, you find the helpers. The people with kind, caring, compassionate hearts who just had so much empathy for what our family was going through.

I could probably write a book just on the helpers in Kendall's journey. There were so many people and organizations that came alongside us and carried us through. Other fundraisers were started for our family and more and more people continued hosting them as time went on. There are many costs that come with a cancer diagnosis, but these fundraisers and foundations willing to help allowed us to have peace of mind and just be able to focus on Kendall's care.

***

One of the first conversations we had with Kendall's social worker was when she explained that we could choose which "wish" organization we would be going with. Because Kendall was facing a life-threatening illness, she qualified for a wish trip through either Make-A-Wish or a local wish-granting foundation, A Special Wish Northeast Ohio (ASW). After talking with some people who have had experience with both, we decided to go with ASW because they would be with us for the entire journey.

Not only would Kendall get her big wish, but she would also get toy drops and special immunocompromised visits to local fun places like Build-A-Bear or Dave & Buster's. Our family would get to go to these places before they opened to the public so she wouldn't be exposed to a lot of people or germs. ASW also did food drops to the hospital multiple times a week, special parties for the wish kids a few times a year, and Kendall could have princess visits anytime she wanted. We were so happy with our choice to go with ASW and the founders quickly became like family to us.

I also found some support groups on Facebook, one of the good things about social media. I was able to connect to cancer parents in my area and to a neuroblastoma support group that was worldwide. It was reassuring to not feel so alone and to have many parents that I could talk with and turn to for advice. Our neuroblastoma group became a wealth of knowledge for us on how to care for Kendall and what treatments were out there and available. We also found so much hope in hearing of kids who had survived this dreaded monster. We were so thankful to have these groups to turn to when we needed them.

***

Kendall was enjoying her new room decorations and her visits from her sister. She would suddenly gain a burst of energy and try her hardest to be a kid when Alexa came around. One Friday evening, Alexa spent the night at the hospital with Kendall. My heart was so full as they snuggled in bed together and laughter and giggles filled our room. Alexa was coming around at the hospital and it helped that Child Life would always bring her a toy too. That made Alexa feel just as important as her sister.

Kendall's counts were starting to rise so she got the okay to leave her room for the first time. We put blankets and a pillow on the wheelchair and gave her a ride down to the big fish tank two floors below us. She was all smiles as she climbed out of her wheelchair and up onto the bench to see the fish up close.

We also took Kendall to see the fountains in the front of the hospital, as well as a trip to the rooftop to get some breaths of fresh air after days upon days of being inside four walls. We were all so happy to see Kendall out of her room, though it was hard wheeling my sick child through the hospital with her mask on and hooked up to her pump. I tried not to pay attention to all the stares, but I could tell people were. I'm sure they were just shocked to see a young child so sick, and others felt sorry for her and us. By this time, some of Kendall's hair had started to fall out too so you could just tell that she was a very sick girl. I was anxious to get back to our room where we felt safe and loved by our wonderful care team.

As the days went on more of Kendall's hair fell out from the chemo. I would brush her hair and some strands would come out in the brush. I hid it from her the first few times, but then she started to discover on her own that it was coming out. I would catch her pulling it out herself and she would hand it to me as she would crack up laughing. It was breaking my heart to see her lose her beautiful blonde locks, but because she was so young and didn't understand, to her it was funny. The first area you could notice her balding was in the front of her head. She had quite a large chunk she had pulled out, and then on the back of her head, there was a large bald spot as well. She would lift her head off her pillow and the hair would be stuck to it. I teared up every time I saw this.

I was hoping it would take some time before she was completely bald, but it seemed to be coming out rapidly. A friend was coming to visit one afternoon, and I asked her to bring a pair of scissors. We braided Kendall's hair and then cut off the ponytail braid so that I could save some of her hair. I put a little bow on the braid and another friend got a pretty little box to put it in. I still have it tucked neatly into the box to this day.

Kendall continued to pull her hair out and hand it to me. I tried to bag up all that I could. I didn't like seeing this happen to her but I think maybe it was itchy and irritating to her so she couldn't wait to have it gone. I had already ordered a lot of cute chemo hats for her and had them ready. Before long, all she had left on her soft, perfectly shaped head was a thin strip of hair across her brow. I was so afraid of seeing her without hair, but she was the cutest, prettiest bald little girl we had ever seen.

***

Just as I had anticipated, we were going to be spending Kendall's third birthday in the hospital. We had already spent July 4th there, and I knew that this was probably going to be a year of spending many more holidays inpatient. The hospital staff did a great job at making her day special. They made a big poster board for her door that said "Happy Birthday" and it was signed by her care team. The team also came to her room to sing "Happy Birthday" and brought her a cake. Accompanying them was one of Kendall's favorite characters, Peppa Pig. My friend whom I had spent many years with in the PTA happened to have a Peppa Pig costume and offered to come to surprise Kendall.
    She was so excited and smiled so big when she first saw Peppa. Then she said in her sweet little voice, "Me want hug Peppa Pig." I told her to go ahead but then suddenly, she seemed afraid. She then wouldn't even look at Peppa, or anyone else in the room. I don't know if she realized all the attention was on her and she didn't like it or that I was filming her or what changed her mood. She did love her cake though and actually took some bites of it. Some of her best friends had come up to help her celebrate so she enjoyed opening gifts, a lot of which were Peppa Pig toys. She took wheelchair rides around the hospital with them in her special *Trolls* hospital gown that a friend sewed her, and a turquoise turban. Kendall seemed to be doing well and it felt like we were getting closer to discharge.
    Prepping to be discharged brought a lot of excitement, but also fear of being on our own taking care of Kendall. Luckily the team was making sure we had all the supplies and meds needed to take care of her. A home health care order was being placed so we could have feeding pump supplies, gloves, syringes, gauze, dressing change kits, etc. sent to our home. We slowly began to clear out our hospital room in hopes of going home soon.
    It was Day 28 when we were finally discharged. I dressed Kendall in a floral dress with a turquoise tutu, her *Frozen* Velcro sneakers, and her turban. She had lost so much weight from her hospital stay and looked so frail as she sat in the wheelchair holding a balloon and grinning ear to ear. She couldn't wait to

get home to see her dog and sister and open all the other gifts that were waiting for her. It was a joyous occasion as we wheeled her down the hallway of M50, with all of the nurses congratulating her and saying their goodbyes. So many emotions go through you as you fear what could happen being away from her care team. We didn't live terribly far from the hospital, but far enough that it would seem like forever if something went wrong, and we needed to get her back there. Frankly, I was terrified and feeling stressed over making the transition to home.

We got into the elevator and headed for the parking garage. We exited the hospital and got our first breath of freedom upon stepping outside. Kendall was so excited to be in her car seat and finally free from the hospital. She was due in for her second round of chemo in just three days, but we planned to make her weekend at home amazing. Our family was finally going to be reunited again under one roof and we were going to enjoy every minute, even if we were terrified.

Chapter 5

Home at Last

Pulling into our driveway with our little girl in tow was the most wonderful feeling. This was our new life, living between home and the hospital. I was so happy for Kendall that she could enjoy the comforts of home again.

As soon as she got in the door, she suddenly had so much energy! She was getting around pretty well, surprisingly. She was a little hunched over, but she was so eager to run around her home and into every room. She found all the gifts waiting for her in our dining room and began tearing into them. I could barely keep up as tissue paper went flying everywhere. We all had the biggest smiles on our faces. It felt so good to see Kendall laugh and be so full of life again. I had hope that she would regain all of her strength and the weight that she lost over the last 28 days.

Wes did a great job prepping our home for Kendall's arrival. Because Kendall would be immunocompromised, we had to do a thorough cleaning of our home, inspect and get rid of any mold, and remove any fresh flowers as they can carry fungal spores. Wes bleached down our house, installed hand sanitizer dispensers at each door, and bought HEPA air purifiers for each floor. He also bought laundry sanitizer to make sure our clothes were free of germs. I am a germaphobe to begin with so I was very paranoid and did as much as I could to keep her safe. You really start to appreciate how sterile a hospital is once you have to try to replicate that environment in your own home.

The three days we were home were hardly enough time to get into a good routine. Kendall had meds to take regularly, lines to be flushed, and formula to be fed through her feeding tube. Wes was so great at making sure we were stocked on her formula, and he bought hospital bed pads so we could use them at home as well. They worked great to put under Kendall when she was on the couch or in her bed. It is harder at home to clean up bodily fluids than it is at the hospital, so the bed pads saved us numerous times.

Wes made us a medication chart and feeding schedule that we hung on the fridge to stay organized. Over time, we learned to also put alarms in our phones to remind us of her medication times. We stored her medications in a basket that continued to grow as time went on.

We had so many medical supplies and toys we brought home from the hospital to sort through, as well as bags to unpack. I had my sister come and help me get organized. She went to the store for me and got some organizing drawers to store all of Kendall's supplies in on each floor of our home. My neighbors also came over and helped us get settled and put together Kendall's new *Frozen* toddler bed for us. I wanted her to be in our room with us so we could keep an eye on her through the night. There was no way I was letting her out of my reach. Before the night was up, our bedroom was resembling our hospital room as her pole was set up, formula hung, and meds and supplies were stocked and ready to go.

Home proved to be so healing for Kendall as she played with her sister and was able to see some of her neighbor friends. She even ate some of her favorite foods while she was home. It wasn't long before she mustered up the strength to go on her swing set. Swinging was one of Kendall's favorite activities. She always needed to be pushed, so everyone would take turns pushing until one of us tired out. She would always shout, "Higher, higher!" Every time she came home from the hospital during her journey she was out on her swing. My heart would be full of joy as I watched her soar through the air. She would tilt her head back and look up to the sky as if she was soaking in every bit of her freedom. Sometimes she would close her eyes as she glided back and forth through the air. It was such a wonderful sight to see and pulled on my heartstrings.

Kendall enjoying her swing

Because Kendall had a Broviac catheter, she was not allowed to be submerged in water. She would be at risk for a line infection if water got through her dressing and into her central line. So that meant no more swimming that summer or baths. Kendall loved her baths so that was hard for her to accept, and she was disappointed that she couldn't take one. After we became more comfortable caring for her dressing and catheter, we would put a tiny bit of water in the tub for her to sit in and gently bathe her, but the majority of her baths were always sponge baths. If I did allow her in the tub, I would put an AquaGuard waterproof dressing over her catheter. She was always good at not splashing and being careful.

We all got some much-needed rest that weekend, free of hospital beeps and the revolving door of people. Alexa was happy to have all her family back home together but didn't understand why we spent so much of our day taking care of Kendall, or why Kendall and I had to go back to the hospital so soon. We tried explaining everything to her the best we could. We made sure we told her what she could expect in her schedule each day we were away, and how long before Mommy and Kendall would be back. We just had to get through another month before she would start kindergarten and have a more consistent routine. In the interim, my friends and family continued to do a great job stepping in and caring for Alexa when we couldn't. They were the hands and feet of Jesus, and I am forever grateful.

***

I spent some of my time that weekend preparing for our next hospital stay. I thought I would get smart and just buy one extra of all my toiletry items. That way I had my bag basically packed for the hospital at all times, besides clean clothes. This allowed me to go back and forth from home to the hospital without leaving anything behind and made for quick packing for those unexpected hospital admissions.

If you are wondering how you can come alongside a childhood cancer family, or any family enduring long stays at the hospital, here are some ideas of items needed:

Helpful Items Needed for Long Hospital Stays

- *A gift for nurses* – Bring some bakery or sandwiches to leave at the nurses' station and say it is from the friends or family of the patient. I can't tell you how many times I wanted to do something nice for them but didn't have access or resources to do so.
- *A journal and pen* – New cancer parents are given so much information and it was nice to have many journals to take notes in. I wrote my questions down so they were ready when the team came in for rounds and jotted down any reminders to myself about Kendall's care.
- *A soft, large towel* – The hospital towels are so tiny, rough, and don't smell the best. I clearly remember longing for a soft, fresh towel and it was one of the first items I asked a friend to bring me during our first stay.
- *Arts and Crafts* – I personally loved it when I could make some art too so try to get creative and bring something for both the parent and child to paint. You could bring a couple of canvases and paint, or some kind of wood object from the craft store to paint and decorate. My PTA made us craft bags with all the supplies needed for us. It was so nice to have so many different crafts to choose from.
- *Books* – Books that the parent can read to their child, along with books for the parents too. Books that provided hope, encouragement, and stories of people who had walked in my shoes were always helpful to me.
- *ChapStick* – The air in the hospital is so dry and takes a bit for your skin to get used to, especially your mouth. I was drinking a ton of water and slathering on the ChapStick for that whole first hospital stay.
- *Cozy blankets/Pillowcase covers* – Blankets can accumulate quickly for the kids, but parents need a comfy blanket for themselves to use. I loved my plush

blanket and I even learned over time to buy a memory foam topper for my hospital bed. I created a comfy sleep space for me that saved my back too. If only I had discovered the mattress topper sooner, I could have prevented myself from many nights of pain from those beds. Pillowcase covers can also be fun and brighten up a room. They are easy to switch out if they are soiled.

- *DVDs/Games/Puzzles* – Kendall loved when she would get a new DVD to watch in her room. Sometimes we had movie nights with Alexa at the hospital. Games and puzzles were always great for keeping Kendall and me busy as well.
- *Gift cards* – You can't go wrong with giving gift cards. Any food delivery gift cards like UberEATS or DoorDash would be great. I always loved Visa gift cards to use in the hospital cafeteria and other restaurants. The food can get quite expensive after a while. Check and see if there are any franchise restaurants in the hospital as well that you could purchase a gift card for. Be sure to check that they accept gift cards as we found some restaurants in the hospital that would not. Gas gift cards are great too as there is a lot of travel back and forth between home and the hospital. Massage or salon gift cards are also a nice treat.
- *Gripper socks/Slippers* – Kendall loved to have her slippers next to her bed to put on quickly when she got up. I also loved walking around our room with slippers on. Fun gripper socks work well too and are a little bit safer of an option.
- *Hospital parking passes* – We were shocked to find out that we would have to pay to park every time we came to the hospital. With the amount of time we were spending there, we thought parking would be included. It cost us $100 for a monthly parking pass! If you can go to the hospital and purchase a monthly parking pass for a

family that would be incredibly helpful. Even individual tickets would be great as well.
- *Inspirational signs/Faux flowers* – I loved having little wood plaques with a Bible verse or inspiring quote on them. I would place them around our room to decorate and also to encourage us. Since cancer patients can't have real flowers, a small faux floral arrangement can really brighten up the room and bring joy.
- *Magazines/Puzzle books/Coloring books* – The parent often finds a lot of time to themselves as their child is sleeping most of the day during treatments, or they have a couple of hours to wait while their child is getting scanned. Providing entertainment for the parent in this way is always a great choice. Coloring books come in kid and adult varieties with fun-colored pencils and marker choices as well.
- *Rugs/Hand towel* – A small bathroom rug and nice hand towel give those stark hospital bathrooms a little touch of home. I couldn't believe how different it felt after Dec My Room did that for us.
- *Sleep masks* – The med pole often has bright lights on the machines attached, or even flashing lights at times. The nurses often need to turn on lights in the middle of the night so a sleep mask works great to keep the light out of the eyes.
- *Snacks* – I loved when someone would drop off donuts or ice cream! Candy, chocolate, and salty snacks were always welcome as well! Trail mix and breakfast bars were also good choices.
- *Spa Night items* – If you are making a care kit for a little girl and her mom, consider making them a spa kit. Kendall and I loved to have spa nights at the hospital. We would paint each other's nails, do each other's makeup, and sometimes use face masks. I would put lotion on Kendall and massage her feet. Some fun nail

polish colors, nail polish remover wipes, face masks, a little handheld mirror, a manicure kit, and makeup would be a great gift idea.
- *Toys/Blind bags/Prizes* – Kendall always loved when someone would bring her a new toy. It brought her joy and was something new to entertain her. I wouldn't recommend stuffed animals as the hospital and many other people give these. Play-Doh, Legos, L.O.L. dolls, and Barbies were some of Kendall's favorite toys to receive. She also loved blind bags, which were small mystery bags with tiny items inside. There was so much suspense over what they might contain. We used these as prizes for achieving things like time out of bed walking, playing on the floor mat, dressing changes, or scans and procedures.
- *Travel items* – Any travel items are a great choice and need to be replenished frequently. Shampoo/conditioner, dry shampoo, bar soap, body wash, lotions, toothpaste, toothbrush, hairbrush, manicure kit, face wash, hand wipes, sanitizer, Lysol wipes, deodorant, shaving cream, razors, Q-tips to name a few. I also loved bringing in my own fragrant hand soap.
- *Water bottles* – One of my favorite gifts I received was a water bottle that kept my drinks cold for days. This was so helpful, especially during transplants when I didn't have access to a fridge and had to limit my time out of our room.

    I hope this list is helpful and you can reference it in the future for ideas when you know a family who is in need. Offering to clean the family's home while they're away, mow their lawn, pull weeds, do laundry, or grocery shop for them are also nice gestures.

***

After a wonderful weekend of enjoying some normalcy, the time had come to an end. We were as prepared as we could be to face the next week. Wes would head to work that Monday, Alexa to the neighbor's, and Kendall and I to the hospital.

Kendall was scheduled to be inpatient Monday through Friday and we hoped that would hold true. Kendall and I both dreaded another hospital stay but tried to make the best of it. Day by day, hour by hour, we would make it to the finish line of each treatment. I was learning to focus on just one part of her treatment plan at a time and to find the joy in the journey. To just let myself be in the moment, to not fear the future, and to keep believing that she would beat this. As Kendall would often say, it was time to head to the hospital and "Get this cancer out!"

Chapter 6
The Ups and Downs of Chemo

Kendall was a rockstar in chemo round 2. She had minimal side effects, was continuing to eat some food by mouth, and was up out of bed and walking around her room. We had tea parties with her stuffed animals, painted more with the art therapist, and even had a dance party. Kendall was in good spirits and I had my silly little girl back. We were actually having fun inside the four walls of her hospital room; something I didn't know was even possible.

Being back at the hospital offered some relief for me as I still didn't have it quite together as Kendall's home nurse. I used my time there to make sure I got all my questions answered and watched the nurses closely to make sure I was doing everything right. It was always good to have help taking care of Kendall as there was a lot to tend to. We had become quite fond of some of the nurses and bonds were being formed.

Not only were new friendships being made with the nurses, but I was getting to know more parents who were staying on our floor with their child. It was so reassuring to know I wasn't alone, and that other people knew what this felt like. I loved hearing all the tips and wisdom they had for me and was grateful to have people to talk to who just got it. It was a club none of us wanted to be in, but there was so much beauty and love in it. There were even parents who had heard about Kendall whose child was on the other side of treatment now. They came alongside me and answered my questions, comforted me, and brought us hope that there was light at the end of the tunnel.

As we continued to journey through treatments, we were beginning to have a better understanding of the roller coaster ride we were on. One minute we were up, the next we were down. It was around this time that more bad news was sent our way. We received results from a test that was run on Kendall's tumor. It showed that she had a MYCN gene amplification. Her diagnosis was now Stage IV MYCN amplified neuroblastoma. Kendall had an aggressive tumor and would need to follow through with the most aggressive treatment. Her prognosis was then lowered from 65% to a 40% chance of survival because tumors with this gene amplification were tougher to fight and more probable for relapse. It seemed like the bad news just kept coming. Just when I thought our hearts couldn't break any further, they were shattered some more.

Tears and fear came as I processed the news. Her doctor reassured me that there was still hope and that we didn't know how her cancer would respond. She said we had many treatments to try and that we would continue the course. I immediately went right to my neuroblastoma Facebook support group to find stories of hope. I did indeed find many parents with surviving children who had a MYCN gene amplification. So that is what I tried to focus my mind on. I kept believing and hoping that Kendall too would beat the odds and with God on our side, nothing was impossible.

There was a song on the radio at this time by a Christian band, Tenth Avenue North, that spoke to my heart. It was titled, "I Have This Hope," and it always seemed to be on every time I drove to or from the hospital. Tears would stream down my cheeks as I listened to the words. The lyrics spoke of the hope we have in Christ and how he is always with us and will never let go. The writer expresses that they don't want to be afraid and that they have a desire to trust God even in the storms of life.

Jesus was and is my living hope and he spoke to me through songs like this. I knew that I had to continue to keep my eyes fixed on him and not focus on all the negatives and fear. I needed his help to repair the shattered pieces of my heart.

Everyone kept telling me I was so strong, but it was not my own strength. I had supernatural strength from God through his Spirit to carry me through. Apart from God, I am hardly strong at all. Every day, I had to immerse myself in scripture and prayer and ask for his strength, peace, and guidance (and I still do). After I made that time to spend with God and asked for his help, I was fueled and ready to take on the day. It was like I was walking hand in hand with Jesus, and I could face the trial before us. That doesn't mean I wasn't scared or full of sadness, but knowing God was with me in every moment gave me the strength and courage to go on. I had put on the armor of God, and I was ready to fight.

***

As we continued through chemo rounds, we quickly learned that time at home would be few and far between. Shortly after being discharged on time from round two, we were at an outpatient appointment. Kendall had around two or three of these a week on her off weeks from treatment. They would check her weight and vitals, and draw her blood to check on her counts. This particular outpatient visit landed Kendall back inpatient for a possible G tube infection. She then spiked a neutropenic fever, which left her in the hospital up until her planned admission to collect her stem cells for her future transplant. I felt so bad for her, but Kendall handled it with such grace. She was getting used to hospital life and knew how much fun she could have there, so she didn't seem to mind. Her response helped me as well to just let go and enjoy the journey. I was not in control anymore. I used to be a planner, but there was no way to know what our next day would look like. We were living day to day at this point.

God was teaching me so much during all these setbacks and disappointing days. He continued to speak to me through songs with the perfect lyrics for what I was going through that particular day. Sometimes, I would wake up in the middle of the night and hear a song in my head. I kept a journal right next to my hospital bed on the windowsill so I could quickly write down some of the lyrics in my tired state.

Another song that was so comforting in those early months of her treatment was by Casting Crowns and it was titled, "Just Be Held." The lyrics talked about needing to find strength when you are shaken. They talked about when life falls apart and you don't have the answers, surrender to God and let him hold you up. You can see how these lyrics felt like God was speaking right to me. I couldn't get over how meaningful all these songs had suddenly become. On the really hard days, God spoke the loudest. He would give me all the uplifting words I needed at just the right moments. It was just the coolest thing and I had never experienced hearing from God like this in my life before. I felt so close to him.

***

The girls' great-grandmother (G.G.) came to stay with us at the end of summer as Alexa's school year was approaching. G.G lived out of state at the beach, so we were thankful she had the time and was willing to come to help us care for Alexa and our home while we were away. G.G stayed for a few weeks and got to enjoy the times we had with Kendall at home as well. One day, Kendall had good counts and was cleared to go to the zoo. G.G. came along and we had the best day with the girls seeing the animals and eating ice cream. Kendall fed a giraffe that day and that story became one she told over and over at the hospital.

She would tell everyone how the giraffe licked her with his long, black tongue.

Kendall also received her first of many princess visits during her time at home. Elsa and Anna were the first to come by the house and it warmed my heart to see her and Alexa so happy. The girls dressed up in their Elsa and Anna costumes and had fun dancing, blowing bubbles, swinging, singing, and telling stories together.

These were the kinds of days we cherished and never wanted to end. Normalcy never felt so good. Things I once took for granted, like the space I had in my home, Kendall's footsteps through the house, or the fresh breeze blowing in through the windows meant so much more. It was the little things that I treasured the most.

***

I was getting better at caring for Kendall at home and quickly adapted to being "nurse mommy." It was far from easy though as I still had to care for Alexa and our dog when I was home, on top of the demanding care for Kendall. Every time I turned around it seemed that Kendall needed a feed hooked up, meds, a diaper change, or her catheter tubes flushed. It was very overwhelming. Alexa was a good helper to me and I loved seeing her care for her sister. My heart melted one day when I saw her wiping Kendall's mouth after she had thrown up. She looked out for her sister and helped protect her.

Kendall was used to her catheter tubes at this point, and she even named them after two of her close friends. The blue was the boy, the red was the girl. She called them her "tubies." She loved to show them to people and liked to help me push the flushes through them. She was always so proud of herself afterward. We used a fun jingle to sing while I cleaned and flushed her "tubies" that went like this:

Me – "Red tubie, red tubie, where are you?"

Kendall – "Here I am, here I am, how do you do?"

She would pull the appropriate color tube out from under her shirt and wave it as if it was singing to me. It was so special and cute! She would encourage me by telling me, "You did it" after I would finish or hook up her feeding pump successfully. It made me smile every time. She was always there to pick me up and tell me it would be okay on days I wanted to cry. One time after a rough day at an outpatient appointment, she wrapped her little arms around my neck and said, "It be okay, Mommy". She was such a compassionate child and made my heart melt. I was so glad we had each other.

***

After a few days of rest at home, Kendall would return to the hospital for more treatment, or more antibiotics if she spiked a fever. We were told that chemo round 3 would be a little harsher on Kendall. This chemo was known to cause more nausea, along with hearing loss and kidney damage. After seeing how she plowed through the first two rounds with flying colors, I was keeping a positive mindset that this round would be better than expected as well.

Well, that did not end up being the case. Kendall completed the five days of treatment, was discharged, and once home the throwing up began. It was pretty often and we had a lot of messes to clean up. Alexa became upset and locked herself in the bathroom. Once I got to her, I held her in my arms and just cried with her. She expressed that all we did was take care of Kendall and she just wanted her mom and dad to herself. I felt so defeated and wondered how I could make this better for her.

Kendall spiked a fever a few days later and back to the hospital we went. She continued to throw up for the next 11 days. It was so hard having to see her like this. Kendall though would throw up in the bucket and then go right back to playing. This is the resiliency of children.

I continued to pray and worship as I had nowhere else to turn. God continued to give me uplifting songs to strengthen my faith and comfort me during this time. Lauren Daigle's song "O'Lord" was my heart's cry and I continued to hope for better days ahead.

***

It had been a few months into living between two places and we were all feeling the negative effects of it. I was missing my husband as we were barely seeing each other. I missed my friends and playdates. I missed out on summer and all the fun activities we usually do. I missed Alexa, my dog, my bed, exercising, and sleeping. I was tired of packing and unpacking, then loading it all into the car, and then from the car to the hospital room. There really needs to be a service at the hospital for families who live in and out of the hospital. Someone that you could call when you arrive to come with a large flatbed cart to help bring all of your things in. Instead, I had to load everything onto a wheelchair and make multiple trips. It was like packing for a vacation every couple of days. It was all starting to wear on me.

Wes was so busy trying to work and take care of my duties at home, all while caring for Alexa and worrying about his baby, that he started losing weight. That was the first thing people noticed and commented on when they saw him. Stress and hardly any time to eat will do that to you.

One of the first pamphlets our congregational care pastor gave us during one of his visits was about how many marriages fail when going through something like we were. I was thankful to be aware of the statistics and then knew we needed to make time for each other somehow. I wanted to do all that I could to protect and fight for our marriage. Wes had always been my rock and someone I never wanted to go through life without. I needed him by my side now more than ever.

Alexa was also struggling with all the disruptions in her

routine. She had so many different caregivers, Kendall and I were away for days at a time, and now full-day kindergarten was starting (she had previously been signed up for half day, but we needed her to switch to full day). We were so caught up in Kendall's care, that Alexa was feeling abandoned. The psychologist on our team recommended a local support center for families affected by cancer. There was a counselor there that worked specifically with children. Wes and I were not around enough to be able to help Alexa process her feelings, so setting her up for counseling seemed like the best thing to do.

    Alexa started out going weekly to counseling. I was so impressed with their facility. It was so peaceful and a safe space for Alexa to express her feelings. She was able to make artwork while she talked to her counselor. She loved going and I absolutely loved her counselor. I still say to this day that she is an angel on Earth. Her gentle voice, beauty, and porcelain skin emanated an angelic vibe. Alexa continued with counseling services from her for the next couple of years to come. I think it made Alexa feel special that she had something that was just her thing. Someone was focusing on just her.

***

    Kendall wrapped up chemo round 4 just in time to be home for Alexa's first day of kindergarten. She barely made discharge in time. Her doctor knew how important it was to me to have us all together for Alexa's big day so she made sure it happened. G.G. was still staying with us and able to soak in the joy of that morning too. Kendall was pretty tired, and we had her wrapped in a pink blanket in her daddy's arms as we waited at the bus stop. G.G. took pictures and we all were able to witness Alexa's first steps onto the bus. Alexa was happy that morning and full of smiles. Another sweet moment to cherish. Our little girl was growing up and off to school.

    Kendall was doing really well for a while after that round

until I heard her throwing up at 3 a.m. one morning. By the time I got the light turned on, she was done throwing up and all I could see was blood pouring out of her nose like a faucet, and a pool of blood between her legs on her bed. I was horrified. I was trying to stay calm, but it was near impossible. I had never seen so much blood.

Before long the whole house was up, and I was trying to keep Alexa from seeing the horror. Luckily, I got her back to her room before she saw anything. My concern was that Kendall was throwing up blood. I called the on-call line and spoke to the intern. She thought it was best to take Kendall in right away because she probably needed platelets. So, there we were packing up and rushing off to the hospital again in the middle of the night. Oh, the adrenaline rush. I had no idea her cancer journey would be like this. I never could have imagined the terror and intensity of it all. Nothing can prepare you for it.

Wes took her to the hospital this time and sure enough, her counts had dropped quickly on this round. She needed a blood and platelet transfusion. This was probably the worst nosebleed I saw on her journey, though she did have one where blood came out of her eyes as well. That too was a horrible sight to see.

Luckily, it didn't appear that she had thrown up blood; rather it was all from her nose. They said she would be able to come back home later that day, though I learned to never count on going home until you are actually signing the discharge papers and heading for the door.

Surprisingly, she did end up coming home after a 12-hour stay. She enjoyed another couple of days at home before she spiked another fever and landed herself back inpatient for a week. So, you get the idea of what a toll this takes on a family.

Alexa became very emotional every time Kendall and I returned to the hospital, and rightfully so. This time she was upset about the cancer ribbons, shirts, and bracelets that were showing up everywhere. Everyone we knew was wearing a bracelet or t-shirt in support of Kendall. I also made cancer ribbons with my grandma for our neighbors to hang on their mailbox posts to light the street gold for Kendall. Alexa told me one morning while I was getting ready that she didn't want anything with a cancer symbol in our house. She also expressed again how she felt that no one cared about her, and my heart broke some more. I tried my best to explain why the ribbons were on the mailboxes. She asked me when the ribbons were coming down almost every day. I was so thankful we had a counselor for her to help with tough feelings like these. I had to start asking people to bring gifts for Alexa too if they were going to bring one for Kendall. This helped her to feel like she mattered too.

***

We were at the point in Kendall's treatment when we were starting to have conversations with the team about the next steps. Kendall was due in to start chemo round 5, which typically was the last round before tumor resection surgery. I was not looking forward to this chemo round as it was the same drugs from round 3 that made her throw up for 11 days. The team had come up with some options though to hopefully avoid that this time, such as continuous Zofran (anti-nausea med) and slow continuous feeds.

The plan was to finish round 5, then scan her to see how her tumor responded to the chemo. Her doctor seemed hopeful that it had shrunk significantly based on other tumor markers they use, such as urine markers. Hers had decreased quite a bit just after one round of chemo. After scans, surgery would be planned, then the 6th and final round of induction chemo, and then onto stem cell transplants.

We had learned from our neuroblastoma support group about Memorial Sloan Kettering Hospital (MSK) in NYC. Many parents transferred their child's care there because they treated so many neuroblastoma patients. They also were the only hospital in the U.S. that did not follow COG treatment protocol and did not have stem cell transplants as part of treatment. They also had one of the top neuroblastoma surgeons in the country on their pediatric surgical team. His name was Dr. La Quaglia, commonly referred to as Dr. L., and we heard nothing but great things.

We had already seen the horror stories of transplants on the neuroblastoma Facebook page, along with other children who got through it with minimal complications. The horror stories scared us though and made us start to question what the next best course of action would be for Kendall.

We addressed our concerns over transplants with her doctor. She explained the similarities and differences between the two hospital's treatment plans, and her desire for Kendall to have her transplants because of her MYCN amplification. She and other doctors on Kendall's team told us it was her best chance of survival. We trusted in our team and knew they would continue to give her the best care and treat her as if she was their own child.

***

Chemo round 5 made Kendall very sick again just as we had suspected it would. She was home for two days before she was right back in the hospital again, which was a recurring pattern with her. We had plans that weekend as a family and we were all so sad and crying over the sudden change. Well, at least us girls were!

Kendall struggled to keep any solid food down. She ended up having to be put on TPN this round, which is IV nutrition feeding. The doctors wanted to give her gut time to rest. She had low electrolytes, potassium, magnesium, platelets, and blood so transfusions were aplenty. Bad nose bleeds continued this round as well. We were so close to scans that the team thought it was best for her to just continue to stay until then since it would be easier than discharging and returning.

We were a week into October at this point. Her surgery was planned for the end of that month, so back home our neighborhood was starting to plan an early Trick or Treat for Kendall. It was something all of us could look forward to and we hoped to get released from the hospital in time.

A lot of these long days in the hospital Kendall just slept. Especially when she would be receiving sedating drugs. I learned how to keep myself busy by reading books, watching Netflix, showering, and putting on my makeup so I could feel normal. I also took a lot of walks outside or even jogs sometimes. I found a nice grassy area outside of our building where I spent a lot of time sitting under trees praying and reflecting. I loved getting visitors to break up our days and I started journaling in all the journals I had received. One journal was for all the funny things Kendall said, one for the joy we found in each day, and one for what God was teaching me in this journey.

Mealtimes were always a favorite of mine because it was a chance to get out of my room. I sometimes would stop at the various stores on the way to the hospital cafeteria to browse. Cleveland Clinic has a lot of decent food options, and I grew to love the salad bar in the cafeteria. Many times, I would pass people I knew along the way like doctors, nurses, and other parents. It was a nice chance to stop and chat but also was a realization that my life was there in that hospital. You know you have been there too long when you are on a first-name basis with the cafeteria lady and parking attendant.

Facebook was a blessing during this time. It was my connection to the outside world and the only entertainment I had some days. I enjoyed keeping everyone updated on Kendall's status and sharing cute photos of her. I loved reading all the comments and having a way to converse with everyone while we were stuck in the hospital. I could ask for specific prayers, share praise reports, raise awareness for childhood cancer, and even post videos of Kendall when she was having fun. It truly was a community for me and a way to give others a glimpse into the life of a cancer family.

***

Scan day came for Kendall and they revealed exceptional tumor shrinkage. The main mass was about half the size it was at diagnosis and the other spots the cancer had spread to were now clear. There was a spot lighting up on her scan though between the aorta and vena cava that was concerning. The surgeons were not sure they would be able to remove that section of the tumor without putting Kendall at great risk. More discussions were yet to be had, and there was talk of bumping up her last chemo round and administering it before the surgery in hopes to shrink that spot more.

The tumor board met that next day and the radiologist pointed out another spot that was wrapped around many vessels. He stressed how difficult it would be to remove. If we proceeded with the surgery at Cleveland Clinic, the surgeons were telling us there was a chance they would not be able to remove all of the tumor. Wes and I did not like what we were hearing and asked for her scans and medical records to be sent to MSK for a second opinion. Our team got to work on sending them over. Then we waited.

We met with one of the surgeons at Cleveland Clinic in the meantime to go over everything and get our questions answered. He explained that the other pediatric surgeons on his team would be in the operating room and between the four of them, they would equal one Dr. La Quaglia. That didn't settle well with us, and we couldn't wait to hear back from MSK. We stayed up late researching, thinking, and praying.

I went to church while we were in the waiting and just happened to get a chance to speak with our senior pastor. I explained our situation to him and he had some great words of advice that stuck with me as the days continued. He asked me, "If the two hospitals were side by side, which would you choose?"

***

After some time had passed, we finally heard back from MSK. We found out a date that Dr. L. could perform the surgery and learned that our insurance was in network with them. We couldn't believe it! It was a clear sign for us.

Kendall's oncologist had spoken with Dr. L., and she called us one evening to go over everything. She explained what the plan for surgery was at Cleveland Clinic again, and then told us that Dr. L. said he was confident he could remove 90% if not all of her tumor. We had done our research on him, and he had an amazing reputation for taking on cases that other surgeons wouldn't touch. He operated on many difficult tumors like Kendall's and his confidence had us sold. The Cleveland Clinic surgeons said they could remove 90% as well, but they mentioned needing the vascular team present to help rebuild vessels that may be damaged from removing the tumor from them. Dr. L. had said nothing of the sorts.

We then read a quote from Dr.L. on the *Humans of New York* Facebook page that happened to be circulating while we were trying to make our decision. He talked about going to church and the bond he had with his patients. After reading that, we knew in our gut that he was Kendall's surgeon.

After prayer, sleepless nights, and a gut-wrenching decision, we told Kendall's oncologist we were going to go with Dr. L. We wanted only the best for Kendall, and he was the best in the country. We were scared to leave our home hospital and had no clue how long we would be gone, but we trusted that God had led us to this decision. I never thought I could handle traveling for her treatments but we made our decision and all we could do was keep moving forward. Our team was supportive and helped us start to make the arrangements to travel to MSK.

Kendall's surgery was then moved to Nov. 20th. We still went ahead with the early Halloween for Kendall since the doctors had decided to give her chemo round 6 while we waited for surgery. She would be dealing with low counts and side effects on the actual day of Halloween.

Our neighbors came through for us once again in the most wonderful way. They put up their Halloween decorations, dressed up in costumes, gathered in their driveways, and had all of Kendall and Alexa's favorite candies ready to go. It was so nice to see everyone, and the girls had the best time. Kendall dressed up as Snow White, and Alexa as Alice in Wonderland. We had to bring a wagon along to carry their haul, as there were many gifts for the girls along with the candy. I was so glad all the neighbors were able to see Kendall before her big surgery day. These were the moments that kept us going. The moments of knowing we were loved and never alone in this fight.

Chapter 7

Welcome to New York

As scared as I was for what may be waiting for us in NYC, I also found myself excited to explore the city as Kendall and I had never been. We would have some time for sightseeing before her surgery if everything went as planned.

While we waited for our time to depart, we celebrated Alexa's sixth birthday. Kendall was home and feeling well so she was able to join the party. We didn't keep her there long and she wore her mask to protect herself. The party room was full of sweet little girls in their fancy dresses and hats for the tea party themed occasion. Kendall felt so special wearing her pretty pink dress and was excited to see all the kids. My girls had recently received their first American Girl dolls from the Radiate Gold Foundation and they brought them to the party to partake in all the festivities.

The dance party was a big hit and Kendall loved dancing with me and the kids during a couple of songs. She also enjoyed pouring "tea" (which was lemonade) into her cup and spooning some to her doll, Ella. The guests were all so happy to see

Kendall as they gathered around her. Kendall sat next to her sister as everyone sang Happy Birthday to Alexa. I felt such immense joy that day. Both my girls were so happy, and it was a magical birthday party filled with people we love.

Kendall then headed back to the hospital and completed round 6 of chemo, but not without an extra hospital admission for a neutropenic fever. She was discharged in time to enjoy a week at home before our departure. I had a lot of phone calls back and forth with MSK during that time to get all the details and paperwork in order. Our church was so gracious to us and held prayer services for Kendall and our family. There was a service before we left to pray for our upcoming travels and for a successful surgery. With a lot of work and planning, everything came together.

I had arranged for my grandmother to come back and stay with Alexa while we were gone. My mom planned a few days to stay with us out in NYC to help support us with Kendall, and Wes got the time off approved that he needed at work. With the help of our social worker at Cleveland Clinic, we were connected to Wings Flights of Hope. This organization offers free flights for patients and their families who need medical treatment. Their pilots are all volunteers, which is amazing. I gave them a call and after some paperwork was in order, we were all set up for them to fly us out to NYC on our own private six-seater jet.

I also called the Ronald McDonald House (RMH) in NYC to see if they had room for us. After speaking to a couple of different people, we were all set up for our stay with them. We also connected to a childhood cancer foundation, Candlelighters NYC, who offered to have a stroller waiting for us at the front desk at the RMH so we didn't have to worry about packing one (not that we would have had room on the tiny jet for it anyway). They also had passes to various attractions in the city and would be there to support us in any other ways we needed. All these things that were falling into place confirmed for us that we had made the right choice.

That still didn't make me feel any less nervous though about going to a new hospital. The Cleveland Clinic had become like family to us. We were comfortable there so we had a lot of emotions with leaving and with never visiting the big city before, I was nervous about navigating and learning the ways of life there. I was thankful Wes was able to travel with us and that his boss was so accommodating.

My heart also broke for what I was about to witness my daughter go through. I feared seeing her after surgery and even had some fear that she might not make it through surgery. I was so thankful to have God to cast all my fears and anxieties on. I don't know how I could have gotten through without him. I was experiencing something with God that some may never get the chance to. I was completely dependent on him. Every chance I got I was on my knees in prayer begging, pleading, and desperate for Kendall's life to be spared.

Wes and I had started visiting the chapel in the hospital. Usually, no one was in there and it provided a quiet space for us to come together and pray for our daughter. We would get on our knees, fold our hands in prayer, and take turns talking to God. I knew the verse in Matthew 18:20 well, "For where two or three are gathered in my name, there am I among them" (ESV). I wanted to make sure we were praying together as I had seen the power of group prayer in the past.

I was full of worry, fear, and anxiety, but was trying my best to release all of that into the Lord's hands. In Matthew 6:30-34 Jesus says, "And if God cares so wonderfully for wildflowers that are here today and thrown into the fire tomorrow, he will certainly care for you. Why do you have so little faith? So don't worry about these things, saying, 'What will we eat? What will we drink? What will we wear? These things dominate the thoughts of unbelievers, but your heavenly Father already knows all your needs. Seek the Kingdom of God above all else, and live righteously, and he will give you everything you need. So don't worry about tomorrow, for tomorrow will bring its own worries. Today's trouble is enough for today" (NLT).

I was keeping these verses at the forefront of my mind and trusting that God would provide everything we needed in NYC. It's not easy to let go of fear and worry. I am a continual work in progress on this. Even Jesus' disciples who were with him in the flesh had doubts, fears, and worries (see Mark 4:35-41). I think it's just a natural human response to hardships that arise. But then we have to retrain our thoughts to focus on the God who never changes. Our rock, our constant. The God who is faithful and with us in all things. This is why reading the Bible is so important so that you have these verses stored in your mind to pull from when difficulties arise and you need guidance on how to face them. You can say to God, "Okay I am terrified, I don't want to do this, but would you please let me feel your presence and provide what I need to walk through this."

***

One last thing we did before our departure was to buy a gift for each day we were away for Alexa. This was an idea given to us by Kendall's psychologist and I loved the thought of her having a little note and gift from us to look forward to opening. We were not sure how long we would be gone exactly, but I had enough gifts for 12 days. I wrapped each one individually with a love note or some encouraging words for her. The items were mainly from the dollar store, nothing big or expensive. Kids just love to open things! And with that all set, it was time to depart.

Leaving that morning was so emotional. Our jet was due to arrive at Burke Lakefront Airport in Cleveland around 11 a.m. We would be arriving in the city on a Wednesday. We were so excited for Kendall and so was she since this was her first time on a plane! We had to pack light because there was not much storage on the jet. I literally could only pack three outfits, one pair of pajamas, and one pair of shoes, which was extremely hard for me. I layered on as many clothes as I could that day so I would have some additional clothing.

We arrived at the tiny airport and were greeted by the nicest receptionist. She gave us some water and warm cookies as we waited for our jet to arrive. We felt like royalty! I was a bit nervous as I had never been on such a small aircraft before and hoped my stomach could handle it. I worried for Kendall too, so I had a motion sickness wristband for her to wear and air sickness bags on hand.

Meeting our pilot (who actually was the founder of Wings Flights of Hope) was one of the highlights of our journey. He was like an angel that had come to our rescue to fly our daughter through the sky and toward our destination of hope and a cure. The kindness that poured from this man was just not something you get to experience often in life. He had so much empathy and love for the patients that he flew. He even had a binder full of photos of kids he had flown over the years. He could remember their names as he shared some of their stories with us. This is the kindness in the world you don't realize exists until you are fighting for life.

As he led us out to his plane, Wes and Kendall were hand in hand behind him and I was in the back snapping photos of them walking out to board. I wanted to capture every moment of our baby's first plane ride. There was joy, fear, and anxiety all filling up inside of me. I was so happy we could get her the care she needed but feared what was to come.

We got all settled and buckled in and had to put headsets on to help filter out the noise from the jet. We looked so official! And then we were off!

Riding in the jet wasn't as scary as I thought it would be. It does feel completely different than a commercial plane, but I felt safe. At one point during the flight, Kendall was able to move around. She took off her seatbelt and went over by Wes to see out of the window. He placed her on his lap, and she took her first peek out into the thick, cottonlike clouds. I was able to capture the moment on camera and share it on social media with everyone following her journey. She had the biggest smile and her face lit up. She kept saying "Wow, Wow!" as her jaw dropped. I was so glad she finally got her plane ride. Her first plane ride was supposed to be to see G.G. at the beach. We had to cancel that trip though because it was scheduled for just weeks after her diagnosis.

A short couple of hours later, we could see the New York City skyline out of the front window. What a sight to see! We arrived safe and sound, (without any upset bellies), at another small airport in New Jersey. Our pilot took some photos with us outside of his plane after we exited and hugged us goodbye. He left us with some encouraging words and told us to give him a call when we were ready to come home. We then called for an Uber and waited inside the airport for our next ride.

I was not thrilled about us riding in other people's cars, subways, or taxis. But, after speaking with many MSK families on a Facebook support group for the hospital, it seemed to be the best way to get around the city. They all had taken their children on these means of transportation, so it helped me feel a bit more comfortable. We just masked up and used a lot of hand sanitizer.

Kendall looking out of the plane
window for the first time

Our Uber arrived and surprisingly provided us with a nice clean car to travel in. We had a little bit of a drive into the city, along with traffic. Loads of traffic! I would never have been able to conquer driving there. It's a whole different kind of driving. My chest was so tight as I held on for dear life while our driver was weaving in and out of traffic. I could relax a little once we exited the bridges and were closer to the city. I pulled out my phone and put on a song Kendall and I had been listening to in preparation for our trip. It was "Welcome to New York," by Taylor Swift. We listened and sang to it as we approached the city. I may have even cried a little as I couldn't believe we were there, ready to take on a new chapter of her journey.

***

We pulled up to the Ronald McDonald House on the Upper East Side of NYC. The street looked just how it did in movies with all the brownstones and tall buildings surrounding us. We entered the house and got checked in at the counter, picked up our stroller, and then were walked to our room. We were pleasantly surprised at how nice the amenities were at RMH. Our room was updated with nice flooring and a tiled shower. It was pretty spacious as well for NYC. It came complete with a window seat that looked out into the city. I loved seeing Kendall sit there gazing out the window, taking in the new bustling scenery.

We had two full-size beds and a pull-out couch. It would be a little tight but cozy for the three of us plus my mom, but she wasn't due to arrive until the weekend. It ended up being only one or two nights where all of us were in the room since someone would be sleeping overnight with Kendall at the hospital.

There was just enough space in our room for Kendall to still have space to dance. She was fearless and just enjoying her life and being silly as usual. She would sing at the top of her lungs and twirled and spun herself while looking into the large full-length mirror on the wall. I wished that it could stay like that, how we were in that moment, but I knew what was awaiting us on Monday. I took Kendall's lead once again and tried to focus on just having fun and time with family until her surgery on Monday.

The first night we got settled and went to the Walgreens on the corner to get some items we needed. I loved seeing Kendall walk the streets of NYC in her custom Peppa Pig shoes a friend painted for her. We then unpacked and set up all her medical supplies in our room. Knowing how much of those to pack was a challenge without knowing how long we would be there.

Next, we explored the RMH and discovered the array of

amenities we had there. They had a nice lounge area on the first floor if you just needed to get out of your room and stretch or meet up with other families. This was the room they also hosted their events and parties in. The kids' playroom there was amazing and had so much to do. There was even a whole music room with a complete band set. Kendall enjoyed making music on the drums...actually more like banging - lol!

Another wonderful perk to staying at the RMH was that dinner was served every night. Different organizations or families would come in and serve. Sometimes they cooked, and sometimes it was catered. There were always different options, and we certainly ate well. We also had our own drawer in the refrigerator and freezer to store some food in, and we could use the large kitchen to cook or heat up food in the microwave whenever we wanted. We would be spending our Thanksgiving in the hospital, so I was happy to know there would be a dinner for us available at the RMH. It was just a short walk a couple of blocks down between the hospital and our room at RMH so that made it convenient.

***

We had a long day ahead of us that Thursday. We woke up and walked to the hospital and found our way to her CT scan. The doctor wanted to take one more scan before her surgery to see how chemo round 6 may have affected her tumor. We had to do a lot of waiting that day. The hospital was very busy. There were so many people everywhere, which made me cringe because we didn't want Kendall to be exposed to any germs.

After her scan, we headed up to the pediatric oncology floor to meet one of the doctors on the neuroblastoma team. The floor was decorated so fun and with color, something we weren't used to at the Cleveland Clinic. There was so much to look at and a fun playroom for Kendall to play in. Unfortunately, Kendall had a little runny nose and they swabbed her when we got there. She tested positive for rhinovirus (common cold) and had to be put directly into a room. The playroom had to wait, which was disappointing for all of us.

The rooms on the outpatient floor were divided by curtains, which seemed so odd, especially with trying to keep cancer kids safe. No walls, just curtains. They also had an open area with reclining chairs in a circle where kids would sit to get their chemo like you often see in movies. We could hear everyone in the other rooms while we waited and waited. There was not much peace. We had some fun entertainment from a clown and the music and art therapist, but the day still dragged on. We met some of their team and spoke with one of the many doctors. We were supposed to meet Dr. L. that day, but he ended up getting caught up in surgery and couldn't see us. After being there most of the morning and afternoon waiting, they finally let us go. We were exhausted and now had to return the next morning to meet Dr. L.

I don't remember doing too much that evening. We did have family in NYC and met up with Wes' cousin and her husband for dinner. It was nice to have them there to show us around and support us.

We made sure Kendall got her formula feeds that night in our room. We were so thankful for her G tube since chemo made food taste funny to her, and she couldn't handle some of the smells. Her formula was giving her the nutrition she needed and keeping her weight on. She actually had some decent meat on her bones going into surgery. She looked great and her skin was glowing. Her nutritionist had us increase the amount of formula she was getting a bit before we left for NYC so she could have a little extra weight since she would lose some during the surgery recovery.

The next day, we traveled back to MSK and got to meet the long-awaited, Dr. La Quaglia. He was so kind and great with Kendall. She took right to him. She had had a dream the night prior that she was swimming with dolphins and she didn't hesitate to tell him all about it.

We went over her scan, and he showed us all of the locations where her tumor was wrapped around vessels, as well as what organs might be affected. Something else he shared that we were not aware of was that she had cancer in her pancreas on her last scan, but it appeared that chemo round 6 may have cleared it. He explained that there was a chance he would have to remove the top part of her pancreas if he opened her up and still saw cancer there. This would then make it a more complicated surgery.

He explained that he would make a U-shaped incision on the right side of her abdomen to access her tumor. He also said he might have to do the same on her left side at a later time if he couldn't reach the tumor from the right side incision. We asked on a scale of 1-10 how bad her tumor was since he had seen many cases. He told us he had seen worse, but hers was an 8. He stressed how risky this surgery was going to be and how aggressive he would need to be to ensure he got it all out. It was going to be a long surgery day, but we were confident in our surgeon and our choice to travel to MSK after speaking with him. Our daughter was in good hands and God had led us there.

We were out of the hospital by lunchtime that day and had a few days to explore the city before her big surgery on Monday. We updated our friends, family, and Kendall's pages regarding our meeting, and asked for prayers that cancer would not be on her pancreas and that the surgeon could completely remove the tumor. Kendall also couldn't get worse with her little cold or else the surgery would have to be rescheduled. I was worried about that, but luckily Kendall's runny nose cleared up quickly.

We had a lot of sightseeing we wanted to fit in but knew Kendall could only do so much. Plus, there were so many people in the city and we wanted to keep her healthy too. We decided a trip to the Central Park Zoo in the open air was a good choice. The weather wasn't too cold yet and we were comfortable with our winter coats and hats on. Even better, we received tickets from Candlelighters NYC to go to the zoo for free! Kendall had the best day seeing all the animals and spending time with Mommy and Daddy. We loved the sea lion show and the beautiful sights inside Central Park. Afterward, we stopped to enjoy some NYC-style pizza and made a trip to the cute candy store across from the RMH for a sweet treat.

The next day we planned to go to Times Square to take Kendall to the Disney store. We put a face mask on her and managed to make our way through the packed store and long line. She loved looking at everything and picked out a unique *Frozen* Anna doll to take home with us. She hadn't been shopping since her diagnosis, so this was a real treat for her. We didn't hang around Times Square too long as it was just too crowded for our liking.

We headed to Macy's next, which wasn't terribly crowded. It was a Christmas wonderland there already and we had so much fun looking at all their displays and taking pictures with all the photo ops. Kendall even got to write and mail a letter to Santa. It was so amazing to walk through and see the hundreds of glittery paper snowflakes hanging from the ceilings. It was just how I had pictured it to be. The city was preparing for the Macy's Thanksgiving Day Parade, so they already had started setting up outside of Macy's. It really was a magical time to visit the city.

Later that evening, the RMH was hosting a Christmas party for the families. Santa was coming and our ticket to the party was that we had to wear matching Christmas pajamas that the RMH provided earlier in the day. I loved all the creativity and the memories they were providing families while we all were away from home. The night was full of fun, gifts for Kendall, crafts, and food. We were able to meet some other parents and cancer warriors at the party. We also were able to connect with several of the parents we had talked with in our neuroblastoma support group on Facebook.

***

Sunday of that weekend my mom arrived in NYC. I was so happy to see her and to have her with us. Moms just make it all better. I immediately felt more at ease.

We got Mom settled into our room and then headed out for a day of sightseeing since she had never been to NYC either. On her must-see list was the 9/11 Memorial and Museum. So, we all hopped in an Uber and headed there. It was a sobering experience as we walked through and saw all the lives lost that day. It is a day we Americans will never forget.

After I dried my tears from viewing the museum, we took Mom to Rockefeller Center to see the ice skating rink and giant Christmas tree. We also walked by Saks Fifth Avenue to watch the Christmas characters in the windows. We then went inside to browse all the expensive clothing. That in itself was mind-blowing that an article of clothing could cost nearly $10,000!

We headed back to the RMH for dinner and then settled into our room for the night. We had to be at the hospital bright and early Monday morning for Kendall's surgery. My worries and anxieties were creeping back in again, but Kendall wasn't worried. She knew she was going to have surgery to get her "boo-boo" out, but she wasn't letting that stop her from playing, dancing, and cracking jokes. She was once again being my brave, strong girl and choosing to find joy.

I wanted so badly to respond like Kendall, but I was a bit of a wreck. My chest hurt from my anxiety, and it was hard to sleep that night. I stayed up late talking to God and reciting scripture until I could find myself in a better state of mind. We had no other choice. We had to go through this to get closer to the end of this journey. It was one step closer to getting Kendall healed. All I could do was trust God to take care of her, pray for the best possible outcome, and continue to turn over my fears and worries to him.

My fears were still there the next morning, but it was okay to be scared. That just meant that we were about to do something really brave. And brave was the word for Kendall that morning. She was having so much fun in the pre-op room with the nurses and the new toys they brought her. She even made a FaceTime call to one of her best friends while she waited to get wheeled to the operating room. They were making themselves turn into animals with filters while getting some giggles in. Kendall was just so calm and all smiles. I know she really had no idea of how extensive this surgery would be, but she still inspired me with the courage and attitude she had.

And then the time had come. Dr. La Quaglia was ready for Kendall.

Chapter 8

The World's Longest Surgery... (Or So It Seemed)

Watching your child get put to sleep and knowing that when they wake up and you see them again, they will be forever scarred and intubated is a feeling I wish no parent would ever have to feel. As hopeful as I was to get Kendall's tumor out, I was still so worried to see my baby after she came out of surgery. Kendall was going through more than I had ever gone through in my life and I wished so badly that I could endure the pain and recovery for her.

The nurse told us she would give us updates throughout the day and after we kissed Kendall goodbye, she escorted us to the waiting room where we would end up staying for the next 10 hours, minus a break for lunch.

In addition to having my mom in the waiting room with us, Wes' cousin also came to the hospital to spend the day with us and to be there for emotional support. I prayed every chance I could while I waited and knew that so many were praying with me and standing in the gap when I couldn't. I had some devotional books with me to comfort me and give me hope as we waited. We would receive a message on our pager every couple of hours and they all said that Kendall was doing great.

The day was coming to a close, so we were surprised we hadn't heard that she was in recovery yet. My worries were kicking up a notch and I feared something hadn't gone as planned, or that Dr. L. indeed found cancer in her pancreas.

After many hours of waiting and waiting, we finally got the page that Kendall was in recovery and that she did great. Her surgery started a little late, hence the delay. So many emotions went through me as I read that update. It was such a sense of relief to know our baby had made it through the surgery. She was still with us. I don't know how these surgeons operate on a patient for so many hours. I can only imagine how drained they must be afterward.

We were told to head upstairs to meet with Dr. L. to go over the details of the surgery. Once we arrived to the floor, we had to do more waiting. And then finally we were seated in the room where Dr. L. would be out shortly to talk to us. My nerves were shot, and I was exhausted and worn from the emotional toll of the day. It was nearly 10 p.m. at this point. Wes' cousin and my mom had hung in there with us all day. We were all in the room anxiously awaiting the news.

Finally, we heard a knock on the door, and in he came. He reassured us right away that she was doing great, and that she made it through the surgery. He explained that she had no complications and only one incision on her right side. She only lost her right adrenal gland and was able to keep her other organs. There was not any cancer found in her pancreas. Her tumor was wrapped around many vessels and major arteries, so it took a lot of time to remove it all. The main tumor he removed was around the size of a softball. As he spoke, I was feeling more and more like I could breathe again. So many prayers were answered.

"So does this mean you were able to remove all of the

tumor?" I asked. Dr. L. explained that from what he could see from the incision made, he had removed all of the tumor! I repeated back to him what he said just to clarify. He said we still needed to continue on with treatment and refrain from using the term "NED" (which meant no evidence of disease) until we had her scans in another month. But for now, he said we had every reason to celebrate. We all immediately burst into happy tears and hugged each other. I was overjoyed with our decision to come to MSK. I remember pacing the room back and forth, unable to stay seated, almost in disbelief that we got the news we wanted. I had so much hope at that moment. Hope that my baby had a chance at life again. We were celebrating, praising God, and had so much faith that Kendall was going to be okay.

I thanked Dr. L. over and over but he stopped me and said, "Don't thank me," and then he pointed to the sky. Hearing him give God the credit verified even further that he was the right choice for Kendall. He treated each child as if they were his own and dedicated his life to saving others. He is a truly special person to spend so much time away from his own family and to endure such long invasive surgeries. I can only imagine the toll that takes on a person. I am forever grateful for his time, knowledge, and gift.

We had a little more time to wait before the nurse would take us to see Kendall. We all started calling our family members in the meantime to get the news out. I also updated our Facebook pages so everyone could join in the celebration. It was such a joyous moment to share our good news with everyone.

***

When I saw Kendall for the first time in the PICU after her surgery, it took the breath right out of me again. Tears (sad tears this time) formed in my eyes as I saw her intubated in her bed with all kinds of tubes coming out of her. She was so puffy and didn't look like herself. My heart hurt for her. I just wanted to be able to make her all better and save her from all this pain, but I couldn't.

Her eyes were closed, but Wes and I told her that Mommy, Daddy, and Nana were there now (Wes' cousin had gone home to give us time with her). Her incision was what I was so anxious to see. I lifted up her gown gently to take a look to see how bad it was. Dr. L did such a great job with her incision, and it looked much better than I expected, though it was about 14 inches long.

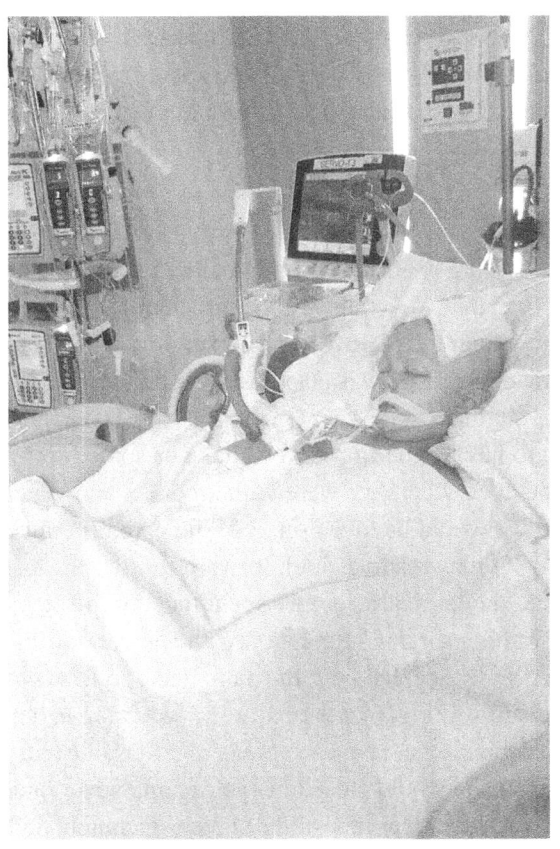

Kendall after her tumor resection surgery

The nurses in the PICU were amazing. They were so kind and gentle and took good care of Wes and me as well. Only one of us could stay the night in the room with her. I did not want to leave her but decided that Wes could stay, and Mom and I would head back to the RMH. I needed a good night's rest anyway after the long day we had. We stayed as long as we could before visiting hours were over. I stroked her soft, bald head and kissed it over and over. She had a tube down her throat, and drainage tubes coming out of her sides. They told us she would probably need around 10 days to recover. All I could do was continue to trust God that he would see her through this, and my little girl would be laughing and smiling again before I knew it.

***

Thanksgiving was quickly approaching, and we knew before we left home that we would still be inpatient for the holiday. The hospital was planning a lovely Thanksgiving dinner for the families and the RMH was also hosting a big dinner. A Special Wish had a connection in NYC with the NYFD, so they too were planning to have some firefighters make us some food. We were so blessed everywhere we went with kindness and generosity. Knowing we would be loved on, fed, and cared for during the upcoming holiday made us look forward to it.

On Tuesday of that week, we spent most of the day at the hospital waiting for any interaction with Kendall we could get. She was heavily sedated with the pain meds, so it was a lot of watching and waiting. Occasionally she would open her eyes and we would quickly get up and approach her bedside and talk to her, but then she would close her eyes again. Never once though did she try to tug at her tubes. She stayed so content and calm and laid there like the wonderful angel she was. She amazed us, along with the staff.

Kendall was such a good patient that the nurses didn't want her to leave the PICU. I loved staying there because it was fairly quiet, and the care was exceptional. Plus, I was dreading having to share a room once she was discharged from the PICU, which was one downfall to coming to this hospital. I loved having our large room and plenty of space in the PICU. I would stay there as long as they let us.

At MSK, not only did they feed the patients, but they fed the parents too. And they actually had really good hospital food! I looked forward to mealtimes and calling in my food order. It's the little things! They also had a candy cart that they wheeled to each room. It was filled with all kinds of treats, and you could pick a few items from it. Kendall, unfortunately, didn't get to enjoy it with the state she was in.

On Wednesday, Kendall was starting to stay awake for longer periods. It was harder for me to see her awake because I could then see how uncomfortable she was with being intubated. The only way we could communicate with her was through her eyes and any head nods she gave us. She always enjoyed getting her feet rubbed so we would ask her if she wanted us to rub them and she would nod her head yes. It was a precious way to care for her and be close to her while she was bedridden. Occasionally, I would see tears fall from her eyes and I would wipe them for her. Each tear broke me a little more as that told me she was feeling pain or sadness. I can only imagine what thoughts were going through her head and how scary all this was for her.

When we began our journey with Kendall, the palliative care nurse on our team told us that the parents that do the best through their child's cancer journey are the ones who take breaks. Wes and I had been good through the months with taking breaks when we needed it and as hard as it was in NYC, I knew we still needed some time away. The days can be long and draining in the hospital, especially when you are watching someone suffer.

Since Kendall was still sleeping most of the time, I decided to take the RMH up on a trip to see the Macy's Thanksgiving Day parade floats lined up the night before the parade. My mom came along with me, and we had a nice couple of hours together having a once-in-a-lifetime experience. It was so nice to have a change of scenery and share laughs with my mom. Laughter is such great medicine and healing to the soul! It was a special night viewing all the floats and getting to walk the VIP side, which allowed us to be up close to the floats. Just those couple of hours lifted my spirits and refreshed me enough to be able to face more long hours in the hospital.

***

You would think spending Thanksgiving in the hospital would be miserable, but it actually was a very special time for us. We had so much to be thankful for and I was overwhelmed with gratitude that day for all God had done for us and for Kendall in her journey. I could have easily looked at our situation, and my daughter hooked up to tubes in her hospital bed and deemed this the worst Thanksgiving ever. But God was working in both Wes and me and our hearts were softened, not bitter. We were celebrating every small step Kendall took in her recovery and were so grateful for more time with her. Plus, we needed to maintain a positive attitude for Kendall to help keep her spirits up and for her to feel love, not negativity. Kendall had always been so great up to this point with finding the joy, so that is what we would do too.

On Thanksgiving morning, my mom and I arrived at the hospital and put on the Thanksgiving Day parade, which felt like a bit of holiday normalcy. I still felt so bad for Kendall though that she still was not able to talk with the tube down her throat. I couldn't wait to be able to hold her again tube-free.

Wes had to head back to the RMH that morning to meet the NYFD firefighters. We were so grateful that A Special Wish Cleveland had arranged this special meal for us. Another once-in-a-lifetime opportunity! The firemen cooked the meal themselves and two of them met Wes to deliver. It was such a good meal, and it gave us leftovers to have over the next couple of days. We only snacked on it a little bit for lunch because back at the hospital, a big meal with all the fixings was being served on the pediatric oncology floor. We were glad we had the meal from the firefighters because we weren't thinking the hospital meal would be too tasty. Boy, were we wrong! That will forever go down as one of the best Thanksgiving meals I have ever had. Who knew? MSK knows food there. The spread was huge! They had everything you could want in a Thanksgiving meal and more! Mom, Wes, and I enjoyed it so much.

Not only were we so thankful for good food that day, but later on Kendall was able to get her tube out of her throat, some IVs out, and her urinary catheter removed! They continued to keep her drainage tube in. She could move her arm freely now and she held Wes' hand for a while, a sweet moment for them. Her face was pretty puffy, and I could tell she wasn't feeling so great. She was so strong though through her discomfort and even got out of her bed for the first time since her surgery that day! She sat in a chair for half an hour. We were so proud of her that she made the effort.

The nurses were falling in love with her, and one even said that she was one of the most amazing patients she had ever had. She was in awe over how calm she had been and how sweet she was. That was our girl, stealing hearts out in NYC. Amidst all the pain and suffering, our hearts were beyond full of thankfulness that Thanksgiving.

***

The next day, Kendall tried to talk a little and had two popsicles. She got out of bed multiple times and sat in a chair. Before the day ended, she gave us a big smile! I was able to capture it on camera to share on Facebook. I can't tell you what that did for my heart. Kendall got knocked down so many times but would always get back up and pull herself through. I knew from her smile that my little superhero was turning a corner and would persevere like she always did.

Dr. L. would come and check on her occasionally those first few days. He stressed how important it would be to continue with her treatment plan. We knew that MSK did not do transplants and we wanted his opinion on which route we should go…head home for stem cell transplants or continue on to radiation and more chemo at MSK. He asked us if we were happy with our care back home, which we were. He felt that the transplant would be beneficial to her but of course, she was welcome to stay at MSK under their care as well. He seemed to support both options which didn't help us with making our decision.

With any decisions we made for Kendall, we prayed and took time to think them through. We talked with other neuroblastoma parents and looked up statistics and other research. My stomach was in knots over having to make the decision. We talked it through together and with our parents as well. It really didn't matter which route we chose though because I would forever wonder if the other path we didn't choose would have been better for her. It felt so unfair that we had to make a choice.

After losing many hours of sleep sick over this, we decided that we would return to our home hospital where we had entrusted our daughter's care to from day one. We knew that we could come back to MSK if she relapsed in the future. They were the place to be for relapse. Our thought process was to throw every option we had at her cancer. We were told that if we skipped the transplant now, we couldn't go back later and give her that treatment. But we could return to MSK in the future and try some of their treatment options. We wanted to take the most aggressive approach.

We decided to go ahead with the transplants while we had the chance and then if she didn't reach NED after we had completed her full course of treatment, we would go back to MSK so she could receive their immunotherapy, which was called 3F8. This treatment was only available at their hospital at the time and was achieving great results in children. So, we decided to keep MSK in our back pockets and knew they would be there for us if we needed them.

Once Kendall got her drainage tube out and showed more improvement, our time in the PICU was over. We knew it would come to an end eventually, but we were sad to go. I didn't know what was waiting for us on the pediatric oncology floor. I hadn't heard the best stories from other parents about the shared, tiny rooms and single-person bathroom for the whole floor! Thankfully, God came through for us once again and answered my prayer that we would not have to share a room. I thought we just got lucky our first night there, but we had the room to ourselves the entire stay. I couldn't believe it!

The nurses were just as sweet on the inpatient floor as they were in the PICU. It was hard though being at a different hospital with different policies and care instructions. There were definitely a lot of differences, but we didn't make too much of a fuss and trusted that she was getting the best care and that they had good reason for their protocols.

Each day Kendall got a little stronger and was a little more herself. She would interact with the art and music therapist a bit and play with her toys for short periods. Our room was tiny with minimal storage and only a pull-out chair for the parents to sleep on, a far cry from our accommodations at Cleveland Clinic. Our room there felt like a mansion in comparison. But that is NYC for you. They have to fit as many patients as they can in there. You can imagine how stir-crazy we were getting.

***

My mom was going to be heading back to Ohio soon, so Wes and I took advantage of her being able to stay with Kendall so we could have a night out. We went to dinner and to the Empire State Building. We also took in some other sights along the way like the Radio City Music Hall and The Today Show. I was so thankful we were able to experience so much of the city while we were there. And my NYC adventures weren't even over yet.

Wes and I both took turns each day taking breaks from the hospital. I was able to meet up with Wes' cousin again and have dinner with her, and I also took a walk to Central Park and got lost on the way back, so I had to hail a cab. I had wandered so far away from the Upper East Side. I have the worst sense of direction!

I also enjoyed some window shopping and picking up groceries in their small grocery stores. I enjoyed so many of the excellent restaurants surrounding the hospital and the RMH. It was such a different way of living there than I was used to. The city started to grow on me in that second week of us being there. I would walk the streets with a smile on my face and a skip in my step. I loved feeling like a New Yorker for a bit and was trying to make the best of our situation, even though I was really starting to miss home.

One day, I was able to meet up with a fellow neuroblastoma mom and her warrior daughter for lunch. I was so excited to meet her in person, as we had only previously spoken on Facebook. We also were able to enjoy a night together with Candlelighters NYC. We took the subway to Rockefeller Center for the Christmas tree lighting. We were able to spend the evening in the Channel 3 News studios, which gave us a perfect view from their windows of the tree. It was such an amazing night and I teared up when we counted down to the lighting.

I was extra emotional for my friend that evening as she had found out earlier that there were no more treatment options for her daughter. This was the reality I was living in. I continued to hope for the best but prepare for the worst too as I was seeing cancer take so many children's lives. I was so grateful for the time I got to spend with my new friends.

Candlelighters NYC had been so good to us while we were there. Not only did they give us once-in-a-lifetime opportunities, but they also provided gift cards so we could get groceries and I even got to spend an afternoon in the director's New York City apartment. She allowed me to shop for Kendall and me in her closet full of goodies, and I left with all kinds of items that I wasn't sure we would have enough room for on our tiny jet home. One thing she said to me that will always stay with me is that I would always have family in New York City now. That made me feel so special and loved.

***

Back at the hospital, Kendall was getting closer and closer to discharge. Day by day she got stronger and stronger. I was able to take her to the playroom on the inpatient floor one afternoon. There wasn't a whole lot to do in there for her, but she enjoyed playing with some Barbie dolls and getting out of her room for a while.

She was finally discharged on a Tuesday. We had a follow-up appointment with Dr. L. on Thursday of that same week. Until then, we tried our best to care for her back at the RMH and enjoy the time we had left in NYC.

Kendall had a lot of extra meds to fit in and we had to take her tube feeds slowly, which meant she was hooked up most of the day. On her breaks, we ventured to the playroom at the RMH and walked around the house enjoying all of the Christmas decorations. Kendall was a little paler, weaker, and thinner than when we first arrived in NYC, but her smile was still as big as ever as she posed in front of the Christmas trees for my camera.

We had her follow-up appointment and got the okay from Dr. L. to head back home. Kendall was able to finally play in the awesome playroom on the outpatient floor that day as well and she loved it! We called Wings Flights of Hope to let our pilot know we were able to go home. He said that he was coming back from vacation, but he would fly over to get us Friday evening. Talk about kindness and putting others above yourself! The heart he has for helping people is just incredible. He literally got off a plane from his vacation and hopped on his jet to come to get us. Now that is what serving others looks like!

While we waited for him Friday evening, I was getting texts from my mom asking when we would be home. She wanted to know the exact timing and her questions seemed suspicious. I knew back home our friends and family were up to something. My mom told me to text her when we landed in Cleveland. We were supposed to be home around 8 p.m. Friday but our pilot was running late.

Seeing NYC from the plane window at night as we flew home was super emotional. NYC had been so good to us, and I was sad to leave all our new friends there. I also still had some anxiety over whether we had made the right choice to return home. But I believe that God guided us in making that decision because we asked for his help and we made the best decision we could with the information that we had.

We ended up arriving at the airport an hour later than we originally thought. We thanked our pilot and said our goodbyes, then got in our car and headed home. As we turned down our street, luminaries in white paper bags were lined on both sides. We came around the slight corner to see a crowd of neighbors, friends, and family in our yard awaiting our arrival and holding up signs. Our home was decked out in Christmas lights and decorations that our neighbors put up. I felt so bad they had to wait so long for us since it was cold outside. We exited our car to hear everyone cheering Kendall on and celebrating her successful surgery and recovery. It was truly a heartwarming moment that I will never forget. It was such a warm welcome home after being away in NYC for two weeks. We were so grateful to have so much support.

Alexa ran outside to reunite with us and hugged us all. Kendall stayed in her daddy's arms and was a bit shy in front of everyone. She gave them some smiles and then we got her inside pretty quickly since it was cold, and she had had a long day. My grandma was inside so Wes and I stayed and conversed with our neighbors on our front lawn for a while. It felt so good to be home and surrounded by our tribe once again.

We had survived what we feared in NYC and were another step further in her treatment plan. We were proving to ourselves that we could do hard things after all.

Chapter 9

A Christmas Miracle Gone

A sign hangs in our home today that says, "It's so good to be home." I had someone make it for me during Kendall's journey because the time that we did get to be home was so very precious. That December we spent the most time home since her diagnosis. Things almost felt normal as we were all home together as a family and starting to prepare for Christmas.

Kendall was recovering well and looking so good. She was having the best time being with her sister and they were up to their usual shenanigans again. They frolicked around the house together in their princess gowns while singing and dancing. They played dolls and house, watched movies together, and we baked lots of cookies and cupcakes. Laughter and joy filled our home, and it was a wonderful time of restoration for all of us. Kendall still had multiple checkups in the outpatient clinic each week but being able to return home after was a blessing.

The next steps in her treatment were to get her scans and then begin the first of two autologous stem cell transplants. She was scheduled to go in on Christmas evening and to begin chemo that next day in the morning. We had a meeting with the transplant team to go over all the details and what we could expect. I was absolutely dreading this part of treatment even more so after finding out more about it. We knew we were facing around a 30-day hospital stay and if Wes or I became sick with any little symptom, we couldn't stay with her as she would be at a high risk of infection during this time. No visitors would be allowed, not even her sister (insert sad face emoji).

We learned that we also had to be careful about the food and items we brought in her room. We couldn't have any fresh fruits or vegetables as they can spread germs, who knew!? Kendall also would not be able to eat fresh fruits, vegetables, or any restaurant food for 100 days after her transplant because of bacteria.

Some other disappointing side effects were that she would be at risk for developing a secondary cancer, leukemia, and that she would have a low chance of conceiving naturally later in her life. She also would be getting a chemo called Thiotepa, which could cause burns to her skin. Because of that risk, she would have to receive sponge baths every six hours while she was receiving the chemo to help prevent this.

As you can imagine, this was a lot of information to take in and prepare for. So even though we were getting lots of time at home, I was still busy getting ready for our upcoming extended stay at the Cleveland Clinic.

The girls were receiving so many gifts throughout the month and enjoying playing with all their new toys. The hospital had a special Christmas party for the pediatric oncology patients with Santa and lots of gifts. Kendall was so spoiled and received some of the items on her wish list. She was so happy and smiling so big as she opened them. I had her all dressed up in a fancy Christmas dress and a beautiful headband. She was glowing and full of joy!

There were also other organizations that blessed our family during this time. Our family was adopted through A Special Wish and Jeremy Cares. The girls got to submit their wish lists, as well as Wes and me. A family shopped for us and then came to our home to deliver the gifts. It was such a special moment for them and for us. Kendall received her pink ride-on convertible, which took some time for her to learn how to drive. It was hilarious letting her practice in our basement as she would bump into everything and crack herself up. Joy, joy, joy! That was what was filling our home that holiday season.

***

As much fun as we were having at home, we still had in the back of our minds the upcoming scans and the anxiety that came with them ("scanxiety" is what us cancer parents call it). We were asking everyone to pray so hard for clear scans. That would be the best Christmas gift we could receive. We were so hopeful and praying and trusting that God would make this possible. Her doctors were expecting good scans, so we went into scan day feeling good.

I once had a boss who would say, "It's a Christmas miracle," anytime something went our way during the season. I was hoping that I would be able to say those same words after we received her scan results, but sadly that wasn't the case.

We had an appointment with Kendall's doctor down at the hospital to go over her scans. Wes came with me that day as we felt this was an important one for him not to miss. Another doctor on our team also joined us in the room and we all sat down to talk. I immediately knew something was up.

Once again, we were completely crushed and devastated to hear that there was still significant tumor showing up on her scans. While the right side where Dr. L. had made the incision was clear, the left side still was showing tumor uptake. This meant either Dr. L. couldn't see it from where he had made the incision, or that the tumor grew while she had been off treatment and recovering. Our team consulted with Dr. L. and he declined to perform more surgery on her at that time and suggested we proceed with the transplant. The tumor was wrapped around many major vessels and arteries and he feared he would have to remove her left adrenal gland as well, leaving her with none. The hope was that Kendall could return for more surgery in the future once the tumor had shrunk more.

It was the nightmare that just wouldn't end. Any glimmers of hope we got were just that. A glimmer. We could never seem to bask in good news for long before it was snatched up from us once again, leaving us in utter despair. I felt like such a fool for celebrating the possibility of her being tumor-free just weeks earlier. *How was I now going to tell our friends, family, and Facebook followers that after all that, the tumor still resided?* That is cancer. So many highs and lows. A rollercoaster of emotions. I was left so perplexed.

I couldn't help but skip back to Dr. L.'s words to us about how important it was going to be to get most, if not all of her tumor out for her survival. We addressed our concerns about continuing on while she still had so much tumor left with our team. We had heard from our support group that ideally, you shouldn't proceed with a transplant if there is still significant tumor remaining after chemo and surgery. But our doctors from both hospitals felt it was crucial to get her to transplant and high-dose chemo ASAP to stop any more growth. We had faith that the doctors had made the best decision for her so we made plans to arrive to the PICU where her transplant would be held on Christmas evening at 8 p.m. Her doctors were hopeful that the transplant would clear her cancer or most of it, and explained that neuroblastoma responded well to radiation which would be the next step after.

This was the point in her journey where it was really hard to hold onto hope. We were in the waiting. The waiting for our daughter's healing. It was discouraging to beg and plead with God day after day to heal her, only to receive less than good news time and time again. I was realizing just how difficult this monster was going to be to beat. I was beginning to wonder if it was God's will for her to be healed here on Earth or not.

The enemy was trying to shake me and have me turn my back on God after unanswered prayers. But I didn't choose to follow Christ only if he answered all my prayers and gave me a perfect life. I chose to follow him so that I could have eternal life in the promise of Heaven. So that I could have a relationship with him and get to know him and his Word. So that I would never have to walk alone. So that he could be my guide on how to navigate this difficult life here on Earth. Everything I needed to know is in the Bible. His words have taught me how to live and have given me the ONLY hope that can NEVER be just a glimmer.

While I waited for Kendall's healing, I continued to seek his presence and continued to hope and trust. MercyMe's song, "Even If" kept playing through my mind during this time. It was about holding onto the hope we have in Christ even if he doesn't answer our prayers the way we want him to. Christ was speaking to me again through this song. My friend gifted me a necklace that had a charm that said "Even If" on it. It was my reminder that even if God chose not to heal Kendall here on Earth, we would still trust and have hope in Jesus.

***

As we were getting hit with this devastating news, back at home Alexa's Christmas concert was the next day. I didn't know how I was going to pull myself together to go while I was breaking into more and more pieces inside. But we had to wipe our tears and be Alexa's mom and dad too. She needed us equally as much.

It was a real challenge that morning to keep myself composed. We were so proud of Alexa and her participation in the songs. She even had a special part that we didn't know about which made us smile. One of the songs they sang was so pretty and touched my heart. It ended up making me cry. Wes and I held each other as we both felt emotional. We were being the strong parents we had to be, while utterly breaking inside. We were secretly wondering if we would ever see the day that Kendall would perform at her school concert.

I scanned the room and realized that most of the people there had no idea we had a child fighting for her life at home. You have no idea what people walking amongst you might be going through. Life can be so cruel and unfair and there is great suffering in our broken world. In fact, we were about to head into some of the worst suffering we would see with Kendall's next part of treatment.

Chapter 10

The Pure Evil That is Transplant

The time had come. It was Christmas Day, and we were due at the hospital later that evening to get Kendall prepped for chemo, which started the next day. This was the part of the treatment I had dreaded and feared something terrible. I had seen children on our neuroblastoma support group page suffer from painful sores on their bodies and horrible burns from the Thiotepa chemo. I even saw death as a result of stem cell transplants. I wished so badly that I could have just rescued my daughter from all this suffering and taken her to a beach to run free and be a kid. But I also wished for healing and there were no other options on the table but to start this next phase of her treatment.

We spent that morning celebrating Jesus' birth with our usual traditions. We sang "Happy Birthday" to Jesus and blew the candles out on his cake that we baked. We read about his birth in the book of Luke and then we opened presents. The girls had fun playing with their new toys that morning and we made the most of our last day all together before being separated for an extended time. I had been packing prior to Christmas for the hospital so that we could enjoy our day, but I still had to sneak away to pack some last-minute items.

It was such a hard place to be. I was grateful we could spend most of our Christmas day at home, but it hardly felt like a normal holiday when I knew we were hours away from our longest hospital stay yet. I was trying to cherish my last moments that day with my girls as I knew they wouldn't see each other for a while, and I would hardly see Alexa through this next phase. We were so blessed to have had all that time home together in the month of December before our time of separation. It gave us the restoration and strength we needed for this next leg of the journey.

I packed up the car that evening which was quite a heavy load this time. Kendall and I said our goodbyes and we headed off into the fear of the unknown.

The great thing about the hospital was the people there that cared for us. We were always welcomed like we were family when we arrived at our floor. It did feel like "home" sometimes and I was always grateful for the support we had there and all the hugs. That said, of course, we were spoiled by our team since we had to go in on Christmas Day! They had presents waiting for Kendall in her room, Christmas decorations up, and excitement on their faces to see us and care for Kendall.

That evening was spent getting settled and unpacked. This was our first time staying for an extended time in the PICU, and our room was huge! Kendall also would have only one nurse to tend to her care for each 12-hour shift (I seriously don't know how nurses can work such long shifts and be coherent enough to administer lifesaving medications. Nurses are heroes in my book). Kendall would have to be monitored more closely and required a lot of round-the-clock care for this treatment which is why it was done in the PICU.

I brought Kendall's big *Frozen* rug that she received from Dec My Room, and she played for a while on it that night. She played with her games and made cute bracelets. Even one of her favorite nurses stopped by to paint her nails for her. Then Kendall returned the favor and painted hers. I decorated her room in Shimmer and Shine decorations this time and set out all my inspirational signs on the window mantle. Pre-hydration for chemo was started and we were ready to battle the beast.

***

The next morning, the bags were hung, and chemo was started. They track this day as Day -7. Then it counts down to day 0 and then Day +1 starts the stem cell transplant. Kendall's team made me a helpful calendar to track the days.

I had everyone praying so hard against any Thiotepa chemo burns. Our hospital seemed to have the best plan and protocols in place to prevent Kendall from getting these awful burns. They removed the dressing around her port and wrapped gauze around her instead to prevent burns in that area. She received a sponge bath every six hours while receiving Thiotepa chemo, as well as a gown and bed change to prevent the chemo from settling on her skin. I can't remember exactly how long we had to do this, but I believe we could stop 24 hours after the last bag of Thiotepa chemo was administered.

She received the Thiotepa chemo for two days and then received a different chemo for four hours each day for the remainder of the days in that week. She had one day to rest and then on a Tuesday, she would receive her cells. She had been doing fairly well up to this point. A little sleepy, a little pukey…the usual.

Kendall's child life team had gifted her a Little Tikes food truck for this stay. Her basketball hoop from her first stay was also back in her room. They had been storing it for us in the hospital all this time. Kendall just loved playing with her new food truck and serving food to me and the nurses. It was such a wonderful gift and we had plenty of room for it in our large PICU room.

I was thankful that I was able to still switch out with Wes, as well as go to the cafeteria to get food or meet someone who had made a meal for us. Some hospitals pretty much lock you in for the entirety of the transplant for fear of bringing germs into the room. We only had to wash our hands outside of the hallway to the PICU upon leaving and entering and just make sure we ourselves were not sick. We also had to abide by the food restrictions in our room that I had mentioned earlier.

***

The time had come for our little girl's rebirth. They make it a big day for these kids in the hospital as their immune systems have been completely wiped out from the strong chemo, and then they are given back their healthy cells to replace the ones destroyed from treatment.

Outside of her room on her window was a large poster board with princesses on it and "Happy Transplant Day" written across it. Then as the day went on, the nurses, doctors, and other staff wrote messages to Kendall on the sign. We had quite a full room as they got her ready for her cells. The team gathered around Kendall, many wearing their Kendall Strong shirts. We had asked a chaplain to come and pray a blessing over the cells and for healing in her body. This was the prayer she prayed:

"God of life and creation who fashioned Kendall after your likeness and who knows all her needs, bless these cells for Kendall's healing. May your spirit and power oh God flow through every cell to bring healing, health, and renewal. Kendall, may the divine love and Word of God be healing to your body and marrow for your bones. May your body accept these cells, may your immune system be strengthened, and may you be relieved of unnecessary reactions. May your health be renewed, and your strength be restored. Amen."

The music therapist then played "Happy Birthday" as Kendall's cells began to transplant into her body. The nurses and other team members in the room sang along and celebrated this chance for healing in Kendall's body. Kendall had a Moroccan shaker in her hand that she shook to the music as we all sang. She lay there expressionless as this all went on, just looking like the angel she was with her perfect bald head. She didn't complain at all. She was a trooper and did what was asked of her.

The doctors had warned us that as the transplant took place, it would smell like creamed corn. Well, they were not kidding. The smell of creamed corn permeated through our room! I am not sure I can ever eat creamed corn again. Kendall's breath even smelled like it for days after!

The cells themselves were not what I expected. They were in a bag of blood and if you looked close enough you could see the tiny cells swimming around in it. Once her cells were infused, we had to wait 10-14 days for engraftment to take place. This is when the transplanted stem cells begin to make new white blood cells, red blood cells, and platelets.

Kendall did not get too sick from the cells going in. She threw up one time that day and that was really the only reaction she had. But I knew the storm was coming. Her counts would continue to drop as the days went on. We still were not in the clear from Thiotepa burns for at least a few more days and I knew the mucositis was on the way. I soaked up all the playtime I could get with her while I still could.

The days then started to count up. Day +1, +2, etc. Waiting for engraftment is not a pleasant time. By Day +6, Kendall was miserable. Imagine having the stomach bug for a week. That is what it was like. Puke, poop, sleep, repeat. Add in mucositis and drooling as well. I felt so bad for her. The sores from the mucositis were all over the inside of her mouth and most likely all down her digestive tract too. Her cheeks were so swollen. She could barely talk or swallow, so we had a stack of drool cloths to switch out as she soaked through each one.

Day after day would pass, and Kendall wouldn't get any better. She had no counts which meant no healing from the sores until engraftment. Her heart rate monitor would be going crazy because her heart rate was so high from all the pain she was in. They had to start her on morphine to keep her comfortable. She also was showing some discoloring on her skin at this point from the Thiotepa chemo. It was mainly on her arms and it was nothing like I had feared. This was also the first time since she started chemo that her eyelashes fell out. My precious girl looked the sickest and was the sickest that she had been yet on this journey.

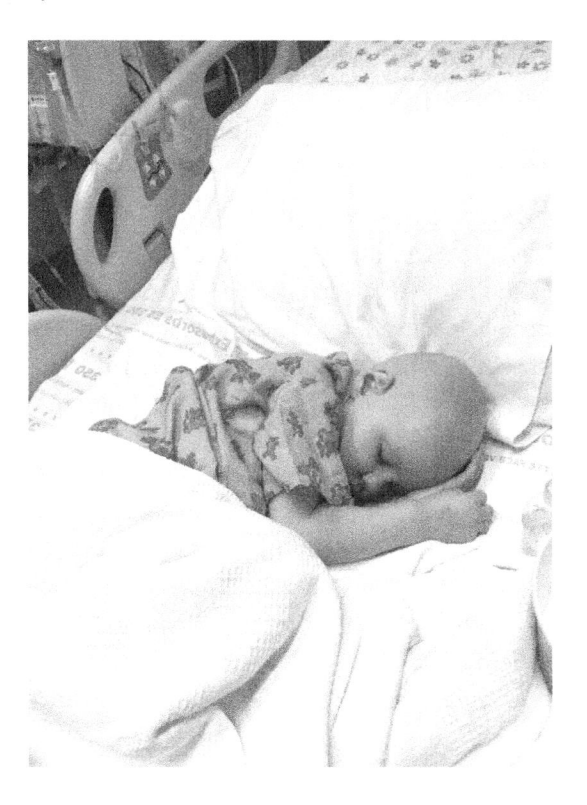

The days were long as I waited for my smiling, silly girl to come back. I would have traded places with her in a heartbeat if I could. It was so hard to hang on as day after day passed and Kendall continued to lie there in pain. She would hold onto the side of the bed as she slept as if it helped her handle the pain. No child should have to endure this amount of suffering.

I watched a lot of Netflix that stay and since I had a larger room, I was able to do some workouts. I would leave on the weekends and go see Alexa just as I always did. Before Kendall got so sick, she made Alexa a card and had me write in it, "I hope I get better soon so I can come home and play with you." Alexa's counselor had suggested the girls write back and forth since Alexa couldn't come to see her on this stay. Alexa wrote the cutest response back. She said, "I love you. You are the best sister. Keep up the work." How sweet is that!? They had such a special bond and they missed each other deeply when they were apart.

***

By Day +16, Kendall was engrafted, counts were up, and she was back to feeling like herself. She had been on TPN because of the mucositis sores in her digestive tract so she had to be able to tolerate her G tube feeds again before we could go home.

At this point in Kendall's journey, I was starting to feel a bit off. I couldn't seem to feel rested even if I did get some sleep. I had this strange pain in my neck as well so I made an appointment to go see a doctor there on campus. I was tested for mono which was negative and then didn't get any other answers that day. I thought maybe my stress and worry about making sure I was healthy during her transplant was just making me imagine that I wasn't well.

Soon after that, Kendall met all the requirements for discharge, and we were able to go home, but not without a set of instructions on how to care for her after the transplant. For the next 100 days, we had to still be very careful and continue to restrict certain foods. We also had to log every stool, urine, fluid, and food intake throughout the day just like when she was a baby. On top of all that we added more meds to her schedule. The basket we kept of her meds was overflowing now. I knew I would have my hands full adjusting to being nurse mom again, as well as normal mom, and dog mom, and managing multiple trips to the outpatient clinic for Kendall each week.

I made an appointment while I was back home with my primary care provider as I still was not feeling so well. She fit me in right away as she knew my situation. She sent me for bloodwork and was concerned I had a thyroid disorder.

Meanwhile, Kendall was happy to be back home earlier than we expected and we had some warm January days where she got to be outside and on her swing set. She was running out to it one afternoon and she stopped herself and said, "Ouch my leg hurts." I picked her up and carried her to the swing and pushed her. She got off the swing and was running around again so I didn't think anything of it.

She continued to complain of leg pain off and on the next couple of days, but again was still walking and dancing around on it. At our next clinic appointment, I mentioned the leg pain. The nurse practitioner took a look and noticed her right leg was swollen. So, yep, you guessed it. Admitted again. We had nothing with us. Kendall and I were so incredibly sad and disappointed. I couldn't bear going back to the hospital room after we had just been confined for so long. We were only home for five days! I was so incredibly tired. I couldn't help but just sob.

The team started with an X-ray and ultrasound and found nothing. But they still kept her because she was complaining of pain. More tests were run the next day and low and behold, she had a fracture above her knee. She originally had cancer there so they were concerned it could be back in that spot again. They wanted to keep her to find out the cause of the fracture. It was either more disease or weak bones from all the chemo.

I was such a wreck again and so upset. *How could it possibly be disease when we just pumped her full of high-dose chemo!?* You can imagine the toll it takes on your body from the stress of a cancer journey. I got a call while we were inpatient from my doctor and she said that my thyroid levels were way higher than they should be. She explained that the kind of stress I was under can trigger this type of disorder in my body. I was so relieved to know that there was medicine to help me feel better, but I was also overwhelmed learning how to take it and coming to terms with this new diagnosis of hypothyroidism. Of course, this was nothing in comparison to what my daughter was going through, but it was a realization of what my body was going through trying to weather this awful storm and be her caregiver. It was also just one more thing to add to my full plate.

Thankfully, the tests run on Kendall's leg showed no new disease. So, she got herself a pretty, blue cast all while having a big smile on her face. She laid back all relaxed in the chair, with her arms behind her head, while her leg was wrapped. In true Kendall fashion, she showed us her bravery and how to respond well to disappointments once again. Then we headed back home for what we hoped would be a longer stay this time.

Chapter 11

The Never-Ending Transplant

Our time home with Kendall ended up being many weeks. She was learning how to get around the house with her new cast and I would have to remind her often to not put pressure on her casted leg. She found new ways to dance while being seated and she didn't let the cast stop her from having any fun.

Carrying her from floor to floor in our home was hard on me because the cast added weight to her. It was quite the workout and strain on my weak knees. Kendall continued to visit the outpatient clinic three days a week during this time. During one visit, the art therapist came and drew a big unicorn on her cast. Kendall helped and did some scribbling of her own. I wrote Super Kendall on it for her because she was our real-life superhero.

The weather was good to us during our time at home. We were blessed with more 50 and 60 degree days during the dreaded winter months we were home. That allowed the girls to get more play time outside with the neighbor kids and swing time for Kendall. All the fresh air and sunshine lifted everyone's

Kendall with her casted leg

spirits too.

Kendall went in for her checkup one morning and I had mentioned that her diaper changes had been excessive. They tested her for C.diff and of course, it came back positive. This is common with cancer kids because of all the antibiotics they receive. So, another med was added to Kendall's growing basket of prescriptions and tons of handwashing! I was terrified of catching it and we wore gloves and masks with every diaper change. This also meant that she was put back on precautions because of how contagious C.diff is. When we visited the hospital, she had to be taken directly back to her room, which meant no toys in the playroom. Everyone had to gown up to come into her room and so you can see how it added a whole other level of stress to her already overwhelming care.

This also meant that Kendall could not go into her second transplant on the date we had planned. It was pushed back a week in order to give her body time to heal. Giving her more chemo would only make her tummy hurt more from mucositis and it also would cause more loose stools. In the meantime, we had positive news that they would be removing Kendall's leg cast before she started her second stem cell transplant!

As we continued to wait it out at home, joy came our way. Kendall was nominated by a friend for a Special Spaces dream bedroom makeover. She was accepted and I spoke with the Special Spaces director to get the process started. I had to get approval from her doctors, and then paperwork sent with a description of Kendall's diagnosis. Kendall would be able to choose a theme for her bedroom and the plan was to start on it while we were away for transplant.

The director and designer from Special Spaces came over to look at Kendall's room and talk about our wants and needs. They also wanted to meet Kendall of course. They felt like family right away and the director was wearing shoes that said "Joy" on them. It delighted me! They brought with them some delicious mini cakes and bright smiles that instantly made us feel loved.

Much to our surprise, Alexa was going to get some things made over in her room too. We were all so excited! Alexa chose a unicorn/rainbow theme and Kendall chose *Frozen*. One of the biggest wishes from the girls was either a trundle or bunk bed so they could have sleepovers together. I had seen some of the other bedrooms the Special Spaces team had created on their Facebook page and they were absolutely stunning. We couldn't wait to see what they came up with and we were so happy to have something to look forward to.

***

Early in March, Kendall and I gathered our belongings as we had done countless times before and headed to the PICU for her next transplant. Kendall had spent so much time at home that it was harder to go back this time. She didn't want to part from her sister and wanted to keep having the freedoms she did at home. I too felt the same but reminded her of all her friends at the hospital and having Mommy all to herself. When this was done, we would be one step closer to completing her treatment plan. The scary transplants would be behind us, and we could move toward what we were told were the less harsh treatments.

There was an opportunity to place Kendall on a clinical trial during this transplant. It was for a drug that may help prevent VOD (veno-occlusive disease) of the liver. VOD is a serious complication and can lead to liver damage. Since she qualified, we were more than happy to place her on the trial in hopes to help future children fight cancer. There wasn't much she had to do for it other than getting weekly ultrasounds of her liver all through the transplant, and then 30 days, 60 days, and 100 days post-transplant.

Kendall and I got settled into her room so the nurses could start the prep work for the clinical trial drug. I got her room all decorated in a Moana theme this time. The decorations were mostly donated by a friend, and this was probably my most favorite room I decorated. I took grass skirts and hung them flat above the windows and cabinets in the room. It quickly helped it to feel bright and tropical. I hung flowers on the walls which made it feel like spring in our room. We had life-sized Moana posters for the walls and a few decorations I hung from the ceiling. The nurses loved coming to our room!

Kendall took her chemo like a champ as it was administered that week. We were having fun and getting a lot of play time together, which she always loved. She also had lots of time with her music and art therapists. I took a picture of her painting with her art therapist one day, which later was used several times by the Cleveland Clinic on their social media pages, as well as on an art therapy tribute wall in the main building of the hospital. They even allowed me to write a little blurb about what art therapy meant to Kendall. The photo truly showed the relationship between them and the joy her art therapist brought to her room each time. Kendall had the biggest smile and looked so happy and radiant in it.

After a few days had past, she was starting to feel the effects from the chemo. The pain meds were started which in turn made her sleepy. I had bought her a new panda sleep mask and she loved to wear it to block out the light during the day. She looked so cute and peaceful sleeping in it, along with her little hairs sprouting up on her head. It had been so long since she had chemo that her hair was growing, but I knew the sprouts would soon be gone again.

Kendall had a break from any treatments for a couple of days after all her chemo was administered. Then on March 13th, 2018, she received her cells back. Her art therapist drew a special sign on the window outside of her room that read, "Happy Second Transplant Kendall." There were Moana characters on it which she drew by hand! She was simply amazing. Her team came by and wrote encouraging messages on the sign, just like they did during her first stem cell transplant. Kendall hadn't felt well and was pretty much asleep most of the day. She even was asleep most of the time while the bag of cells went into her. It was an uneventful day, but she did get sick once.

Kendall had some rougher days as we waited for her cells to engraft. Multiple blood and platelet transfusions, multiple pukes a day, and mucositis with lots of drool and mouth sores. Luckily, she did not get sores as bad as the first transplant and she was up a little more trying to play than the first time around. She had to go on TPN earlier this time since she was throwing up so much. It wasn't long before she was back on her tube feeds though at a slow rate. By Day +9 the doctors thought her counts were trending up and she was doing very well at this point in the transplant. By Day +10 she was fully engrafted, and we were so excited! We were hopeful this stay would be shorter than the first transplant stay, but we were in for a rude awakening.

Every day seemed to hold its own set of challenges. Her counts would be okay one day, then drop the next and give her terrible nosebleeds from the low platelets. Kendall looked great though and was up playing and laughing. It had seemed promising that we would make it home for Easter, so I began clearing out some of her toys to make discharge easier. Unfortunately, her vomiting started increasing and I wrote a post on her Facebook page desperate for prayers after 19 days straight of vomiting multiple times a day. I had counted around 40 times at that point, but that still was not the end of it.

Because Kendall was throwing up more, the doctors didn't feel that she was well enough to go home just yet. Her gut needed more time to heal. The end of March was upon us, and we learned we would spend Easter in the hospital. As disappointed as we all were, I had to jump into action and make plans to have the best Easter that we could in the hospital. I was hoping they would let Alexa come up and we could all be together as a family.

***

Meanwhile, back at home, the girls' room makeovers were finished and just waiting for Kendall's discharge. Alexa though couldn't wait any longer and she was missing her bed since she wasn't allowed in her room while it was being redecorated. So, we planned to do Alexa's room reveal when I went home for a couple of days from the hospital. It wasn't how we planned or expected the room reveal to go, but we didn't know how much longer we could keep Alexa from peeking into her room.

The Special Spaces team met us at our house and led us upstairs to the much-anticipated room reveal. Alexa and I stood outside her door with our eyes closed. The door was opened, and they told us to open our eyes. The whole scene is on video, and I am so glad because it is such a joyous moment. Alexa was in awe. I was so blown away by how beautiful it was and I just kept saying, "Wow! Oh, my goodness!"

Alexa loved the plush unicorn adorned with flowers above her bed, and the large, standing plush unicorn whom she quickly named Sparkles. My favorite was the pink and white striped walls with gold circles sprayed out from the corner, and the large area rug. The new Ikea light was also a statement piece. There was so much to look at and take in. Every little décor piece was carefully thought out and many items were handmade by Etsy artisans. The dresser we had in her room was painted a pale yellow and custom shelving was made for her wall. Her room was now so bright and colorful. Knowing that the room was done by all volunteers made it even more special. Beautiful souls who wanted to bring joy and smiles to one hurting family. Based on the design elements of Alexa's room, we knew Kendall's would be just as incredible, if not more.

***

The next day, I gathered Easter clothes for all of us so we could make the holiday special. Kendall loved her fancy dresses, and she had some beautiful new dresses from her great-grandmother to choose from. Radiate Gold was at the hospital with Wes and Kendall bringing fun toys and decorating her room for Easter. A Special Wish was bringing the Easter meal and Alexa was cleared to visit. As much as I would have preferred us all home, I was pretty excited to spend the holiday at the hospital. As long as we were all together then my heart would be happy. The girls hadn't seen each other in weeks so I was so thrilled for them to reunite.

I brought the girls' Easter baskets with us to the hospital, along with my usual load of clothes and food for the week. Kendall was in good spirits that day and smiled so much. It was so good for her to see her sister and have a little change in her monotonous days. It wasn't a long visit, but we were grateful for any time they were allowed to have together.

Our Easter meal was probably one of the best I ever had. I couldn't stop raving over the mouthwatering flavors of the food. What can I say, I am a foodie! I put Kendall's Easter dress on, and the nurse took a nice family photo of us together on the couch in the room. Kendall looked beautiful in her lacey white and green dress with pink ribbon. The hospital was always so good at making holidays special for these kids and families.

Celebrating Easter together at the hospital

Three days after Easter, Kendall's platelets and RBC counts continued to drop. She also had high blood pressure and high LDH numbers. The doctor believed she was showing signs of TMA, Transplant Associated Microangiopathy. This is a tough one to explain so feel free to Google it. Sometimes chemo can irritate the blood vessels and cause TMA to happen. It affects the red blood cells, and platelets, and can cause organ damage. The doctor didn't think she had a severe case, but a moderate one. He felt it was caught early enough that the medication they would infuse, Ecluzimab, would treat it quickly. They could treat her outpatient, but she still could not go home until her vomiting subsided and she didn't need daily transfusions.

I took this news how I usually take disappointing news. I let worry and fear consume me and was screaming inside because I just wanted my little girl to get back home. I myself wanted to go home! It was Alexa's spring break, and we were missing it. I was so grateful to all of my friends though who rotated taking Alexa each day to do something fun. She had a great spring break with her friends, even though I couldn't be there. I took the news hard, but I knew I had to pull myself together and try to stay positive. It was just so difficult to do when there was setback after setback. Kendall was also really missing home at this point. My heart was breaking for her, especially the day she stood staring out the window with her arms crossed and resting on the sill, saying how she wished she could go home. This was going down as our longest stay yet.

Since we had been in the PICU longer than expected, we had to move rooms and head back to the pediatric oncology wing because our room was needed for the next transplant patient. Kendall cried, and I did inside too. It was already hard staying in the large room we had, but now we had to go back to a smaller room. We quickly felt right back at home though on M50 and it was nice to not be so isolated. We had more freedom there and were also able to have Alexa in her new room, so we couldn't wait for Friday when Wes would come and bring her.

Things continued getting worse before better. Kendall's kidney function had decreased which is a side effect of TMA. This started a slew of tests that had to be done to monitor her. Every time I turned around someone else was coming in to do something else to her. She also started physical therapy during this time to help her gain her strength back since she had been hospitalized for so long. You can imagine how busy it was in our room some days.

On the days when it wasn't as chaotic, I had to get creative. We played with every toy we had, and I even bought every toy I thought she would like in the hospital gift shop. I went daily hoping something new would jump out at me. I started doing puppet shows in her room with the dolls we had. I used the privacy curtain and had the dolls peek out from the bottom of it. I put on a comedy show for Kendall and she would laugh so hard. She'd say "Mo (More) puppet show" when I stopped. She never wanted it to end. I loved being silly and making her laugh. Her laugh was the best and it made me laugh too.

We also made the minutes go by playing I Spy and set up bowling pins in her room for bowling. Kendall had a visit from the hospital magician one day, and she acquired some magic trick skills. She loved to show everyone that came to her room the new tricks she had learned.

When we would play with her dolls, a lot of the narrative she would create would be medical play. That is what she had come to know so you would often see her putting a Band-Aid on her doll or she would use gauze lying around in her room to make a pretend cast on her doll's leg. Sometimes she would pretend to be the doctor and use one of the various toy doctor kits she had. I would be her patient and she would fix me right up. She would tell me to take my medicine so I could get all better. It even went as far as her care team creating her very own Cleveland Clinic doctor badge for her, complete with a rainbow poop emoji on it. They knew her so well!

Kendall and I had some sweet moments together while we waited for the days to pass. She loved for me to read to her at night and we had a good bedtime routine going. I would read her a book, along with a story from her children's Bible, and then she would ask me to rub her back and sing to her as she fell asleep. "Sing to me Momma," she would say in her sweet voice. No matter how tired I was, I couldn't say no to her. I would sing song after song until she was sound asleep.

By this time, we had had many visits from our congregational care pastor. Kendall had taken quite a liking to him and enjoyed his visits. He would come by to check on us, see what our needs were, pray for us, and he would read Kendall's children's Bible to her. She would get down on the floor with him while he read to her, or sometimes even crawled right up in his lap. She was always attentive to each story and she had her favorites. She loved to read the story of Jesus' death on the cross because she couldn't wait to shout out, "But Jesus didn't die!" She would hold her little index finger up in the air, waving and pointing it while she said it. Oh, the faith of a child!

Every day was a waiting game. Would her counts come up on their own, or would another transfusion be needed? They continued to check her liver and kidney function. I was so scared she would end up on dialysis, but day after day her kidney function continued to improve.

We never saw TMA coming. I turned once again to my neuroblastoma support group and low and behold, I found many other kids who also dealt with this side effect. It was always nice to hear other children's stories, but it could scare me too. Some parents explained that the TMA set back their treatments and others shared how long their child had to receive Ecluzimab transfusions. Now today, TMA is mentioned to the parents before going into transplants because it is such a common complication.

Every child reacts differently to the aggressive neuroblastoma treatments. One child may get through with very few complications and reach NED (no evidence of disease). Others may have many complications and struggle to get to NED. Kendall started off great and I really thought she would skate through, but transplants were so very hard on her.

The amount of suffering I had seen from each transplant was inhumane. I had such a hard time understanding how these drugs could cause so much harm and toxicity, but yet save my daughter. Sadly, some children do die during transplants because it is so harsh on their little bodies. Most of the chemos and therapies given to pediatric cancer patients are the same ones given to adults with cancer. Treatments for childhood cancer are outdated and haven't changed much in decades. Since childhood cancer is considered rare, there is not enough funding allocated to childhood cancer research, which is unfortunate. These kids deserve more.

***

As we anxiously awaited discharge, Kendall was allowed to

have some freedom throughout the hospital. Her neutrophil and white blood cell counts were good, so her doctor said she could leave her room in the evenings after it wasn't so busy in the hospital. I would wheel her outside for some fresh air, or to the multiple fish tanks throughout the hospital, and also to the hospital gift shop. She even would stop at the nurses' station and sit at the desk with them, pretending to be one of them. Just those quick trips out of her room refreshed us and lifted our spirits enough to make it another day.

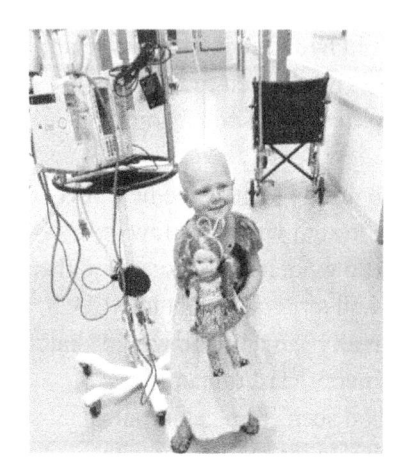

Kendall enjoying time out of her hospital room

As another week went by, Kendall improved day after day. The doctors caught the TMA early and the infusion was working. After 40 long days inpatient, on April 13th we finally were able to bring Kendall home! I thought the day would never come!

The Special Spaces team was waiting for her arrival at our home and Kendall could hardly wait to see her new room. She didn't waste any time and headed right up the stairs to her bedroom. The team had her close her eyes, and then they opened the door to her magical princess room. She ran in and got right up onto her new bed. There was so much to look at and she took it all in. She also knew they had a special surprise waiting in the playroom for the girls, so she didn't stay in her room too long. She took off heading for the basement while I was still in her room admiring its beauty.

    The *Frozen* theme was done so tastefully and elegantly. She had beautiful white furniture with ornate detailing. She got a trundle bed so the girls could have sleepovers together and so Wes or I could sleep with her. There was a beautiful chandelier hung and wainscoting on the bottom half of the wall. Snowflake wallpaper hung above on one accent wall, and the other walls were a light *Frozen* blue. Her bedspread was a beautiful grayish/light blue color with *Frozen* pillow accents. There was even a pillow cover made with Kendall's name on it and our motto "Choose Joy" with the *Frozen* characters. A beautiful area rug took up most of her room and large paper snowflakes hung in the corners. She also had a beautiful tiara wall decoration hanging above her bed with white tulle draping that hung from it and swept over her bed. It was truly a room suited for a princess. Every detail was done so thoughtfully and with love.

    Downstairs in the playroom, the girls were thrilled over all the fun changes. Someone had donated their time to turn an armoire into a *Frozen* dress-up wardrobe. It was painted blue with snowflakes on it and had fancy knobs. Inside held tons of beautiful Disney dress-up clothes and shoes. There was just about every princess costume available hung neatly in it. Kendall didn't waste any time either putting one on. Of course, she chose the *Frozen* Anna costume.

    The girls also had many other toys and items donated to them. They were most excited about their new ice cream truck for their American Girl dolls. There were beautiful, crocheted hats, costumes, and other hand-made décor items to personalize their space. I was blown away by the fact that someone out there was so kind to use their time to make something so special for a little girl they didn't even know.

Seeing the girls' room makeovers was definitely a highlight of Kendall's cancer journey. I was so happy that Kendall had a quiet, healing space to call her own. A safe, comfortable place for her to rest and play while she was on breaks from the hospital. Special Spaces will always hold a special place in my heart. They brought us joy and peace during some of the most difficult days of our lives. We will never forget such a beautiful gift.

Chapter 12

Radiation Days

Peace, rest, and healing never felt so good. Kendall was enjoying her time home and getting a little better and stronger every day. Though we had some weeks at home to enjoy before radiation, we still had many appointments, Ecluzimab infusions, meds to administer at home, and round-the-clock tube feedings. It was never truly a complete break.

Kendall's care team at the Cleveland Clinic had recommended for her to have proton beam therapy for part of her treatments. This is a targeted form of radiation that would help to protect her important structures and organs such as the liver. It was needed because of how intertwined her tumor was in her organs and tissues. Because they did not have the machine to offer proton beam therapy at their hospital, we had to have her radiation done at University Hospitals (UH) Seidman Cancer Center, another nearby hospital. We were so grateful to have a hospital with proton therapy close to home as many neuroblastoma patients end up having to travel out of state since there are very few centers that offer it in the U.S.

So not only did we have to do our usual checkup appointments at Cleveland Clinic, but now we had a whole new team to meet, a new hospital to navigate, and many appointments to get Kendall set up for radiation, which included a fitting for the molding to keep her in the same position daily.

It was kind of refreshing to have a change in hospital scenery. The food in the cafeteria was all new to us, colorful walls were new, as well as the beautiful historic area the hospital was in. We quickly fell in love with our new team at UH. They had a special sedation unit that would administer her sleepy meds (anesthesia) and be there by her side for recovery. These nurses were so extra kind and caring, and the child life specialists that came along with them were phenomenal. The love for their patients just flowed out of them.

I remember pulling up one day to the UH Seidman Cancer Center and I thought to myself, *Wow I never in a million years would have thought I would be coming to this place with my daughter*. Yet there we were about to embark on another leg of Kendall's journey.

There was something so special about this cancer center and I could feel it as soon as I walked through the doors. One great thing was that this hospital campus was much smaller and easier to navigate, which meant fewer people to have to wheel Kendall past and receive awkward glances from. Upon entering the office, we were always taken right back to her room and greeted with a warm welcome. On the walls of the cancer center, there were beautiful, framed photos of cancer patients with a quote from them about their journey or some words of wisdom they could pass on to others fighting. I stood there reading them all one day, even taking photos of some so I could remember the hope in their words. I felt such a sense of peace and had confidence that my daughter was in great hands.

Kendall was set to start radiation in the middle of May. Radiation treatments were Monday through Friday for four weeks straight. She would receive 12 rounds of X-ray based radiation, and then eight rounds of proton beam therapy. The whole process with sedation and recovery would take a few hours every day.

Kendall was healing so well at home and even her TMA had resolved, which allowed us to stop her Ecluzimab infusions. I was able to push a lot of extra nutrition like kefir and smoothies through her G tube at home and she looked great because of it. She had good color and was gaining weight and strength. She was headed into radiation in great shape.

***

We continued to be so blessed during our time at home. We found out that Kendall was the next recipient of a Lowe's Hometown Heroes swing set build. Our dear friend referred her and the next thing we knew, there was a volunteer crew in our backyard building Kendall her dream swing set! It was truly one of the most amazing things I ever witnessed. A group of people who had never met us came together to build our little girl a Backyard Discovery swing set.

Kendall patiently waited and watched while they assembled each piece. She would come outside for a while and mingle with everyone, then return inside for a bit before coming out again to check on the progress. Never once did she complain it was taking too long. She just kept looking out the windows excited as can be. She was so happy that day and spread her joy to all who were there.

By the time Alexa was home from school the swing set was ready, and Kendall couldn't wait to show her. I was so glad that the girls had a nice, large swing set to make memories together on. Kendall enjoyed swinging so much and this gift couldn't have come at a more perfect time as she was able to spend more time at home during this next phase.

***

As the radiation start date grew near, Kendall had a fall on the sidewalk. I was worried as her bones had become so brittle from the awful chemo. She was still using her arm as usual though, so I was hopeful she was okay. She then started to tell me her arm hurt so I brought it up to the doctor at her next visit. He sent her for an X-ray and sure enough, it was broken. Not just one bone, but she had a both-bone forearm fracture. Because her arm touched her radiation mold, she had to have a removable splint put on. This way I could take it off each day before she went into radiation. I was just thankful we didn't have to postpone her treatment and that the splint was an easy solution. I felt so bad for her that she had more broken bones and it was concerning how easily her bones were breaking.

Then, radiation day was here. I was told this was the easy part of treatment and there would be minimal side effects. All was going well that morning until I accidentally fed some millimeters of yogurt through her G tube. I had been in such a habit of doing so each morning that I didn't even think about her needing to fast, even with getting up at 3 a.m. to shut her feeds off and switch over to water. I was kicking myself, but I wasn't sure who to call at the hospital to tell of my mistake. I thought since it was just a tiny bit I would go ahead and head down to the hospital.

I remember that morning being quite a train wreck. I was really hard on myself and called myself the worst cancer mom for my mistake. I hated that I could be the cause of a delay in her treatment.

We had about a 40-minute drive to the hospital, and we had to be there at 8 a.m. I gave myself extra time to get downtown with the morning commute traffic. Then once we arrived at the hospital, we had to wind our way through the floors of the parking garage until we found a spot, which could take a few extra minutes. When I parked and went to remove Kendall from the car, I realized that she had had a massive blowout in her car seat. So now not only did I already mess up, but I had a huge mess to clean up too. I was in tears as I hurried to get her changed and into the hospital.

I came in looking like a wreck that first radiation day. I was frantic, stressed, out of breath, and crying. I shared with the nurse all that had happened that morning and to add to my sadness, my mistake had indeed caused Kendall to not receive her radiation that day. I was so mad at myself and embarrassed because I knew that at her checkup at Cleveland Clinic later that day, I would have to reveal to our team that I messed up. Luckily everyone was so gracious to me and the nurse at UH gave me a package of wipes and some plastic bags to help me clean up the mess in the car better. She hugged me and told me that we could try again the next day. Kendall's care team at Cleveland Clinic also was gracious to me and made me feel better. They helped me to see that beating myself up over it wasn't going to do any good. The mistake had been made and we just had to move forward the next day.

Each day got better from there as we journeyed through radiation, though seeing Kendall sedated day after day was hard for me. Just think about how you feel after being sedated and she had to endure the effects of it five days a week! Because of her age and inability to hold still for an extended time, it was required for her to be sedated daily. She would fight it and cry in those first few days, I assume because she was scared, but she adjusted and became a pro over time. Kendall grew fond of the two child life specialists at UH and would ask them to hold her hands as she was put to sleep. It was the most precious thing, and I am sure it made them feel so special. Kendall was good at doing that.

Each day that I saw the big, heavy radiation doors closing, I entered into a time of prayer and declared healing over Kendall. The radiation itself was only 10 minutes, but the whole morning was usually around two to three hours with sedation and recovery. It grew to be exhausting doing this day after day through the week. I was so tired from shutting her feeds off in the middle of the night and all the driving between hospitals. Thankfully Kendall had good counts during these weeks and only needed to be seen at Cleveland Clinic once a week. It was still tiring though to walk all over these hospital campuses and lift my almost four-year-old in and out of the car and stroller. This part of treatment certainly had its own set of challenges.

Kendall moved through these weeks with minimal side effects as expected. She did begin to have some vomiting halfway through but overall, this was a nice break for her. She had a month of returning to her home each day. She would usually be tired after radiation and sleep on the drive home. We had to work hard to get her feeds in once we got home since we couldn't feed her the entire night. But we were home! That in itself was healing for her to just have a break from hospital life and be able to do some normal kid stuff. She enjoyed more time playing with her sister and the neighbor kids, and of course, swinging on her new swing set.

She also enjoyed sleeping in her bed in her new dream bedroom. She looked like a princess curled up in her bed. I often would visit her room in the morning before she woke to watch her sleep, and her chest rising and falling from breathing. Each breath she took was a precious gift. Sometimes we don't stop to think of how miraculous each breath is that we take.

***

We were starting to near Day +100 from her first transplant which meant that she could return to eating some of her favorite foods again, like strawberries. It was something to look forward to and another milestone in her journey. While Kendall had been home every afternoon, she had started having home visits from physical, occupational, and speech therapists. She was not happy about it at first and didn't want to spend her time at home working, but after a few weeks she warmed up to them and the leg she had broken was getting stronger.

As the radiation wrapped up, I was firmly believing that God had healed Kendall with this treatment. She looked good, she felt good, and continued to improve each day. I was looking forward to the next scan to see the progress made.

On the final day of radiation, Kendall wanted to dress up in a fancy yellow sundress and white dress shoes. She had taken these weeks during radiation to show her personality through her clothing and the staff always looked forward to seeing what beautiful dress or costume she would be wearing each day. When we arrived that morning, she was greeted with parting gifts from the nurses and child life specialists. They had come to know Kendall well and that showed in the items they had chosen for her, like the poop emoji pillow and pink cone princess hat.

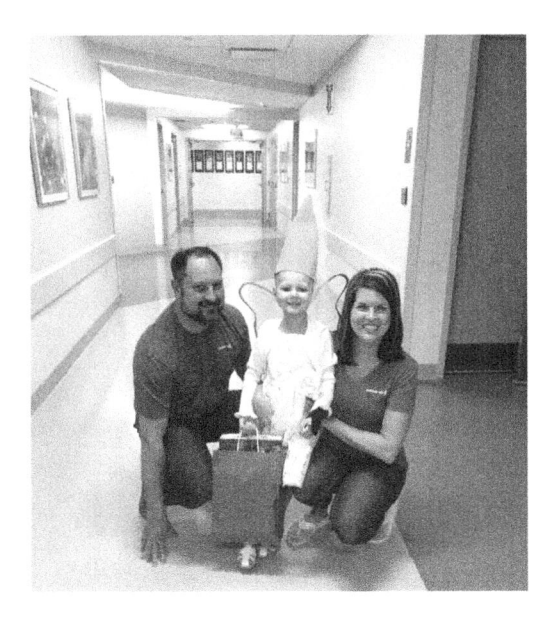

UH made the last day of radiation special by allowing the patients to ring the bell and place their thumbprints on the tree mural on the wall. Her whole care team gathered to cheer Kendall on as she gave the bell a ring to signify the completion of her radiation treatments. She had a little trouble giving it a good ring, so her radiation tech lifted her up to help her give it the victorious ring it deserved. Everyone clapped, congratulated her, and exclaimed, "Way to go Kendall! You did it!" My heart swelled with emotion as Kendall was one treatment closer to the end. It was such a joyous moment, but also sad to have to leave this wonderful care team we had all grown close to in such a short time. We said our goodbyes and walked out of the radiation wing for the last time, filled with joy and hope.

Chapter 13

Back Down the Roller Coaster We Go

It was now mid-June of 2018, and we were coming up on one year since Kendall had been diagnosed. She had scans scheduled to see what her disease burden was like after radiation and transplants. We wanted more than anything to hear the three letters, "NED". Kendall had fought so hard, and we really needed some good news to give us that push to keep going through this strenuous battle. I really believed that good news was coming our way.

Still, I was dealing again with "scanxiety." The fears and worries can start to come about in the days or weeks before a scheduled scan date. It can be hard to sleep or think about anything else as the nervousness sets in. Then, once the scan is done there is more anxiety and worry over waiting for the results. "Scanxiety" is not fun and all I could do was pray my way through it.

After Kendall's scans, one of the doctors on her team called me. He had her results, and I began to feel my heart race. He asked if Wes was around, which he wasn't, so he asked us to call him back when we were both together. That gut feeling in my stomach made me fear that this was not the news we wanted to hear. I began to frantically pace the house as I called Wes to see when he would be home. More waiting. More time to let my mind wander and for my body to be consumed with fear.

Wes returned home when he could, and we called the doctor back. My gut was right. This was not good news. Kendall's cancer had progressed. They found two new tumor growths, one on her left adrenal gland, and one on the back of her abdomen. The tumor that was still left from her original tumor hadn't budged. I began to feel nauseous, and my body was shaking. This was so unfair and made no sense when Kendall was looking and feeling so great. For cancer to grow right through radiation told us that her cancer was a beast to fight. The doctor said our team would meet and come up with a new plan while involving other hospitals to look at her case. More waiting.

We had no idea at this point if we were going to head back to Memorial Sloan Kettering or a different hospital out of state to try to cure her. We were told she still had many treatment options once her platelet count came back up. It was such a helpless feeling knowing that we had this treatment plan a year ago and we were nearing the final round of it, but now that was all out the door, and we had no clue if and when there would be an end.

Just like in other times throughout this journey, we pulled ourselves together over time and found the strength to continue to fight. The doctors consulted with other hospitals and came back with a chemo plus immunotherapy plan that would keep us at our home hospital. I had heard of great success with this treatment for neuroblastoma from other cancer parents so I was happy with this plan and ready to battle yet again. That is cancer. A roller coaster of emotions.

***

Immunotherapy was supposed to be a less harsh treatment than Kendall had previously been through. Since we had to now add chemo in with it, she would have to endure more pain and suffering. Luckily, the plan was still to admit her on a Sunday evening and then have her back home by Saturday. She would then repeat the cycle every few weeks and have another scan to see if this treatment was working.

I never quite understood how immunotherapy worked but knew that it was to help Kendall's body recognize cancer cells and destroy them. She would receive this treatment in the PICU once again and have more attentive care due to the possible side effects such as nerve pain, fluid buildup, increased heart rate, blood pressure issues, and high fevers. Her nurse would be checking on her every hour throughout the week, so I was not expecting to get much sleep. We also had to give her injections at home to help her counts recover quickly after she received her treatment. She would get one shot a day for a period of time and it never got any easier.

At the end of June, Kendall started her first round of this new treatment. It was nice to see all our nurse friends on our floor again as we hadn't been inpatient through radiation. They were excited to see her, and Kendall was feeling the good vibes and energy when we entered her room. She decided it was dance party time, and we now had a disco light to add to the fun. A bunch of the nurses gathered in a circle around her and laughed and danced with Kendall to some fun dance tunes. Kendall was showing off her latest moves as the nurses chanted, "Go Kendall, Go Kendall." Oh, the fun we had! She loved all the attention.

Kendall was admitted on a Sunday and by Tuesday she had already started feeling pretty crummy from the treatments. She then basically slept from Tuesday to Saturday. She battled with high heart rates and fevers as high as 103. She also broke out in hives a few times and her vomiting increased. The nurses kept her pretty comfortable with the morphine pump, hence the sleeping. I never heard more beeping from the machines than when we entered that week. They would tell me that when her heart rate was high, that could mean she was in pain. Every time the monitor was beeping my heart broke a little more for my sweet baby.

Overall, everything went as expected that week, and as planned, she was discharged on Saturday. It took a few days before she had much strength to do anything, and it took some time before she could work back up to tolerating all her feeds. I went back into nurse mommy mode and did my best to help her recover and be comfortable at home. She, unfortunately, came down with C.diff again during this treatment so there were a lot of extra diapers and precautions I had to take at home. You give an antibiotic to prevent diarrhea from the chemo, but then get C.diff from the antibiotics. It was a vicious cycle.

Day by day Kendall felt better and was starting to be able to enjoy her summer again. By July 4th she was ready to party and enjoyed a day poolside at her Nana and Papa's pool along with her aunts, uncles, and cousins. Though she couldn't swim, she enjoyed dipping her feet in the refreshing, cool water. We even put on a good song for her to have a poolside dance party with the family. Our girl could dance!

The summer fun continued back at home through the next few weeks. Aside from a few checkups, she was able to stay out of the hospital and heal at home. We were getting to do more that summer than we were able to the first summer she was diagnosed. We had bonfires, put up a tent in the backyard, caught lightning bugs, went out for ice cream, and Kendall even enjoyed her blow-up pool a couple of times with just a few inches of water. We were doing our best to stay positive and choose joy every day. We were living each day the best we possibly could and cherishing every sweet moment we had as a family. We knew firsthand just how quickly it could all be taken away.

Chapter 14

Kendall's Fourth Birthday

Kendall's fourth birthday was approaching, and it was looking like she would be home to celebrate it. While we were excited, we were still apprehensive and didn't want to get our hopes up. We lived day to day and knew we could return to hospital life at any moment.

Being the planner that I am, I still began to make some calls and get some special things together for Kendall's birthday. We were pleasantly surprised that Kendall was doing well enough to enjoy her birthday celebrations at home, a big step up from the year prior. And boy did we celebrate! Kendall didn't have just one party, but four!

First up, on her actual birthday, was a trip to the Disney store at the mall. I called and spoke to the manager and explained Kendall's immunocompromised position to see if we could come in before they opened. We were able to come in an hour earlier to have the store to ourselves. It had been a long time since Kendall stepped foot in a mall so I was so happy she could experience this outing on her special day.

Kendall dressed up in her Disney Elena dress and fancy shoes for the occasion. She had birthday money and gift cards to spend so she was excited to shop! It was such a magical morning watching the girls try on princess dresses and load up our stroller with all their toy selections.

I had also asked A Special Wish to contact their princesses to see if one could come to our home for a visit. Kendall had requested Cinderella. Of course, her wish came true, and Cinderella was scheduled to arrive for a special birthday tea party at our home that afternoon. Kendall invited her best friend and her sister to join her and Alexa for the party. Once home from the mall, I got right to work setting the table, putting treats out, and helping the girls get dressed up for the occasion. They both had the latest beautiful, dazzling blue Cinderella dresses with butterflies stitched on. Kendall wanted to add her clip-on heart earrings, black sequin bracelet, and pink frilly headband to her attire. Both girls looked darling as ever.

Kendall's first guests arrived dressed also in Cinderella gowns. Her friends came bearing presents and Kendall didn't waste any time unwrapping them to discover some L.O.L. Surprise! Dolls, one of her favorites.

Next, the guest of honor was knocking at our door. The girls ran into the foyer, barely containing their excitement. I opened the door to the most beautiful Cinderella impersonator I had ever seen. This was the same girl that had previously come to our home as Anna, and she would later come as Ariel. She was very talented and played every character so well. She had made her own Cinderella costume and it was stunning from head to toe. She adorned a sparkling blue headband in her hair, a black rhinestone choker (which matched Kendall's bracelet she chose so well), and a beautiful Cinderella blue ball gown with a lattice laced back. The girls were all in awe of her beauty.

Cinderella greeted the girls and then kneeled down to Kendall's level to give her the best, long hug. My heart swelled with joy. Cinderella took over and led the girls to our playroom for a dance party. It was the sweetest moment seeing four sweet girls jumping, twirling, and spinning in circles with Cinderella. Kendall got out her Cinderella castle for them to play with as well.

Then, it was tea party time. The girls enjoyed pouring their "tea" (actually lemonade) into their tiny teacups. Cinderella laughed and told them stories. It's not every day you experience this level of joy! We sang Kendall Happy Birthday, and she blew out her four candles on her four, tiny, blue-frosted cupcakes.

After the tea party, it was time for some outdoor fun. I had thought it would be fun to set up Kendall's bubble machine in the backyard. It was such a wonderful sight to see all these beautiful princesses in my backyard with Cinderella. The girls ran and twirled through the bubbles, attempting to catch each one. We got some incredible photos throughout the day, but some of my favorites are the bubble pictures and the girls twirling their dresses with Cinderella in the yard.

Photo Credit: Kimberly Lane Photography

Then, of course, Kendall had to show Cinderella her swing. The two of them chatted and swung together for a while. That too made for great photos to forever treasure. Kendall dressed in her special gown on her swing is probably my favorite photo of her during her journey. It was a moment of pure joy. I was so happy that A Special Wish could make this amazing day happen for her birthday.

***

The following weekend, we had another party for Kendall with neighbors and my family. She had requested a poop emoji-themed party. Yes, you read that right! Like one of Kendall's rainbow poop emoji shirts said, "Being normal is boring!"

I wasn't quite sure how I was going to pull this off, but a quick Google search brought up plenty of poop emoji-themed birthday decorations to choose from. Who knew? I bought poop emoji banners, tablecloths, headbands, plates, napkins, swirl decorations, straws, and other party favors. I also ordered poop emoji cupcakes from a local baker and they turned out so cute! Some were unicorn poop and the other ones had cute little pink bows. I found a rainbow poop emoji birthday shirt for Kendall to wear, along with a pink rhinestone poop emoji headband. So based on all I had found, it couldn't be just my child that loved the poop emoji so much!

To add to the humor, I found some games called *Don't Step In It* and *Gas Out*. It was too funny seeing the guests blindfolded trying to dodge the piles of Play-Doh poop on the *Don't Step In It* game mat. *Gas Out* had the same concept as the game *Hot Potato*. You passed the game piece around in a circle and had to press the green blob of gas a certain number of times. If it passed gas on you, you were out. Needless to say, there were plenty of laughs throughout the day. I was thankful her guests got just as much a kick out of it as Kendall did. She loved the potty humor.

Kendall with her poop emoji cupcakes

Kendall couldn't wait to open her presents and I could barely keep up as she tore through each bag and box. One of the gifts that stood out from that day was from her nana and papa. She got the American Girl Doll Wellie Wisher named "Kendall" that she had been wanting. She thought it was so neat that she had the same name as her. Kendall was so happy, and she hugged the box she was neatly stored in tightly.

That evening the girls wanted to have a sleepover with their neighbor friend. We were starting to wind down for the night and got set up in the basement for the sleepover. It was time for Kendall's meds, so I attached her tubing to her G tube button and then ran upstairs quickly to get her meds. In that short amount of time, the girls were jumping around and the next thing I knew Kendall was crying, and Alexa was calling for me to come quickly. I still don't know how it happened, but because her tubing was hanging, it got caught on something and pulled out the entire G tube button.

Because the hole into her stomach can close up quickly, this required an ER visit. Since this was the second time this had happened, we knew how urgent it was to get it back in to prevent another surgery. Kendall was so sad she couldn't have her sleepover. I was so sad for her too. With every high, there was a low. She, unfortunately, was admitted and had to have a sleepover at the hospital instead, not what any of us wanted. The ER was unsuccessful in getting her tube back in so surgery was scheduled for the next morning. Luckily Kendall was back home the next day with no complications.

That was another time when I was hard on myself for making a bad decision to leave her unattended with her tube hanging from her stomach while she was up running around. I felt so bad that her birthday party had to end that way. My heart broke for her that she had to go back to the hospital when it could have been prevented.

Since my in-laws were not free for the poop emoji party, we had another party a week later with that side of our family. Kendall had a great day playing with her cousins and opening more presents. We then had another small gathering with my dad, his wife, and my brother to celebrate her birthday. It was an incredible couple of weeks celebrating Kendall and enjoying time at home with our family. We all wished it could last, but another round of treatment was on the horizon.

Chapter 15
It Wasn't Supposed to Be This Way

It was the end of July when Kendall and I lugged our belongings into the hospital once again for another round of misery. Kendall had been throwing up at least once a day since her birthday and then once her treatment started, it only increased. We met with her nutritionists often to try to adjust her feeds and solve the issue. Over that summer, we had ordered an organic, plant-based formula for her to try. We had heard great things from other neuroblastoma parents about how it helped heal their child's gut and slowed diarrhea. We had seen improvements for periods of time, but Kendall would often face a setback.

Kendall dealt with all the same symptoms from this round as the first. Sleeping and puking were what I remember most from those awful weeks. Kendall made it through though and was discharged again close to what was planned. Her scans were scheduled for mid-August and the "scanxiety" started all over again.

Kendall had many days in the month of August to play at home. She still had her usual outpatient checkups and an X-ray of the arm she broke to see how it had healed. She was doing great, had recovered from the last round of treatment, and didn't have any casts or splints on her body parts, which was a win.

Her doctor gave her the okay to take a trip to Target since she was doing so well. She had a bunch of gift cards stacked up to use once again and she was excited to go on a toy shopping spree with her sister.

She put on her pretty pink heart dress with a white tiered lace bottom, along with her fancy white dress shoes and tan hat. We went first thing in the morning when less people were out. She had a blast perusing the aisles and choosing carefully to get the most out of her gift cards. She purchased the Barbie ambulance and camper that day, along with some L.O.L. dolls. From that day on, she would ask me in her cutest voice, "Mommy we go Target?" I was so happy for her that she was able to have a little bit of normalcy and a fun outing to the store. We were able to take a couple more Target trips that summer with her. I was more than happy to buy the girls anything they wanted.

***

The day before Kendall's scans, she was scheduled to receive her injection which helped to light up the cancer on her MIBG scan (this is the full body scan). Kendall wasn't cooperating that morning and it was time to go. She was on our living room couch and would not get up to leave. I tried to pick her up, but she was resisting and yelling "No" at me. This was very unusual behavior for Kendall. My momma instinct told me to feel her forehead. Sure enough, she was burning up.

Since she had a fever, we had to change our plans and head to the outpatient clinic instead. Upon arrival, the nurses drew her blood and started antibiotics. Unfortunately, Kendall had to be admitted while we waited for the bloodwork to come back and ran the course of antibiotics. Fevers were to be expected after the treatment she had, but it was typical to have to stay at least 48 hours when feverish. Because of this setback, her scans had to be postponed to the following week. Her bloodwork came back good and the doctor on call that weekend thought she would be okay to head back home for us to monitor her there. So, 48 hours later and she was back home.

Once home, Kendall was still just not herself. She was resting a lot, barely playing, and had woken up with a fever the next day after her discharge. The doctor had told us we could treat her at home with Tylenol, but Kendall just didn't seem right to me. She was moaning in pain and vomiting more. So, after just two days at home, she was readmitted. Worry began to set in.

A prayer service had been planned through my church for the next week at the beautiful sunflower field called Prayers From Maria, named after a local little girl who had passed from DIPG (brain tumor). The field was a place to bring awareness to childhood cancer and DIPG, as well as to share the children's photos who had passed from cancer. We had family pictures taken there early on in Kendall's cancer journey and they are just stunning. Kendall had been at that field every year of her life and I would walk through the rows of sunflowers with the girls and look at the children's photos who had passed, not once thinking that could be us someday. The sunflower field seemed like a symbolic, peaceful place to come together to pray over our daughter.

While Kendall was admitted, she was able to get her scans. They were having trouble scheduling the MIBG scan, but they went ahead with the CT scan since Kendall had been vomiting so much. They wanted to rule out a bowel obstruction, which she didn't have. I mentioned that I was worried about going into scans. Anytime a fever was involved it gave me flashbacks to her diagnosis. Kendall hadn't quite been herself either, so I was preparing myself for less-than-desirable news.

All our family, friends, and Kendall's followers were concerned for her and anxious to hear the results. I remember getting several messages from people asking for an update. I still didn't have the whole picture but went ahead and gave an update with the information I did receive on Kendall's page. I explained that the CT scan showed there was progression and of her two new tumors from the last scan; one was unchanged, and one had grown by .9 cm. The CT was also showing a spot on her liver, but we would have to wait for the MIBG scan to have a better picture.

It was August 25, 2018, when we received her MIBG results. We were ushered into a hospital room across the hall from Kendall where several of our team were waiting for us. I knew walking into that room that this was not going to be the news we wanted. It felt so awkward knowing that they all already knew her results, and a bit intimidating having so many there when the doctor gave us the news. I know they were all there for support, but I was shaking.

Kendall's doctor pulled up her scan on the computer monitor and started listing off all the places Kendall's cancer had spread. She was lit up like a Christmas tree. I just wanted to sink into the floor and cry, but instead, because so many in the room were waiting for our reactions, I put on a brave face and tried to stay positive. I didn't want to show any weakness. I had been anticipating the bad news, so I wasn't shocked. I do remember feeling some anger though too. I just wanted someone to fix her. I needed her to be healed. Not that her doctors could have done anything better. Their care was exceptional. But when you are in those most helpless, desperate moments your mind starts to wander. *Did we make the right choice in her care? Should we have taken her back to NYC, or never even come home from there?* That was where my mind was going in that tense hospital room.

This was the point in time when I knew I was going to start taking matters into my own hands. I knew the doctors needed to do what they needed to, but there were things that I could integrate into Kendall's care as her mother, and I was certainly going to fight for her.

I went right into action and started speaking up with the knowledge I had gained from other neuroblastoma parents. I suggested several options for us to investigate, hospitals to call, and different natural treatments I wanted to try. Her doctor agreed to look into the things I mentioned and to start consulting with other hospitals. Wes and I immediately started making calls to hospitals and integrative doctors and made a list of natural supplements to purchase for Kendall's care once we returned to her room.

We consulted over the phone with a highly recommended integrative doctor in Arizona. He was willing to take her as a patient, but he was in agreement with our team that she was in no shape to travel. He did recommend some supplements that we could purchase to help increase her platelet count, as well as some vitamin C powder to help heal her body from the chemo toxicity. This was somewhere to start to try to heal Kendall's body enough to be able to endure more treatment. Meanwhile, Kendall's doctors got to work reaching out to other hospitals to see if there were any clinical trials that she might qualify for.

Here is my post from CaringBridge and my Facebook page from the day we received this terrible news:

"Yesterday evening we received Kendall's scan results. Her cancer has spread again. I can't even believe I am typing these words and that this is happening to our daughter. It feels like we are right back at the beginning all over again. Kendall's cancer is in her lymph nodes, her bones, her spine, and many other areas including the remainder of her original tumor. It is still questionable whether the spot on her liver is cancer or not. She will undergo surgery possibly as soon as Monday to get a biopsy of it and of one of the new tumors as well. Kendall has been very ill this week, ran fevers, and slept most of the week. Also, because she can't tolerate her feeds, she started TPN nutrition today. The other tricky part of this is that her counts keep dropping. The doctors are afraid the cancer has entered her bone marrow as well. A sample has been taken but we still do not know the results. We have been talking with two other hospitals that specialize in neuroblastoma and unfortunately, we cannot go on any trials at those hospitals because of Kendall's

disease burden. If we can gain control again, then she may qualify. So, our hospital, in addition to the two others (MSK and Helen DeVos Children's Hospital) agreed that Kendall needed systemic chemo asap. This would mean giving her some of the chemo's her tumor responded so well to in the beginning, in addition to a chemo her cancer had never seen. Once her disease is minimal and under control, we can pack up and take her to one of these hospitals. But, because of the drop in her counts, specifically platelets, chemo cannot get started right away. An injection was given to try to help them climb. She cannot be transfused because her body needs to be able to make them on her own. We are very sad and heartbroken, but still hopeful. There are still options, we just need to get her stable right now. Please pray for Kendall's miracle."

It pained me to write that update. I cried and shook while I wrote it. It wasn't supposed to be this way. Why was Kendall having to fight so hard? Why had her cancer stopped responding to treatment? How much more was our little girl going to have to endure? We had thought if the frontline treatment didn't work for her, we would still be able to pull other options from our back pocket, but nothing was going according to plan.

Wes and I were so scared and worried. While Kendall slept, we spent hours researching and talking to other doctors in other states to get their opinion. We even made a call to St. Jude's Children's Research Hospital, even though we had heard from other parents that they wouldn't take a child who had started treatment at another hospital. We were desperate and wanted to entertain all our options. Sure enough, we didn't get very far into the call before we were asked if she had already started treatment. We answered yes and that was the end of that. She didn't qualify to go there. I screamed out loud, "Please someone help my baby, why can't anyone help her!!!?" This was the most helpless I had felt yet.

It was around this time that Wes started staying with us at the hospital more. With Kendall being so ill and with me such a wreck waiting for the next steps, I was so grateful I had him there with me to lean on. He too would hear everything the team was telling us about Kendall's care since it was so hard for me to relay to him at times. Kendall enjoyed having both of us there to care for her too. Wes had a wonderful boss who allowed him to work remotely at the hospital and come and go to the office as he could. Kendall was such a daddy's girl and wanted him to sleep in her bed with her every night. I think since I stayed with her mostly, it was a treat for her to get some time with her dad. She loved on him so well and made him feel so special and needed.

Meanwhile, neighbors and friends continued to help with Alexa, but I was sensing it may be time to have my grandmother come and stay again with her since it didn't seem like Kendall would be discharged anytime soon.

Kendall's biopsy was scheduled, and we were wheeled down to the surgery center that morning. I rode in the bed with Kendall and had my arms around her for comfort. I was so sad that she would have to go under yet again for another surgery. Kendall was usually so brave and up for anything, but this time she just wasn't herself. I could tell she was really down and scared. As they were prepping her, she began to cry. Then I cried because I wasn't used to that from her. She was always so strong, which made me strong. But, this time, it was just different. She was tired. I was tired. We were all tired.

Child Life did their best to calm her as she put up a little fight with the nurses and tears continued to stream from her eyes. It is so hard as a parent to watch your child go through such trauma. To have to stand by her bed and not be able to fix it. To not be able to say it would be okay because you didn't know if it was really going to be okay or not anymore.

***

Kendall made it through her biopsy and recovered in her hospital room. She hadn't been out of bed much since her admission, so she was getting very weak. We tried our best to motivate her to get out of bed to play music and paint with her therapists. More times than not she would turn them away. I knew she must have felt pretty crummy to not play with them. One night, I had come up to the hospital after being away at home for a break. I was a little more refreshed and better able to handle Kendall's care. That evening I was able to convince her to get out of her bed to walk to the door and back. She slowly walked with my help and the nurse and I congratulated her for succeeding. It was so hard to see her so weak and struggling to walk, though her willingness to try showed me that fight she had in her and gave me some hope.

It was the day of the prayer service when we received the results from her biopsy. That day I was alone at the hospital with Kendall. She was asleep when her doctor came in and sat at the end of my bed next to me. She gently broke the news to me that the biopsy revealed it was indeed neuroblastoma in Kendall's liver. She explained that in addition to some of the chemo's she had in the past, she would now need a very strong chemo to try to stop this beast. The three hospitals were in agreement and treatment could start as soon as her platelets were recovered. Her doctor told me that she would not survive without this chemo.

She also shared with me the results of Kendall's bone marrow aspiration. For the first time in her journey, the cancer had entered her bone marrow. I was crushed. I feared I was going to lose my daughter. I laid my head on the doctor's shoulder and wept. She put her arm around me and comforted me the best she could.

The options were to give her the chemo with the additional natural supplements through her G tube or to stop treatment and go home and try an all-natural approach. These are gut-wrenching decisions that cancer parents must make. I called Wes to fill him in and we prayed on it, and then agreed to consent to more chemo. We didn't think Kendall was done fighting yet and we were too scared to refuse treatment. We were trusting in her doctors and had hope in their plan.

***

    I left Kendall with my grandma at the hospital, who had arrived in town, and headed to the prayer service to meet Wes. It had rained that day, so I was quite bummed about the sunflower field being wet and muddy. The sun wasn't shining that evening and all the sunflowers were a little droopy, but it reflected the day we were having with the continuation of sad news.

    One positive was that not many other people outside of those we knew were there since it was wet. We basically had the field to ourselves. Unfortunately, we were not able to walk far into the field like I had imagined we would. Instead, we gathered near the front and got started. I hadn't shared the news of the biopsy with anyone yet, so that is where I began. I could hardly get through my words as I began to share what was going on. "We received some unfortunate news today…. the cancer has spread to her liver and bone marrow…".

    We gathered in a circle with all who were there, held hands, and began to pray in the midst of God's beauty. Some pastors from our church had come out, along with one of our worship leaders. I had arranged for some people to read poems and prayers I had picked out. We sang some worship songs, one being "Healer" by Kari Jobe, and opened the floor up to anyone who wanted to pray for us. So many beautiful prayers were said that day, memories with Kendall were shared, and many tears were cried. We felt so supported and loved seeing the crowd that had gathered to pray for our girl. We all were believing in Kendall's miracle and stood firm in our faith.

    In the sunflower field stood a large life-size sign that said "HOPE." It was so suited for the journey we were walking in. No matter what, we always had hope. Hope that the next treatment would work, hope that she would be cured. But if not, we still had hope because of Jesus and what he did for us on the cross.

    We took a group photo by the sign, and many took additional

photos of their families by it. The sun was setting, and the photos came out beautifully. The sun's rays began to shine on the sunflowers and in one photo, the reflection from the sun formed a smile under the word "HOPE." It is one of my favorite photos captured from that evening. We left the sunflower field feeling restored, encouraged, loved, full of hope, and ready for battle. We sure were going to need it.

Chapter 16

The Last Chemo Round

It was the end of August when Kendall received three days of intense high-dose chemo. Her counts had risen enough for the nurses to be able to administer it. I was cringing inside knowing that the side effects were going to be brutal for her. She was already so sick and weak that I feared how her body was going to respond but tried my best to trust in this treatment plan. We just had to gain control over the cancer again.

Kendall had some good moments before the side effects started to set in. She had more fun times being goofy with her nurses, making music on the keyboard with her music therapist, playing with the latest toys she was gifted, and watching some of her favorite shows, such as *Peppa Pig*, on her iPad.

She had days where she was well enough to get out of her bed and come to my comfier bed which had plush blankets, pillows, and a padded mattress topper. She loved the small change of scenery and the privilege of hanging out in Mommy's bed. She would bring all her stuffed animals with her and enjoy the comfort for a bit before having to return to her own bed.

Unfortunately, we couldn't do much with her bed other than a pillow from home and a blanket since she required frequent bed changes. Cancer is messy.

***

As we entered September of 2018, the days grew darker and darker. Kendall had started to suffer from chemo side effects very quickly. Her counts plummeted and other counts such as her liver enzyme level became affected. She was on a pain pump to manage her pain and on IV nutrition to help ease the persistent vomiting. She slept most of the day and we ached for the return of our silly, happy girl.

With every passing day, the symptoms grew worse. Kendall developed a bad cough and had labored breathing. After some tests were run, fluid outside of her lung was discovered. The word "pneumonia" was mentioned, and I went into panic mode. I knew that if she had pneumonia, this could be what would take her life based on what I had seen from other warriors' stories. The waiting and worrying began taking a toll on me and I grew sick to my stomach. I was so thankful Wes was there to step in when I couldn't handle much.

There were so many different care teams involved at this point that there were not many quiet moments. Every time I turned around another person was coming through our door. We also had an increase in friends and family visiting during this time, so Wes and I grew very tired.

One night while I was staying with Kendall by myself, we had quite the scare. Wes had gone home to get a much needed good night's rest. Kendall had been vomiting multiple times a day at this point. I woke up to her violently puking. I don't know how else to describe it. I had never seen anything like this from her. She was struggling to get out more while making these awful, agonizing sounds. When she finally got it out, blood was coming out of her mouth. I hit the nurse's button so fast, and her nurse quickly came and helped me. After this happened a couple more times that night, there was much concern and talk about her being transferred to the PICU.

It is hard for me to remember every detail, but we didn't end up moving to the PICU. More tests and scans were run in the days ahead to check on her stomach. She stopped vomiting blood, and the doctors believed it had been caused by the mucositis. This chemo was absolutely brutal on her. I will never be able to unsee that night in the hospital. It was a horrific sight for a parent to have to see and it caused me great fear as I didn't know what was happening to her body. My own body ached so badly over what she was going through and how scared she must have been as well. My heart hurt that I couldn't fix this for her. All I could do was rub her back and tell her I was so sorry, and that I loved her.

From that point on, Kendall had several more vomiting episodes where she would be trying so hard to get it out. Seeing her struggle and the noise she made that accompanied it broke me. I continued to rub her back and help hold her bucket while she tried with all her might to get it out. Once she finally did, she would breathe a sigh of relief, lean back into her pillow, and say "Ahhh that's better."

Her fuzzy, tiny hairs she had so proudly grown over the summer were now starting to fall out from the chemo. Since they were so short, they were getting in her eyes and mouth and itching her skin. We asked her if she wanted us to shave her head and she did. Wes went home to get his razor and he shaved her head for her, then she shaved his. The plan was that he would shave his head bald like Kendall, but her shaving skills didn't quite cut it. And then I chickened out and didn't want him to shave it. So, he got an interesting haircut but he was able to clean it up okay.

We gave Kendall a warm sponge bath that day and put on her clip-on earrings, and a cute, gray chemo hat. She had fresh pajamas and new bedding and she said she felt so much better. We even took her for a wheelchair ride outside to get some fresh air.

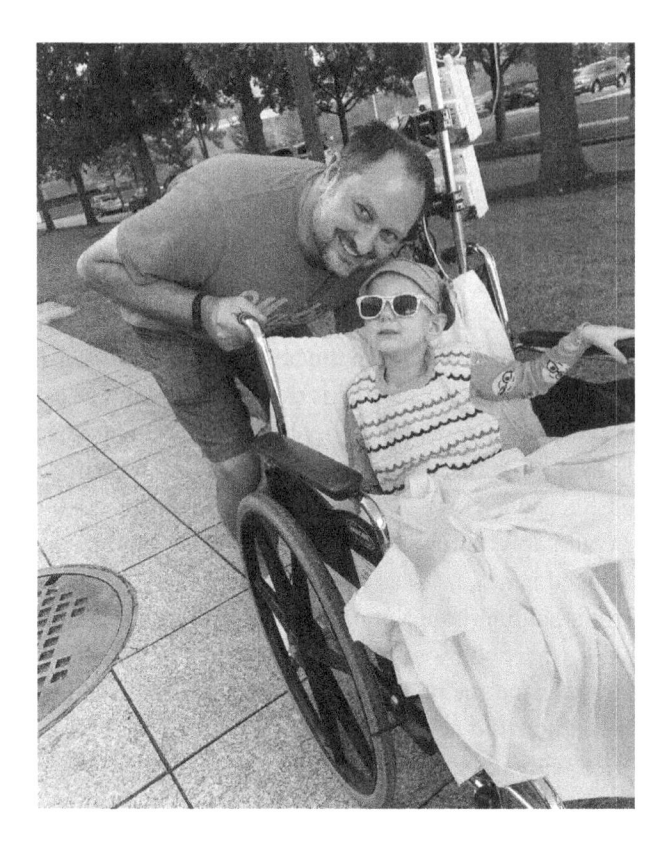

Kendall was never diagnosed with pneumonia, but rather we found out that some of her lymph nodes the cancer had spread to were growing and close to constricting her airway, hence the cough and labored breathing. Kendall became jaundiced from the cancer in her liver and day after day struggled with her counts recovering. The mucositis was so bad that we went and bought her some large bibs to catch all the drool pouring from her mouth. Every so often she would perk up and interact with us, showing us that fight she still had in her. But overall, she was miserable and sleeping her days away. She didn't look good, and I was so scared we were losing her.

It was around mid-September when a meeting was scheduled on the pediatric oncology floor's conference room with some of our team. Kendall's main doctor sat across from us, another doctor on her team sat to our right, and Kendall's nurse for the day, palliative care nurse, and social worker were to our left. When we arrived at the room and saw everyone sitting there, I just wanted to turn around and run away from it all. I knew the news wasn't good. I could see for myself that Kendall wasn't turning a corner and was having a hard time recovering from this treatment. She couldn't break her fevers or make any platelets. Kendall complained of belly pain daily and that wasn't like her to complain, so I knew this was more heartbreaking news.

We took our seats and Kendall's doctor opened the meeting by asking us how we thought Kendall was doing. We said she had been having a hard time with this treatment, but she would occasionally perk up, so we were hopeful. The next thing her doctor said was that Kendall was declining and they didn't think she was going to make it. She told us that she could not give Kendall any more of the chemo regimen she had just been given. It was too dangerous and made her too sick. They wanted to have a meeting set up with hospice to start talking about options and possibly switching care. The palliative care nurse also told us to start thinking about what her wish could be from A Special Wish.

Wes and I were in shock. We knew things were bad but couldn't believe that we were at this point already. I wanted to crawl under the table and hide. I didn't want to have to face this. I didn't want anyone to look at me. How was I hearing these words? Why weren't our prayers being answered? I didn't want to believe it. I felt myself growing angry.

Wes and I somehow found our words and began to ask questions and make suggestions for things we could try. We tried to understand why some things couldn't be done, like a medical flight for her to get transported to other hospitals. We were told it would cost a lot of money and what the other hospitals had to offer her was not going to buy her much time. They explained that they would search the country for other trials for her, but with her current condition and amount of disease, it wasn't looking hopeful. She most likely was not going to qualify for any trials.

Her palliative care nurse stepped into the conversation and brought up the concern that if we did transport her and she died in another state, we would be without our family surrounding us and then would have to pay to transport her body back home. Yes, this really was the conversation we were having. She also asked us a question that we would carry with us as a guide in the days ahead. She said, "At some point, you have to ask yourselves are we doing things to her or for her?" Meaning, is giving her more treatment going to cause her more harm than good?

Tears poured out of us through that meeting. The team was so sad as well and on the verge of tears themselves. Kendall was one of the favorites around the hospital. I imagine it is so hard on them to break such awful news to families. I don't know how they do it with such grace and composure. I remember saying to them through tears "It's not supposed to be this way. I am supposed to have two daughters. I can't lose Kendall."

You can imagine how difficult this conversation was. How were we even talking about this? About my daughter dying. This couldn't be. *She was going to make it, they'll see*, I thought. We would keep researching and making calls. Kendall was a fighter. This couldn't be the end. Wes and I believed that. We were not ready to make the transition to hospice. We declined to meet with them at that time.

One more pressing issue discussed in the meeting was about giving Kendall more radiation on her lung where the lymph nodes were growing. The hope was that radiation would shrink the lymph nodes enough so she could breathe better. We would have a consult later that day with radiology where we would find out that she would be sedated and intubated because of the length of the radiation, which was four hours. She then would be moved to the PICU to recover.

Based on knowing what had happened to other children in our neuroblastoma support group, this didn't sit well with us. When these kids are in this state and get intubated, many never come back from that. Knowing that the doctors didn't think she was going to make it, we couldn't fathom putting her through this with how weak she was. We were afraid she would spend the rest of her days on Earth intubated and we didn't want that for her. But then again, making this decision was awful for us because we sensed the doctors thought we should do it and what if it did help her? More impossible decisions to make as a cancer parent. More time on our knees in prayer.

***

    Walking back to our room after the meeting was the hardest walk. I felt like I could barely pick up my legs again, just like at the beginning of this horrific nightmare. So much was thrown at us, and it was going to take a while to process everything. I had to dry my tears and hold it together for Kendall back inside the room. I was so angry and upset and didn't want to see anyone. All my strength and happiness had been pulled from me and I just wanted to sit in a puddle of tears and feel sorry for myself.
    Wes and I talked a bit back in the room while Kendall was asleep and tried to brainstorm what we could do. We did not want to accept this. We hadn't even had scans yet and I was holding onto hope that there would be a response to the chemo after all the agony it put her through. We decided to look for places near us that could do vitamin C infusions. We thought if we could just get her body healed enough and her counts recovered, we would still be in the fight.
    I needed a break from the hospital before I had a mental breakdown. I headed home to get some fresh clothes and a good night's sleep. I took a walk the next day to clear my mind and spent some time at the pond near our home talking with Jesus. I prayed so hard and with such desperation for him to heal Kendall. For this not to be the end. I feared what people would think of my God now. How was I going to say that God was good if he took Kendall home? I feared I would lose my faith. I

expressed all of this to God that afternoon at the pond and asked him for guidance in the days ahead.

I felt so much better after I had a good cry with God and listened to some praise and worship music. I was ready to head back to the hospital with a renewed spirit and positive mindset. I was believing with all my might that Kendall would get her miracle.

As I drove back downtown to the hospital, I received a phone call from the radiologist. I answered the call knowing how important it was. Kendall's radiologist asked if we gave the approval to start the radiation on Monday. I addressed the concerns we had with her and much to my surprise she agreed. She did not realize that Kendall would have to be under anesthesia for so long. Kendall had started to improve with her breathing as well, so we made the decision to decline.

You would think there would be a sigh of relief after making a decision like that, but when it is a matter of life and death, you just feel sick afterward. Wondering if you made the right decision just eats at you. Luckily, we did make the right decision as we found out on her next scans that her lymph nodes were not any bigger and not constricting her airway. Her cough improved, as well as the fluid around her lungs. I was so thankful God helped us to make the right decision.

***

We met again with Kendall's team to go over her scans to see if the horrific chemo had any effect on her tumors. Her doctor started off by breaking the news that her cancer had progressed again. "Again?" I questioned. "How could it have grown while receiving high-dose chemo?" Her doctor explained that her cancer was chemo-resistant, and it was taking over her body now. Her liver was fully engulfed in cancer and new cancerous lymph nodes were in her stomach. We knew this was very bad.

Her doctor followed up with the other hospitals involved and she came back later that day to inform us that Kendall still did not qualify for any trials. We were losing this fight. Our daughter was slipping away from us, and we weren't sure how much time we had left. We were terrified and so helpless.

Over the next few days, Wes and I made many calls ourselves to other hospitals. We talked to her doctor at MSK and Dr. Scholler who worked at Helen DeVos Children's Hospital in Michigan at the time. She ran many trials for neuroblastoma and helped start the DFMO drug used to prevent relapse in neuroblastoma patients, which was the drug we had fully intended to give Kendall at the end of her frontline treatment. Unfortunately, they said the same things our team was telling us (which we already knew they would). There wasn't anything they could do for her at this time.

We asked for help on our neuroblastoma support group page in finding somewhere close that could help us get Kendall vitamin C infusions. We found somewhere about 45 minutes from our home that would treat pediatric patients. But Kendall was inpatient, and we couldn't bust her out of the hospital. We were stuck. Our hands tied. We begged our team to work with this integrative doctor to get the vitamin C administered to her inpatient. They agreed to look into it.

We spoke to another holistic doctor out in Wisconsin. We had a nice conversation with her, but again there wasn't much more we could do at that point. She offered to take Kendall on as an out-of-state patient and work with us on her nutrition and supplements. We had every intention of trying all that we could. We were very limited with what we could do in the hospital though as a lot was not allowed because it could interfere with the conventional routes of treatment. We did administer what we could through her tube, but we could only do so much.

Kendall continued to sleep a lot, except for the occasions when her sister would come up to visit, or her cousins. She would try so hard to be a kid and play with them, but it was a struggle for her. She couldn't talk much because drool would pour from her mouth, and she was so weak that she would fall back asleep after only playing a short while. We could definitely see she was declining. Day after day she failed to improve.

Since I had kept Kendall's story fairly private, we didn't have as many followers as some of the other cancer kids did. Thoughts filled my mind with fear that we didn't have enough people praying for her. *If I had just had 20,000 followers on her page maybe she would be healed.* The guilt was setting in. I started going back over every part of her journey. All the decisions we had made. All the things we wanted to do for her care but hadn't gotten around to it. If we had just done that or gone here, etc. Negative thoughts were filling my mind.

***

Palliative care nurses would come by our room daily. They made suggestions to get her photos taken and to record as much of her voice as we could. I did not like when they would come by because I did not want to think about Kendall dying. I was in denial and didn't want to talk to them. They would ask us if we thought any more about hospice. We would tell them we weren't ready yet. Kendall would still have moments where she surprised us and gave us glimmers of hope. One day though, they asked if we would at least consider setting up a meeting to see what hospice would be able to offer us. They said we didn't have to make a decision right away, but at least we would have all the information we needed. We finally gave in and agreed to meet.

Grandma G.G. came up to the hospital to stay with Kendall that morning while we met with hospice. I was so angry and still in denial as I walked myself to the conference room. I did not want to believe that Kendall was going to die. Kids were miraculously cured often, and I kept believing that God was going to do the same for her. I did not want to hear anything the hospice team had to say. I had an attitude and was so mad that we had to have this conversation.

Much to our surprise, one of Kendall's nurses from the

beginning was sitting in the room with the hospice coordinator. She had switched jobs and would be one of Kendall's hospice nurses if we chose to go that route. It was comforting to know that we would have this sweet, amazing nurse who was with us at the beginning of Kendall's journey to take care of her. A blessing for sure.

We began talking about the medications hospice would use to keep her comfortable at home, how often the nurses would come out, the med schedule we would have, and the support we would have from the social worker and their grief counselors. They also talked about funeral planning and the help they could provide with that. Again, I could not believe we were having this conversation.

We left the meeting still not able to make a decision about transferring her care. The choices presented to us were to take Kendall home on hospice care, stay in the hospital, or transfer her to a hospice house where she would still have a nurse at all times, but be in a more comfortable setting for her and our family.

We returned to Kendall's room knowing my grandma needed to head out to catch a flight back home to the beach. We shared a bit with grandma about what was talked about, and she left there in tears that day, barely able to speak. I'll never forget watching her heart break before my very eyes. Then came my tears. And they wouldn't stop for a very long time.

***

With each hard conversation we had, my body was broken a little more. I didn't want to eat, I was sick to my stomach, and felt ill from the anxiety and worry. My mind wouldn't stop racing. I couldn't focus. After crying for hours, sick over having to make a decision, and consumed with the fear of losing my daughter, the migraines began. They weren't too bad at first and I could manage them with ibuprofen. But they grew stronger as the days went on and I was in so much pain. I had barely slept in weeks and was feeling so weak.

We had the hospice meeting on a Friday. Shortly after, we noticed that Kendall's abdomen was distended again, just like at diagnosis. It was hard as a rock and Kendall looked so uncomfortable and like it hurt to breathe. Her skin had also yellowed even more from the jaundice.

I had spoken earlier in the week with a friend who lost her daughter to cancer a year earlier. I asked her, "How did you know when it was time to let your daughter go?" Her answer was so helpful to me, and she offered to walk with us through this new chapter. She had nothing but great things to say about hospice and she shared some of her daughter's story with me. There was a defining moment when she and her husband knew their daughter had had enough. As I saw Kendall lying there in pain, unable to do much of anything, I knew we were having that defining moment. Wes and I both looked at each other and we just knew. She was dying and it was time to let her go in peace.

We had the weekend to go over all the options. If we stayed at the hospital, we had round-the-clock care with a team we were comfortable with and whom Kendall loved. But there wasn't much rest for anyone there, the room was so small for visitors, and we had to see many people and patients' families while we were grieving. If we took her to the hospice home, we would have more space, but new nurses and another new space for Kendall to get used to.

While we didn't think we wanted Kendall to die in our home, we also didn't want her to die in the other two places. We had to ask ourselves, "What would Kendall want? What would we want if it was us?" We knew the answer. Kendall would want home. A chance to be in her beautiful bedroom again, to play with her sister, to swing one more time, and to make some final memories as a family. It would also give us a chance to give Kendall all the natural remedies we could and have more control over her care. Most of all, it would give her peace and privacy. There wouldn't be as many beeps, tubes, wires, or other disturbances. She could have a private death at home surrounded by those she loved. When we asked Kendall if she wanted to go home, of course, she said yes.

I had not updated our CaringBridge or Facebook page for days while we were sorting through all of this and processing. Finally, I found the courage to write this post while shaking on September 25, 2018:

"Last week we found out that Kendall's disease progressed right through chemo. There are no more options. We are taking our baby home to enjoy what time we have left with her. Our hearts are shattered. Please respect our privacy during this time as we make precious memories as a family. Prayers for this next chapter are what we need right now."

Chapter 17

Homebound

It was a Monday when we told our team our decision to transfer care. It was a mix of emotions as I felt so defeated and incredibly sad, but I was excited for Kendall to get to go home again and for us to be able to hold and hug her without so many tubes and wires attached. I was hopeful that we would have many more days with her since I had seen some children spend months on hospice.

There was so much to do before we could get Kendall discharged and headed home. We had paperwork to go over and sign, new people to meet from the hospice team, home care supplies to order including a hospice bed, and training for Wes and me. We had no idea that we would be responsible for giving her so many medications at home. We were under the impression that a nurse would be at our home doing most of that. But instead, we were going to be her nurses for the most part, especially through the night. At this point, there was no capacity in my brain to learn anything else. My brain was so foggy, and tears consumed me most of the day, so I was not in any place to comprehend a whole new med plan or learn how to work the pain pump at home. Wes so graciously stepped in to learn what we needed to.

It was also around this time that we had to sign a DNR (do not resuscitate). It came with the package once you switched to hospice. That was hands down one of the hardest things we ever had to do, and we felt sick over it. We were supported by our care team, but feelings of guilt, conflict, and sadness were still there. The cancer was winning in the final leg of this journey.

It took several days to get everything in order. While we were waiting, our wonderful nurses on M50 set up a table in the hall outside our door filled with snacks and drinks for us and those who were visiting to enjoy. It was such a nice gesture, yet so sad because they only provided that for families who were losing their child. I didn't want to be that family.

There were some overwhelming days for both Wes and me, and our girls. Sometimes our room would be full of visitors, and we could tell when Kendall was ready for them to go so she could be in peace. I still didn't want to face our reality and I wasn't in the mood to be social. It didn't help that I was beyond tired and still suffering from migraines. Kendall was also still throwing up so Alexa was having a hard time visiting at the hospital. She would leave the room every time Kendall threw up, which was often. I didn't blame her as the sound Kendall made was frightening.

***

One quiet evening when I was alone in the hospital with Kendall, I had a moment to think about what was happening. All the emotions I was trying to hide from and avoid feeling came to the surface. I lost it and cried my eyes out on my bed while Kendall was asleep. The try to catch your breath kind of cry. I remember crossing my arms over my chest, holding myself, and crying out to God, "I don't want to be a bereaved mother." I feared I would live the remainder of my days broken and sad.

I also was so afraid of how I would be able to go on in life. Would I survive this? Would I ever be okay again? How would people respond to me now? I feared everyone would avoid me because they wouldn't know what to say to me. I feared I would be all alone and left to navigate this next chapter unsupported. I feared I would be the mom in our community that everyone would point out as the mom who lost her daughter, and they would run the other way. I also thought that I wouldn't be allowed to be happy ever again. That if I smiled or found happiness I would be judged. I threw my hands up to God and asked, "What am I going to do now? How could this be your will?" I begged and pleaded with God for this not to be true and for him to heal her.

***

In the days leading up to her discharge, we made some final memories at the hospital. Many from her care team would pop in to see her for one last visit. Even one of her favorite nurses who had moved away came back to see her and it was a special time for them both. Kendall passed out poop emoji stickers to many on her care team, and we even left some on the cabinets in the room for the next child to find. One of the doctors put the sticker on his name badge. A little reminder for him of our sweet, silly girl.

As much as I loved seeing everyone come by to see Kendall, I also was cringing inside and hated that they were saying goodbye. I was still having thoughts of denial and was waiting for her miracle. When Kendall would have those moments when she would perk up and want to play, it gave me hope that this wasn't the end yet.

Our friend from the Radiate Gold Foundation came and decorated her room one last time. Kendall was into superheroes at the end of her life, so the room was decorated with Supergirl and other superheroes, which was so fitting. Kendall even got a Supergirl costume and put it on one day, then got out of bed and sat in the chair. Her doctor was shocked when she came into the room at just the right time to see Kendall sitting there. That was our strong girl, fighting as hard as she could.

Kendall also was feeling well enough one day when Slider, our major league baseball team's mascot, came to the pediatric oncology floor to visit. She happened to have her Wonder Woman costume on and she perked up when he came into the room. I captured a sweet photo of her and Slider hugging.

One last thing we needed to do before we took Kendall home was fill Alexa in on what was about to take place. We had been coached by the hospital psychologist and Alexa's counselor on how to handle this. We were told to tell her the truth and they gave us some books to read with her. How do you tell a six-year-old that her sister is going to die? I knew we had to do it, but it was just so unfair.

Alexa came up to the hospital and we took her down to a lobby area. It was the weekend, so it was quiet, and not many were around which was good. Wes and I sat down on the chairs with her. I explained to her that her sister was very sick, and the doctors didn't think Kendall was going to make it and she would have to go to Heaven to get better. Alexa immediately burst into tears and ran into my lap. She responded, "Now I won't have anyone to play with." I hurt so badly for her. We tried to read one of the books to her, but she was too distraught to focus so we just held her and comforted her the best we could. We told her we would keep praying over her sister and hoped to have many more days with her.

The day came on a Tuesday when all was in order, and we were set to be discharged. Some of Kendall's closest "friends" at the hospital came by to give final hugs goodbye and spent some time with her before the discharge papers were signed. Some of the doctors from her team stopped by and she told one of her favorites that she loved him, which she had told him many times prior as well. She even included a kiss on his cheek a couple of times. It was the absolute sweetest and shocked us all the first time she did it.

Her main oncologist also came by and gave her hugs. Kendall's little arms wrapped around her neck, and I broke a little more. Their bond was so special and Kendall loved her. I could only imagine what her doctor was feeling at that moment. It must be so hard to not be able to save your patient. To work so hard to cure them, just to have to let them go. And to see that happen over and over again. Absolutely heartbreaking.

Kendall had grown very close to the nurse who cared for her often during her last stay. This was the same nurse she had at the beginning of her diagnosis who she once told, "Me not like you." But Kendall loved her now, so much so that she wanted her to come home with us.

This nurse was so motherly to Kendall and gentle in nature. Kendall was attached to her and the last photo I have of them together shows the special bond they had. Her nurse had picked her up and Kendall had her arms around her with her head resting on her shoulder and her eyes closed. It shows the love between them and the comfort her nurse provided her. The picture still tears me up to this day. It takes a special person to place themselves in that environment and provide care to a dying child and their family. She was an angel in our eyes.

Kendall had not been doing too well the last couple of days before discharge day. We were so anxious to get home and feared she wouldn't make it. She was declining quickly, and we were not sure we would have very long with her once we got home. Our reality was setting in. She visibly looked like she was dying.

We had asked Kendall if she would like to have an early Christmas with princesses and Santa. She nodded her head yes with what little excitement she could conjure up. We had planned for A Special Wish to give her this wish as quickly as possible once we got home. We were praying and hoping she would make it long enough to receive it.

***

It was just Wes and me at the hospital with Kendall on the day she was discharged. His parents were at our home helping to get everything ready for Kendall's homecoming. Since Kendall was not in the best shape, we arranged for an ambulance escort home. Once the paramedics arrived, they placed Kendall on the stretcher, unhooked her from the hospital pumps, and she was ready to leave M50 for the last time. I could barely pick up my feet as I felt so heavy and out of body. This seemed so surreal. I couldn't believe I was witnessing this scene. I did not want this to be our reality. I was terrified to leave.

When we reached the hallway, we were surprised to see Kendall's entire care team lined up along both sides of the wall. I am not sure how I didn't lose it again, but I did pretty well maintaining composure for Kendall's sake. We hadn't told her that there wasn't any more treatment to save her. All she knew was she got to go home and be free from the hospital. Wes and I hugged everyone as we made our way through. Everyone told Kendall their goodbyes and gave her more hugs. I am sure Kendall could sense something was up as we had never had this kind of farewell on a discharge day before, and many on her care team had tears in their eyes. It was for sure another deeply emotional moment.

Only one of us could ride in the ambulance with Kendall. We let her choose, and being the daddy's girl that she was, she chose Wes. We exited the hospital from a side door that led right to the ambulance parked outside. The paramedics had asked Kendall on the ride down if she wanted to drive to the airport to see the Cleveland Clinic helicopters. Kendall was excited about the opportunity and agreed to go. I stayed until Kendall was secure in the ambulance and then parted ways with plans to meet back up at home.

I crossed the street to get to my car in the parking garage. I remember nearly collapsing onto the ground as I was trying to get there. My legs felt weak and were trying to give out on me as they trembled. I leaned myself against a wall and took some deep breaths as tears were rolling down my cheeks. I made it to my car and waited awhile before I had enough composure to drive. I really should have had someone there that day to take me home.

    Thoughts flooded my mind as I made the drive to our house, which seemed like forever. This was really happening. We were taking our daughter home on hospice. We were embarking on a new chapter. It was either going to end with Kendall's miracle or her healing in Heaven. Whichever the ending, all I could do was surrender, trust God, and pray the hardest I ever had. Either ending to this next chapter would be a win-win for Kendall. Whether she received her healing on Earth or in Heaven, she would finally be set free. If she received her miracle on Earth, she would have more time with family and get to grow up. If she received her miracle in Heaven, she would be in her new, perfect and wondrous home with Jesus. Only time would tell what her fate was.

Chapter 18

Hospice Days

I arrived at our home first since Wes and Kendall were on a special trip to see the helicopter. I walked into my house to see the hospice bed set up in our living room. *People die on that bed*, I thought. It made me so sick to my stomach. *How could that be in our home?* It was so unbelievable. My head was pounding from the ongoing migraine I couldn't get rid of, which was exacerbated by my tears. My house was in shambles as I hadn't been home in so long and furniture had been rearranged to fit in the hospice bed.

Alexa was at the neighbor's and waiting with the girls' friends for Kendall to arrive home. I was worried the ambulance might scare Alexa, so I allowed her to stay at the neighbor's to observe from afar with her friends. It seemed to be taking forever for Wes and Kendall to get back. I paced the house as I waited and waited.

Finally, the ambulance pulled up. Kendall ended up not getting out of the ambulance to see the helicopter. She just gazed at it from inside, which I kind of figured might happen. The paramedics wheeled her on the stretcher into our home and right up next to the hospice bed to transfer her. Watching all of this take place was almost debilitating for me. The scene made me even sicker to my stomach. I could barely function, and my body was shaking. I so badly wanted to wake up from this horrific nightmare. *This was not how Kendall's story was supposed to end. How can I stop this from happening? There must be something we can do.* "God, please help her, help us, we need you," I prayed in my head.

I went outside to grab some of Kendall's things from the ambulance and I could see Alexa and her neighbor friends perched on the front porch of the house two doors down, peeking over with curiosity. I felt so bad for them that they were having to witness Kendall in this state. I didn't force Alexa to come home. We had enough going on and I knew she would come around in her own time.

We had to wait a bit for Kendall's hospice nurse to arrive to help us get her hooked up to the pain pump. In the interim, Kendall was not happy being in a foreign bed. She mustered up her voice to tell us that she wanted her bed. Since she wasn't hooked up yet, Wes carried her upstairs to the beautiful bedroom Special Spaces created for her for moments like these. A place to rest and find solace. Home to her meant the comforts of home, like her bed. Not another hospital bed that was now the centerpiece in our living room.

We let her rest in her beautiful princess bed for as long as we could. We tried to make her hospice bed as comfortable and cozy as possible in the meantime. My mother-in-law had put Kendall's *Frozen* bedsheets on and we put comfy pillows and blankets on the bed for her to cover up with.

Eventually, we had to take her back downstairs and get her set up on the pain pump and TPN nutrition once our nurse arrived. She needed to be on the first floor where we could keep an eye on her. It was going to be too hard to move her between floors with tubes attached to her. Wes and I went over her care with the hospice nurse and got all her med supplies organized in a three-drawer rolling cart that we placed next to her bed. It seemed that her med schedule was heavier than we had ever experienced. She would be getting medicine every couple of hours around the clock. We were already so exhausted that this felt impossible.

Alexa decided to come home that evening and took quite a while before she had the courage to get close to Kendall's bed. I am sure she was fearful, and this was just as uncomfortable for her as it was for me. Kendall was so happy to see her and just wanted her to hug her and be close. Alexa was upset though and having a hard time processing her emotions. She thought it was unfair that Kendall was taking up so much of our time. She was almost seven when Kendall came home on hospice, so she was too young to be able to comprehend what was happening. She felt less important and less loved and it broke my heart.

We explained to Alexa the best we could why Kendall needed so much of our attention and that we loved her just as much. She acted out some over our time home on hospice, but things got better, and she warmed up to Kendall. We were fortunate to have Alexa's wonderful counselor come out to our home to help her process her emotions during the final weeks of her sister's life.

While my in-laws were still at our house, I decided to get some much-needed sleep. I needed to recharge the best I could to be able to help Wes administer meds throughout the night so he could sleep some too. There was no way he would be able to do this on his own. After a couple of days spent with us, his parents returned home so we could have some time as a family making what memories we could with Kendall.

***

First up was Kendall's wish. We had planned to have her wish trip at Give Kids the World Village and Walt Disney World. She also wanted to swim with dolphins. Since we couldn't give Kendall that wish in her current state, A Special Wish did their magic and got her new wish of an early Christmas with Santa and princesses together in just 24 hours! They told us to send them all the gift ideas the girls wanted. Nothing was too big. They wanted to go all out for both of them. They worked fast since we had no idea how long Kendall had left.

The morning of her wish, her hospice nurse came out to get her all set for the day. We had two alternating hospice nurses, both of whom were so kind and gentle in spirit. These nurses are so amazing to do what they do and are angels on Earth. It was such a comfort to us when they were there, and I was grateful that Kendall's pain was able to be managed well.

My good friend, who also was Kendall's best friend's mom, came over with her camera to capture every moment for us of Kendall's special day. I was glad she could be there with us and that we had someone we knew capturing such treasured, precious moments.

The girls wore their matching Christmas nightgowns for the occasion and could hardly wait to tear open all their new gifts. They had been asking all morning with eager anticipation when everyone would arrive. Then finally, the elves from A Special Wish showed up to our home and got to work in our garage prepping everything. Before I knew it, the elves had turned our living room into a festive space donned with Christmas trees, garlands, and lights.

Next, they brought in all the gifts and placed them neatly in front of the fireplace. There were piles and piles all wrapped in beautiful Christmas paper! The level of joy in that room was through the roof!

To make the moment even more magical, the princesses had arrived dressed in their Christmas best. Ariel, Tinker Bell, and Snow White were ready to help make Kendall's day extra special. They gathered around her bed and handed her gifts. They interacted with her and sang Christmas songs to her as she discovered what was in each package. They showed Alexa love too and stood by her side as Alexa's special gift was rolled in…a brand-new bike! Alexa's face was priceless! Her jaw dropped so far!

While all of this was so incredible and special for the girls, my heart ached for Kendall. She looked so uncomfortable, could hardly smile or talk, and grew tired quickly with opening gifts since there were so many. Alexa had to help her finish opening them. The girls had received many accessories for their American Girl dolls, and Peppa Pig toys, L.O.L. blankets, Barbies, princess dolls, and so much more.

Then, the most magical moment of all came. Santa himself was coming through our doors! Santa was in our home! This Santa looked like the real deal. He made me want to believe. He had an authentic, white beard, and a beautiful red and white Santa suit. He was so good with Kendall and as he approached her bed, she perked up and lifted her little arms up to him so she could give him a hug. She had loved Santa since she was a baby. The photos my friend captured of all of this are incredible. They truly capture the magic of Christmas. My heart was exploding with joy and my eyes were filled with both sad and happy tears. A bittersweet moment.

I was so thankful that we were able to give Kendall her wish. We took some beautiful family photos, the last we would ever have together, and then Kendall was worn out and went back to sleep.

***

In the days that followed, we made as many memories as we could. We had family movie nights, played dolls in Kendall's bed with her, and we all camped out in the living room together each night to be with her. Some days, Kendall would attempt to get out of her bed and play on the floor with Alexa with their new doll schoolhouse. She couldn't interact much or play as she once did. She would only make it about twenty minutes before wanting to return to her bed to sleep or watch her iPad. But during the time that she was up, she was still trying her best to be a kid and to make us laugh.

She would pretend that she was a baby and say, "Goo goo ga ga," or she would dance in her hospice bed by moving her upper body and swaying her arms to the music with what strength she still had. One morning at 5 a.m., Kendall woke us all up because she was giggling away over potty talk of course. Being woken up from her laughter was the absolute best! How incredible she was to try to get us to laugh while she was so close to death. Those were the moments we lived for during that time. Those sweet, unexpected memories we would forever cherish.

***

Wes was taking great care of Kendall and had our new schedule down. He would tell me what I needed to do if he was sleeping or had to leave. Kendall would often say, "I in pain," and we would hit the button for her to get a dose of her pain medication, which she said helped her feel better. We were continuing to push some supplements through her G tube to try to help buy some time. Kendall liked to have a cool washcloth on her head throughout most of the day and she also really enjoyed taking baths. She couldn't take them for so long during her treatments, but now we didn't have to worry as much. We still used caution, and minimal water, and placed her in the bathtub to feel the warm water on her skin. It seemed to soothe her, and she would ask for one every night. I'm sure she missed them so much.

One thing we were hoping Kendall would get to do was swing again on her beautiful swing set. Unfortunately, she was never strong enough to sit on her swing again, nor had the desire to. We did have one day though that she wanted to go outside and lay in our hammock. We took her outside, laid her down in it, and were able to swing her gently.

Because Kendall was having low platelets when we left the

hospital, we had planned on bringing her back occasionally for transfusions, mainly because we feared her bleeding out at home. We didn't want Alexa to have to witness any more horrors than she already had. Our team had arranged for ambulance transport in order to keep Kendall comfortable on the ride down to the hospital to get her infusions. It was comforting to see our team again, but it was not easy seeing Kendall pushed on a stretcher through the hospital. She did not look well at all, and I couldn't wait to get taken back to a private room.

Kendall was loved on by our team as she mainly slept while getting her platelet transfusion. They would come and kiss her on her sweet head as she lay there like an angel. We only brought her to the hospital twice for infusions while she was on hospice. Of course, she didn't leave the hospital without more gifts. A bunch of American Girl dolls had just been donated so Kendall picked one out for her, and then asked if she could get one for her sister too. That was our Kendall. Always thinking of others and Alexa was so grateful that Kendall picked her out a new doll. It was Kendall's final gift to her sister.

***

We had visitors most days that would pop in for an hour or two. No one stayed too long since Kendall slept most of the day. Everyone was coming to say their goodbyes and it was heart-shattering, as well as overwhelming. Our hospice social worker suggested we have an open house and tell everyone it was their chance to come by one last time to see her. This would eliminate the daily visits and allow us time alone with Kendall and more time for us to rest. The open house worked well but was a very tiring day for us all. While it allowed many people to come by, we still would have the occasional drop-ins. We also had social workers and grief counselors coming by to start to help us prepare for her death, and I didn't want to listen to any of it.

During these days at home, we could visibly see Kendall's

cancer spreading. It had now spread to her face and skull and presented with raised, hard bumps on her skin. She had a tumor on the top of her head, one to the left of her eye, and another above her right eye. Her doctor saw the bumps when she was in for the transfusion and she confirmed that they were most likely tumors. Only a biopsy could tell us for sure, but there was no point in putting Kendall through that at this time. It was awful to be able to physically see these tumors and to know the cancer was continuing to spread. Kendall also said that they hurt so I felt so bad for her.

As we began the second week of Kendall being home, she began to sleep more and more. Our hospice nurses told us this was a sign she was getting closer to her death. They had to turn off her TPN because she was retaining too much fluid, which without nutrition it wouldn't be long. We prayed so hard and had pastors come to pray over her. People brought over prayer blankets, a traveling Mary, and Holy Water. Everyone was desperate to help us save our daughter.

Kendall began to withdraw from us, another normal thing that happens as someone is dying, as our hospice nurse explained. It was hard to have her push me away and for her to tell me she didn't want me in her bed. She just wanted peace and to be left alone, which I couldn't blame her after all she had endured. Sometimes I could sneak in a soft kiss on her little head or whisper an "I love you" to her when she was in a deep enough sleep.

Our hospice social worker had told us that we needed to start planning for her funeral and I wanted no part of that. I wanted to spend every minute I had left with Kendall, not planning for something that I was still not wanting to accept. But she made a good point that we at least needed to pick out a funeral home so that when she died, we would know who to call to come and get her. *Great*, I thought. Just what I wanted to do was research funeral homes.

We were told that many funeral homes give significant discounts for children. She gave us the names of some to start looking into and Wes and I spent an afternoon calling to get quotes for our daughter's funeral. It was just as awful as you can imagine. Even with the discount, we were shocked at how much a funeral cost. Thankfully, my sister had reshared our Go Fund Me page asking for help with funeral expenses and many so generously gave.

We also had to decide where to lay her to rest. Again, I was doing all of this against my will and not wanting to believe for a second that this was happening. It all seemed so wrong. But I did what I was told to do.

We had many family members buried in a cemetery about twenty minutes from our home. Knowing that made it feel a tad bit more comforting that Kendall would be near relatives if we chose that one. It was absolutely beautiful on their grounds so I knew I wanted to look there first. They also had a funeral home on their property so we called them to inquire. We had already called a few other funeral homes, but with this call it was different. They had so much compassion and empathy and offered to come to our home to go over all the details so we didn't have to leave Kendall. That was above and beyond to us and put them at the top of our choices before even meeting with them.

My parents joined us that evening as we met with some of the funeral planners and directors at our home. It felt so weird to be talking about this while Kendall was alive in our home. She stayed asleep the whole time while we told them a bit about Kendall and started going over what they could offer us. They truly seemed to care and even had tears in their eyes as we spoke. A deep connection was being formed and everything they could offer us seemed right.

I was barely functioning and felt out of my body again. It was like I was there in the room, but not fully. All the grief was taking a toll on me with the lack of sleep, not wanting to eat, constant migraines, and a strange pain in my side that grew worse each day. I nearly vomited as a catalog was brought out showing the different casket options they had for Kendall.

Seeing the tiny coffins and having to pick one out for her was just sickening. I was screaming in anguish on the inside and didn't want to believe that this was Kendall's fate.

We arranged to meet again the next day at the cemetery so they could show us the grounds and plots available. My parents met us there, as we were all interested in buying plots together, and a neighbor stayed with the girls.

As we pulled into the cemetery, I knew, at first sight, this was the place. A beautiful fountain greeted us beyond the gates, and tons of trees, flowers, and green space surrounded us as we drove in. It was a large property that stretched out over 170 rolling acres and overlooked a beautiful river. I sensed so much peace as we were taken through the property to look at different plots. There was beauty everywhere. I also loved that they had a tall Jesus statue overlooking one of the sections. We thought maybe that would be where we would choose until we found the section called the "Heart." It was a more private section and backed up to a beautiful, wooded area. The street is shaped into a heart and cherry trees were lined on each side. We were told they were a breathtaking sight when they were in bloom.

We agreed with my parents that though these particular plots cost a bit more in the "Heart", this was where we all wanted to be buried. So that day I did something I never expected to do at age 36, which was to buy my plot to be buried in along with my daughter's. Wes and I bought the two plots to the left of Kendall's, and my parents bought the two to the right. We did not buy one for Alexa because we wanted to let her choose someday and were factoring in that she would have a family of her own and may not even live nearby.

It felt good to have a plan and be able to go back home to be with Kendall. The only thing I had left to do was pick out a dress for her. I knew it needed to be fancy like she would want. A friend had told me how Amazon of all places had the most beautiful dresses for girls. She was right and it didn't take me long before I found the most elegant, lacy, pink gown for Kendall. I found a headband with flowers to match it and made the purchase. I wept as I thought of Kendall wearing it in her casket.

There was a term our hospice social worker shared with us called "anticipatory grief." She explained that we had started grieving the day our daughter was diagnosed. Then when we met with our team a month prior and heard the news that she wasn't going to be healed, we started to grieve over the thought of losing her. We were able to start preparing ourselves and processing our emotions which helped us during these final days of her life. We had already begun moving through the stages of grief, though not in order. We would bounce back and forth between the stages or feel them all at once. Denial. Anger. Bargaining with God. Depression. Acceptance. At this point, we were accepting that her death was imminent, though we still pleaded with God for there to be another way.

**

Kendall ended up being home on hospice for two and a half weeks. One day, near the end of the second week, a neighbor was over visiting with us. Wes had gone out to get more supplements we were out of and was not back home yet. Kendall had been sleeping while my neighbor and I were talking. Then, my neighbor noticed that Kendall was pointing to the ceiling in her sleep. I got off the couch quickly and ran to her side. It appeared she wasn't breathing. Her breathing had been changing and she would go longer in between breaths, but I was still panicked that this was the end.

I shook her a couple of times and said her name. She was still pointing and I continued to try to wake her. I was so relieved when she finally woke up and yelled at me, "Mommy I'm sleeping!" She then turned her head and went back to sleep. I was so thankful she wasn't going to pass while her daddy was out. That day, I think she was pointing to what visions she was having of her new life in Heaven. Maybe she even saw the angels coming for her, but they decided to let her stay a little longer since her daddy wasn't home.

***

Wes had been talking with an integrative doctor back and forth. She was the local doctor who was willing to give Kendall a vitamin C infusion in her office. Kendall had some good days and was up playing a little more when we decided that maybe we should try to take her in.

By the time we got everything in place though with the integrative doctor, Kendall had been back to sleeping more, of course. But we still decided to go ahead with the appointment and take her in. We felt so helpless sitting by her bedside watching her die and we just wanted to be able to say we tried everything to save her. There was a doctor willing to try a treatment for her so we felt we had to at least try. We made sure to ask her if she was okay with taking a car ride and she said "Yes."

We had about a 45-minute drive to get there and Wes said we could look at it as her last adventure. She slept the whole way there and we kept her as comfortable as possible. It was a pleasant, sunny Wednesday and she was able to get some fresh air in the stroller ride from the car to the doctor's office. The doctor was so kind and made Kendall a comfortable space on a recliner to sleep while she received the two-hour-long infusion. Everything went well and she also gave her a drug called Lasix to remove any extra fluid the infusion may have given her.

We asked the doctor if there was anything else we could do to try to save her. She said that she needed nutrition if we wanted her to live longer. So, once we got back home, we started giving her some syringes filled with formula. Not too much though. We just gave her a few throughout the day. Well, that did not go over well. Kendall began throwing up again, which she hadn't done since her TPN was stopped, so we felt horrible that we made her sick again. We were just trying to do everything we could to save our baby. We immediately stopped giving her formula.

It was at this time that we noticed her eye was swollen shut from the tumor above it. It appeared more tumors were popping out on the top of her skull as well. That was when we knew that we just had to stop trying to save her and let her go. She deserved to go peacefully. She had fought so hard but this time she just didn't have any more fight in her. She was knocked down and couldn't get back up anymore. We could see that she was tired and her body had had enough.

We had to surrender the situation to God. Our prayers then changed. We began to pray that God would take her soon and peacefully so she could be released from her pain. We were so scared of what the end might be like for her. I had never been with someone when they died before and I wasn't sure what to expect. I just didn't want her to struggle.

***

The next day, Kendall was not any more energized from the infusion. She was actually weaker and her breathing began to change that evening. I wasn't sure if this was the death rattle I had heard about, and I was so scared. I called our hospice nurse to come out and check on her. She agreed that her breathing had changed and also pointed out that her heart rate was slowing down. She left that night telling us that we were getting closer. I was so thankful to her hospice nurses that they had her pain managed so well and that she wasn't struggling.

I could not sleep that night as I was afraid she was going to leave us at any minute. But morning came, and Kendall was still with us. She would ask for a few sips of water from time to time and she would stick her little feet out of her blanket which meant she wanted a foot rub. Her breathing was still different and a little rattled. The throwing up had thankfully stopped and she was resting comfortably. Our hospice nurse came out to check on her and put on some serene spa music for her. Kendall seemed to enjoy it and it helped her sleep so peacefully.

On Friday, we sent Alexa to the neighbor's because we feared Kendall would not make it through another night. Alexa's counselor had said to let her choose if she wanted to be there for Kendall's death and she did not. This was such an awful, hard, unfair circumstance for a young child to go through and I wasn't about to add any more trauma to her life. Her counselor said that when Kendall passed, we could give Alexa the option to see her before they came and took her away.

Friday night, I decided to head upstairs to sleep in my bed. We had still been sleeping on the couch and air mattress in the living room, but I had been so tired from the previous night that I thought I would try to get a couple of hours of sleep while Wes watched Kendall.

That same evening, Wes's sister had gone into labor and we were expecting another niece to be born. Kendall wanted to meet her so badly as she loved babies so much. We like to think that somehow their souls crossed paths as our niece was born into this world on October 13th, 2018, around 2:15 a.m. That was around the same time Wes had come upstairs to wake me to tell me that Kendall's breathing had changed again and I needed to come downstairs. I woke up and grabbed my phone to see the news that our niece had been born, a sweet blessing God gave us on the worst day of our lives.

Wes and I both sat on Kendall's bed, one of us on each side of her, and she allowed us to stay this time. There was no more kicking us out of her bed. The time was near. We could feel it.

We told her how much we loved her, how proud we were of her, how hard she fought, and how many lives she touched. We told her how strong and brave she was. We told her that her baby cousin was just born and we were so sorry she wouldn't get to hold her. I told her I was so sorry that we couldn't fix her boo-boo, but that she would be all better soon when she got to Heaven and saw Jesus. She nodded her little head up and down the slightest bit as if she was saying okay, I understand.

Through tears, we told her she wouldn't have cancer anymore and we would meet her there in Heaven someday. We told her Jesus would take care of her until we got there and he had a swing waiting for her. I was so glad she knew and loved Jesus since she would be seeing him face to face soon. I played some of her favorite songs softly as I held her hand and kissed her cheeks. And then with the most heartbreaking sentence we ever had to speak, we told her it was ok if she was ready to go be with Jesus now.

***

We didn't know how much time she had left, but we didn't put it past her to hang on until the morning being the warrior she was. Wes wanted to get a little sleep, so it was my turn to watch Kendall. Wes laid down on the couch next to her hospice bed. I laid down next to Kendall in her bed to get some cuddles since she was allowing me to be by her. I switched the music to the relaxing spa music Kendall seemed to enjoy earlier and she settled herself back into a deep sleep. I wanted to place my arm around her but I didn't out of fear of hurting her hard, swollen stomach. Instead, I just lay on my side facing her, watching her breathing become slower and slower.

    The next thing I knew I had fallen asleep. The relaxing music calmed me so much that my body fell into rest. A couple of hours into it I frantically awoke and immediately checked on Kendall. I jumped out of bed quickly and yelled for Wes to wake up. "I think she died!" I exclaimed with fear. It appeared Kendall was not breathing. "I fell asleep, oh my gosh I fell asleep I'm so sorry," I said to Wes as I began to cry.

    Wes got up and grabbed the stethoscope because he thought he saw her chest rise. He listened and wasn't sure if he heard her heartbeat or not. I listened too and heard something but wasn't sure if that was it. We scanned Kendall over. Her mouth was parted open and her eyes were slightly open. It appeared there was no life left. Her soul had left her body. I called our hospice nurse and told her that Kendall had just died. She said she would be right over.

Kendall's body was still warm and not stiff so I must have woken up right as she was passing from this life to her next. I looked at the clock and it was 5:30 a.m. on the Saturday morning of October 13th, 2018, just hours after her cousin was born. There was joy in new life, but sorrow over death. Joy and sorrow are always coexisting. God provided joy for us through our niece while we were experiencing the deepest pain of our lives. We wept uncontrollably over the loss of our beautiful daughter. Her battle was finished.

***

As upset as I was at myself for falling asleep and missing her last breath, I was grateful that she died so peacefully. We couldn't have asked for a better way for her to depart from this world than softly and quietly in her sleep. We had an overwhelming sense of peace now that she was fully healed, made whole, and beginning her new life in eternity with Jesus. The saddest day for us was the best day for her as she met her Jesus face to face and was greeted by our family members who were waiting for her there. She was surrounded by the splendor, beauty, and glorious riches of her new home. It was her Heaven day! She no longer had to suffer through cancer. She was set free. How wonderful that must have felt for her! She was now in the place that I long to be and I can't wait to see her there again someday. I am so thankful that the grave is not the end.

Scripture says that "Our bodies are buried in brokenness, but they will be raised in glory. They are buried in weakness, but they will be raised in strength" (1 Corinthians 15:43, NLT). Because of this truth, we could grieve with hope. We were temporarily separated, but we would be together in Eternity.

One of Kendall's hospice nurses had previously told us that

"Death can be so beautiful." I couldn't appreciate that statement at the time but looking back, I can see what she meant. Kendall was surrounded by love. Over the weeks home on hospice, her friends and family gathered by her bedside to pray, say their goodbyes, and walked her to Heaven's gates. She was comfortable and had minimal pain. Her breathing changed but it wasn't scary, and she didn't struggle. She drifted off to sleep with her parents nearby and when she woke up, she was in Heaven. She indeed had a beautiful death.

Chapter 19

A Celebration of Life

It felt like an eternity waiting for our hospice nurse to arrive at our home. I began pacing the house, shaking, trying to make sense of what just happened and going through the timeline of events in my head. Though I had peace knowing her suffering had ended, I still was feeling guilt over falling asleep and was upset that God didn't answer my prayer of getting to see a glimpse of Heaven as she passed. I had really hoped for that. I kept looking out the windows into the sky that morning searching for anything that would give me a sign. I specifically asked God for a rainbow, but sadly one never appeared.

My husband was so gracious to me and easily could have been upset with me over falling asleep, but he instead comforted me. I was so distraught and he helped calm me down. He told me that this was the way Kendall wanted it. He also reminded me that we were able to say our final words to her and then she drifted off into a peaceful sleep. He joked that she didn't want me shaking her again like I had that day I thought she had passed while he was out. I was so thankful he wasn't mad at me, but I was really beating myself up and saying over and over that I would never forgive myself for missing her last breath.

Looking back now, I can see how it happened just how Kendall wanted. Many loved ones pass away shortly after you tell them your goodbyes and say it's okay for them to go. Maybe she didn't want us to see her die so that is why she waited until we all were asleep. I'm so grateful that I was next to her in the end as she graduated to Heaven. I was the first person in her life to ever hold her and the last person to ever touch her (I would have been holding her if I could). I like to think she sensed me there and was comforted to have her mom close to her as the angels came to get her.

Through my tears and trembling, I began calling family members. Once I notified our closest family, I called our congregational care pastor that had been with us from the beginning of Kendall's journey. I told him through tears that I had fallen asleep and that I was very upset over it. He comforted me in the same way and with the same words as Wes did. That was how she was supposed to go. He said he would be right over. I tried to let it go and just focus on what we needed to do for Kendall at that moment.

I called over to our neighbor's house where Alexa was staying to let them know Kendall had passed. We went over to their home a bit later to talk to Alexa once she woke up. She took the news much better than we expected. We asked her if she wanted to come and see Kendall, but she didn't. Her counselor had told us that it would be important for her to see her sister dead so she understood that she wasn't coming back. But we would have our chance to show Alexa her sister at the wake and funeral so we honored Alexa's wishes and didn't force her to come home.

Kendall's hospice nurse arrived promptly to check her vitals and pronounce her death. She then began cleaning up all the supplies, unhooking Kendall's tubes, and pouring out Kendall's medications. It was comforting to have her there and she told us we could enjoy our time with Kendall for as long as we wanted. I didn't want to wait too long on calling the funeral home as I didn't want to see anything else happen to her body, but we kept her with us for a couple of hours.

It wasn't long before our family and friends started to arrive. Everyone wanted to come and see her before the funeral home came to get her body. I was so in shock that this was our reality. That our daughter was no longer with us. My body ached so badly for her. Literally. I was in so much pain and could barely make it through each minute. It was hard to even breathe. My body was so heavy with grief.

Family and friends gathered around us as we sat next to Kendall in her bed. Our pastor arrived and prayed over us. I put on the song "I Can Only Imagine," by MercyMe. It felt so fitting for that moment as we were all imagining what Kendall was now experiencing in her new life in Heaven. Worship had been such an essential part of her journey so even though we hurt, I knew we needed to sing to God in that painful moment. Kendall was free. Her chains were gone. This led me to play the next song, "Amazing Grace (My Chains Are Gone)," by Chris Tomlin. We praised God for healing her in Heaven and taking away her pain. We knew that Kendall had a whole eternity in Heaven ahead of her. She was more alive now than ever in her new heavenly body and for that, we could worship.

Wes and I gave Kendall one last final sponge bath and changed her into her pink Supergirl tutu dress, which was fitting because she would always be our superhero. After she was cleaned up, I sat in her bed and Wes picked up her stiff, cold body and placed her into my arms. It was then, that her eyes closed a little more and her lips closed together and formed a smile. Everyone in the room marveled at how special that was that she had a smile once she was placed in my arms. She looked beautiful and peaceful as I kissed her cheeks and head over and over.

***

I was absolutely dreading calling the funeral home. I didn't want to leave her side. I knew this was going to be so painful carrying Kendall out of our home for the last time and I didn't know how my body could bear any more pain. Once we made the call, a van from the funeral home showed up quickly. This was just a minivan that had a stretcher in the back. A lady was driving the van and it all just seemed so wrong. She deserved a princess carriage to escort her to the funeral home. *How was I just going to hand her over to this lady to place her in the back of her van?*

Our hospice nurse helped us through this difficult moment. She had our family and friends wait outside so Wes and I could be with Kendall alone. She told us we could grab one of her dolls or other comfort items to send with her. We chose her L.O.L. blanket and one of her American Girl dolls. It made us feel just the slightest bit better knowing she would have something she loved with her.

The time had come to carry Kendall out to the van. Wes wrapped her up in her L.O.L. blanket and picked her up. Our hospice nurse spotted Wes as it was difficult to carry her with how stiff she had become. I was so worried other neighbors or passersby would be around and see this tragic sight. But God took care of everything and we had a private moment with our friends and family on our front lawn.

Wes placed Kendall onto the stretcher and the lady from the funeral home and our nurse took care of the rest. We kissed her goodbye as many times as we could before the van door was closed and they drove away. It was every bit as painful and hard as I imagined it would be. She was gone.

A part of me died too in that moment. I nearly collapsed into the ground but our family and friends surrounded me and held me up, just as they would do for months and years to come. Loud cries and groans were coming from many of our loved ones too as they grieved as well. I'll never forget the shrill cries coming from my mother. She was so broken not only over losing her granddaughter, but also over the sight of her own daughter in pain over the loss of her child.

Grief takes a tremendous toll on your body and the pain was unbearable. Between the headaches, the pain in my side, the tightness and anxiety in my chest, and my broken heart, I was a wreck. I found the strength from within to make my legs work long enough to carry me back into my home where I would be safe from any passersby seeing me like this.

I sat down on my couch, hugging the pillow Kendall had been resting her head on, and worked on taking deep breaths to relieve the chest tightness. I felt so very ill from the grief. I just wanted to go to my bed and hide for days, but there was so much to do and a funeral to plan.

More and more family began showing up after Kendall's body was taken away. Everyone wanted to be there for us, offer condolences, and comfort us. They also all brought food but we had no interest in eating much for days to come. Another person who showed up shortly after Kendall was taken was the man who came to pick up Kendall's hospice bed. I sat on the couch staring in disbelief as he disassembled her bed. He had it done and carried away in what seemed like no time and a large empty space remained in the room. A reminder of what once was, but now was gone. She was just there in that room, but now her body was gone and we were so broken. We would never see her body in our home again.

***

I can't remember much more from the day she died. Just a house full of people and so much aching. Our neighbor kept Alexa occupied that day and took her to the mall to shop. She recalls thinking to herself how they were there in the mall and that no one around them even knew that Alexa's little sister had just died. It then brought to light for her the phrase, "Be kind to everyone you meet for you never know what someone is going through."

I can't remember if I slept much that night, but the next day we had no choice but to get up early and start planning for Kendall's service. First up was calling our church to secure a date for the funeral/celebration of life. October 18th would be the calling hours, and October 19th the funeral. That gave us a short window of time to complete all that we had to do. You can't even grieve because your mind is so focused on preparing for the service and making every detail incredibly special.

My in-laws had arrived from out of town the morning that Kendall passed, but we did not know they were coming and Kendall's body had already been taken away. I called the funeral home and asked if there was any way we could come and see her and explained what had happened. They were so kind and gracious and said while that is not usually something they do, they would make an exception. So, the day after she passed, we took our in-laws to the funeral home, along with my parents, my grandmother, and Wes' sister. Alexa still did not come to see Kendall at that point because we had a lot to pick out for the funeral that day and she preferred to be with her friends anyway.

I have never cared for funeral homes; I mean who does? God bless those who work there. It takes a special person to do that. But they are for sure needed and appreciated. There is just this certain smell when you walk in that I can't seem to get past.

I was so relieved though that we could see Kendall's body again so soon, yet nervous to see what she would look like. The funeral home director told us to take as much time with her as we wanted, which was so kind of him. Much to our surprise, she looked beautiful when we walked into the room. She wasn't in her coffin yet, but was laid out on a stretcher. Her skin looked radiant, full of color, and plump. It wasn't what any of us expected. She looked like the angel she was, lying there peacefully with her doll in her arms. I was so thankful to get that extra time with her and glad our family members could too.

I'm sure this sounds so unimaginable, and you wonder what that would be like to visit your child's corpse in the funeral home. It is hard for me to explain what it felt like, but I think I was in such shock and kind of felt that out-of-body feeling again going through that week after she passed. The shock and numbness shielded me and helped to block out the pain so I could focus on what I had to do in a short time span for her service. It is a whirlwind with a long list of to-dos leading up to a funeral. Even at night while I lay in my bed, all I could think about was all I had to get done the next day and ideas for her service.

After we had visited with Kendall, we met with the team at the funeral home to begin picking out the guest book, memorial cards, poems, and prayers to use for the funeral. It was so difficult to pick the perfect ones in such a short amount of time, all while they are staring at you waiting for your decision. Honestly, I just wanted to crawl under the table and not do any of it. I felt overwhelmed. Looking back, I wish we had taken more time between her death and the funeral. A week is just not long enough to get everything perfect and to be coherent enough to make decisions. Luckily, we did have our parents with us in that meeting to guide us, which helped so much.

We had brought her dress with us that she would be laid to rest in. The director at the funeral home saw her fancy, ball gown dress and he said, "Now that is a dress that we won't want to cover up," meaning he suggested we keep her coffin completely open instead of half-open so everyone could see the pretty tulle bottom part of her dress. I included fancy dress shoes like she enjoyed wearing, and the soft headband I had purchased with flowers on it.

***

Back at home, I was so anxious to get some time to ourselves so we could work on her obituary that was due. Once we finally had some quiet time later that evening, I tried to begin but had no words. I didn't know how to get it started and didn't want to write it. I reached out to another neuroblastoma angel mom for help. She tried to give me some pointers over the phone, and some prompts to get going, but I just kept saying, "I can't do this." I was so drained and barely functioning. This needed to honor her life well. It needed to be perfect. How could I achieve that when I could barely think and felt so numb?

I didn't get anywhere with it that night. My friend sent me her daughter's obituary and the next day, I was able to use hers as a guide to complete Kendall's. I was happy with it, had Wes check it and add what he wanted, then sent it off to the newspaper and funeral home. Another task was checked off, but next up was meeting with our pastors to plan out her service.

My mom met us at our church to join us for the service planning. We met with both our senior pastor and our congregational care pastor. It was comforting to see them and to have their help with getting everything together. They were so kind to let us have the viewing at our church, instead of the funeral home. We have a large church that was able to accommodate all the people we were expecting. With the large lobby area, we would be able to set up many tables to display photos of Kendall and some of her special items.

I had come somewhat prepared for our meeting, as my pastors had told me to think of songs and scriptures we would want to be used. I shared with them our three songs, Laura Story: "Blessings," MercyMe: "I Can Only Imagine," and Chris Tomlin: "Amazing Grace (My Chains Are Gone)." We then went over the order of the service and decided that they would both officiate. It was important to us for our friends and family to hear from our senior pastor, but we also wanted our congregational care pastor who had spent so much time with Kendall and our family to speak too. We felt that he had come to know Kendall well and saw what she faced firsthand as he visited us often in the hospital.

Then my pastors suggested something to me that was not on my radar at all. They felt that it would be meaningful if I gave Kendall's eulogy. My immediate response was that I didn't think I could do that. They told me to think about it and that Wes could stand up there with me for support. They thought my journal entries over the course of Kendall's treatment were so impactful and they thought that people would like to hear from me. Just when I thought I was getting through my checklist, another thing had been proposed. They told me to pray about it and let them know soon.

***

The time was ticking and we still had quite a few tasks to get started on, such as getting photos to the person who was making our video for the viewing, as well as printing photos for the boards we were going to set out in the church lobby. My mom is very crafty and she had already hit the craft store for all the frilly ribbons, flowers, stickers, and other embellishments to adorn the boards with.

It took me hours to go through four years' worth of photos, carefully picking out the ones that showed her personality well and highlighted all of the wonderful memories we made in the years she was with us. My mom, her friend, my sisters, and I worked for hours getting the boards organized into stages of Kendall's life and then attaching the photos and embellishments. They were so beautiful once they were finished, and all in pink and purple, the color theme for her celebration of life.

I also wanted to have a space for young kids to color and craft during the calling hours. I thought it would be nice to have a mailbox marked for Heaven, and then have colorful paper, markers, and stickers for the kids to write a letter to Kendall in Heaven. My mom found a bright pink mailbox and attached angel wings to it. Our church agreed to set up a kids' table in the lobby to place the supplies on. I wasn't sure how many people would bring their children, but with Kendall having so many little friends I wanted to make sure there was a space just for them to express their feelings.

I had been contemplating whether to give Kendall's eulogy or not. After much prayer and consideration, I decided that I would do it for my daughter. I would be brave like her. I didn't have much left in me, and the last thing I felt like I could do was to write anything inspiring, but I had to at least try to attempt it and honor her well. I felt I might regret it if I didn't do it.

The time was getting closer and the last thing I had to do was get my tired, worn out looking self more presentable. The pressure was on since I would be getting up in front of everyone to speak at the funeral. My hair stylist fit me in for a fresh cut and color, and then it was off to shop with my mom and sisters for dresses for the calling hours and funeral.

We were asking everyone to dress formally, but with pink and purple accents for her funeral, Kendall's favorite colors. My thoughts were that I would look for a black dress and then accent it with colored jewelry or a shawl. It was slim pickings at the mall though and just another task that I dreaded doing. I feared running into someone we knew and it just felt awful being out in public. I wanted to hide from the world but I couldn't. I bought a couple of black dresses that I wasn't crazy about, some pink and purple jewelry, and got back home as fast as I could.

Meanwhile, one of my best friends was out shopping for a dress as well and happened to find a black dress with large purple flowers on it that she thought might work for me. There weren't many left, but there happened to be one in my size. She sent me a photo of it, and I wasn't sure about the flowers on it. *Is it too happy?* I thought. She chatted with the cashier and told her what the dress was for. Wouldn't you know it, the cashier happened to know Kendall and me from the hospital. She was one of the hospital volunteers that would come check on us and bring toys from the playroom. She also attended our church. I knew exactly who it was once my friend told me her name. What are the chances of that!? My friend thought it was a sign that she was supposed to buy me the dress and she brought it home for me in case I decided to wear it.

I tried on the three different dresses I had with the accessories. The floral one my friend had bought fit me perfectly, like it was made for me and for this very occasion. I sent photos of myself in the dresses to family and friends to get their votes. Everyone loved the flowers and it was the most flattering on me. The flowers were large and tasteful. It was a classy, form-fitting dress that stopped just above the knees. While it seemed a little loud to me for a funeral, it did seem like a sign that I was supposed to wear this one. I wasn't crazy about the other two, there was only this one dress left on the rack in my size, and it was sold to my friend by someone we knew from the hospital who happened to be working at Macy's that day. Then I asked myself, which one would Kendall choose? Kendall wouldn't want me to wear a boring black dress. She liked fancy and pretty colors. I had my answer. The floral dress it was. Handpicked by my daughter in Heaven.

***

The days were getting closer to the calling hours and I felt like I had barely had a chance to breathe or process Kendall's death. From the moment she left our home it had been nonstop with family visits, planning, and preparing for the funeral. I was so incredibly exhausted and now I had to sit down and write her eulogy. I don't know how I did it, but I was coherent enough to get my thoughts and words together to honor her well. I sent it off to the pastors for review and was finally all done with every task, just in time for the calling hours the next day.

When morning came, I didn't want to get out of bed and face the day. I didn't want to see my daughter lying in a casket. We were expecting many people to come to pay their respects and I didn't know how I was going to be able to stand for so long. My legs were so heavy and had a burning sensation running through them. It was so incredibly painful and I didn't know how I was going to do this. I just wanted to run away from it all.

I have always wondered how people who have lost a dear loved one make it through the calling hours and funeral with such grace and composure. I was beginning to see how. I had cried all the tears I had in me, was barely sleeping, and felt like I was in a haze (which probably was what they call grief fog, which I learned about later). I hadn't really been able to process my feelings yet so I just kept pressing on, doing what I had to do to get through this and asking God to give me strength.

We arrived at the church early to have time with Kendall before people started arriving. All our close relatives also joined us. The funeral home director warned us when we got there that Kendall was a little bit orange after they had put makeup on her. I was really worried walking up to her casket that she wasn't going to look like herself. Wes, Alexa, and I walked up by her side to see her placed so perfectly in her pretty white casket. Though her skin did look a bit tan, it wasn't too bad and didn't take away from her beauty. Her dress looked absolutely beautiful and her lace flower headband fit her little head so perfectly and helped to cover up some of the tumors that were still protruding from her skull.

I leaned down to kiss her sweet, bald head, then ran my hands over her hard, lifeless body that remained on Earth. As a Christian, the beauty in death is knowing that her soul had left her earthly body and she was given a new Heavenly body. While it was her body that I was touching in her casket, I could not feel much of a connection because I knew she was not there.

Wes, Alexa, and I wrapped our arms around each other as we each said a little something to Kendall. Alexa did better than I ever had expected with seeing her. We had read many books on death to her since Kendall had come home on hospice and she seemed to have a good understanding of where Kendall was. It also helped that she had her friends and cousins around to distract her from the awful reality that her sister was gone.

We had asked for some items to be placed in Kendall's casket with her. We asked for some to be buried with her, and some to only display through the calling hours and service. We had her *Frozen* Elsa and Anna dolls with her, one of her American Girl dolls, a note, a picture from Alexa, and a rosary. We also bought a sisters necklace that was a heart in two pieces so Alexa could have one half of it, and Kendall would have the other half around her neck in the casket. Two sisters forever connected.

The church looked beautiful with all the tables in the lobby decked out with the photo boards of Kendall and her special items laid out in front of them. We had big bunches of pink and purple balloons throughout the lobby area as well. We felt the balloons were suited for a child's funeral as kids loved them. We wanted it to look bright and fancy with Kendall's favorite colors, just how she would want. We were celebrating our girl's beautiful life.

It was just about time for people to start arriving so we grabbed some water to take up to the front of the worship center with us and I asked for a chair in case my legs couldn't make it through the hours. Wes and I stood to the left of Kendall, allowing us to be the first to greet those paying their respects. Then our parents and grandparents stood on the other side of her casket to the right. Beautiful pink and purple flower bouquets were displayed all around Kendall's casket. She truly looked like a princess in a fairy tale, softly asleep.

The video slideshow started playing on the two big screens in our worship center. When we were choosing the music to go along with the photos, I suggested the popular sad funeral songs. Wes had a better idea and wanted some of Kendall's favorite Disney songs played. I loved the idea and it was so nice to hear her favorite songs begin to play as we stood by her side. Some were happy and upbeat like "Love Is an Open Door" from *Frozen*, and "How Far I'll Go" from *Moana*, while others were sad like the song we included from *Trolls*, "True Colors." We ended the slideshow with a Hawaiian version of "Somewhere Over the Rainbow" by Israel Kamakawiwo'ole. It was a perfect mix and played on a loop through the entire calling hours.

The 2-4 p.m. hours were steady but not too overwhelming. Still, it was difficult and awkward for us to know what to say, as it was for those coming to pay their respects as well. There really are no words. I had warned people that it would be an open casket because I knew that may change some people's minds on coming. It isn't easy to see a young child in a casket. But we chose to have the casket open to have closure, and we wanted people to see our beautiful girl whom we were so proud of.

We had arranged for a break in between calling hour times to allow us a chance to eat and rest before another wave of people came. I wasn't expecting that we would actually get that time, but I was so relieved when we did. Luckily, the line ended just minutes after 4 p.m. and we were able to eat and I had time to stretch my legs to try to ease the pain. I was on the verge of a breakdown and didn't know how I was going to last on my legs for the evening calling hours, but I did.

The evening was much busier than the afternoon. The line was fairly long, though I am not sure how long the wait time was. We received so many friends, family, co-workers, and hospital staff. There were so many people that it is hard for me to remember who was there and who wasn't unless I check the guest book. I was surprised to see so many of Kendall's little friends and cousins there. I was thankful we had the table out for the kids to craft and write letters to her. It was definitely needed!

At one point during the calling hours, a man walked toward us from the line who resembled the Santa that came to visit Kendall just a couple of weeks back.

"Santa?" I questioned. "Is that you?"

"Ho Ho Ho," he replied.

I didn't fully recognize him at first without the suit. Wes and I both were so touched that he came. It meant so much to us and for a moment, I felt some magic and my spirits lifted. He really was that good of a Santa. I will never forget him.

Alexa had some of her classmates and her teacher come to the calling hours that evening. Alexa took her teacher's hand and walked her up to the casket, proudly showing her sister to her. She did this with her cousins and friends too and I was amazed at how brave she was. When she wasn't at her sister's casket, she was running around the church playing with her cousins while we continued to receive people. Kids are so resilient.

It was comforting to have so many people who loved us come out to pay their respects. That couldn't have been easy for any of them. We had around 500 people come through so that meant 500 people we hugged. My neck was so very sore by the end of that evening. I could barely turn my head from side to side. My legs were so stiff, painful, and heavy that I don't know how I walked myself out of the church that night.

***

The funeral/celebration of life was the next morning at 10 a.m. I didn't want to sleep that night because I wasn't ready for the finality of it all. I was dreading taking her body to the cemetery to be buried and was also very nervous to give the eulogy.

I had thought it would mostly be our close friends and family that came to the funeral, but I was very much surprised to see a full house show up, as well as some people we had never met before. That made me even more nervous to speak with so many people there.

Kendall's service was so moving, touching, and beautiful. My pastors did a phenomenal job honoring Kendall's life and pointing people to Jesus. The music and vocalist were wonderful and she sang every song perfectly. As much as I was trying to take it all in, it was hard to focus and I was cringing in my seat in the front row. I felt like all eyes were on me and I was so worried about speaking in front of everyone.

Before I knew it, my turn was up. I walked up to the podium and took some deep breaths before I began to speak. Wes stood next to me as we had planned, but it didn't make it any easier. I couldn't believe I was actually doing this. I got through it with a shaky voice and many tears. People told me later that they were shocked that I was able to get up there and speak. As uncomfortable as it was, I had to do it for Kendall.

Once the service was over, each row of seats was dismissed

to walk past Kendall one last time. Everyone cleared out except us and our immediate family. We all said our final goodbye to Kendall and I leaned in to give her one last kiss on her cheek. We then watched Alexa give her sister one last hug in her coffin and it was one of the saddest sights.

And then Kendall's casket was closed.

We had six of Kendall's uncles carry her coffin out to the hearse. Wes and I walked beside them as they carried her through the church lobby. I couldn't believe this was my life. Every part of this was so painfully hard.

Her uncles exited the church and placed her in the back of the hearse. The funeral home provided a luxury car for us to ride in directly behind the hearse. The church parking lot was full of cars in the funeral procession lineup. It was so long that somewhere along the drive to the cemetery it got broken up, which caused many to arrive at the cemetery before us and they didn't know where to go. You can't just pull into our cemetery and find your way. It is a whole city in itself with many different paths and winding roads to take. But fortunately, most found their way back to Kendall's grave.

Our pastor gave a beautiful graveside service and even included one of Kendall's favorite songs, "Jesus Loves Me." He asked everyone to sing along and it was just the sweetest sentiment hearing everyone's voices sing out. We had all earlier heard Kendall sing this song from her hospital bed in one of her videos shown during the service. I was hesitant to share videos of her during the service, but my pastors thought it would be nice for everyone to see her and be reminded of her joy.

Another special thing we had planned for Kendall's graveside service was to release doves. There was a company that specialized in this and volunteered their services for Kendall. They for sure made it special with a beautiful poem and the release of doves. My sister-in-laws helped release them from their cages. One dove was released first in memory of Kendall, followed by two separate flocks of doves to represent the angels carrying her spirit home. It was truly one of the most beautiful, peaceful sights and I was so glad there were so many people who came out to her grave to experience it. I had never seen a crowd so large graveside before. I was glad our girl and our family were so loved.

The day continued with a reception luncheon back at our church, and then more time with family. We had made it through another one of the hardest days of our lives. I didn't know what was next, but I did know that what I needed most was to be alone and to sleep for days to let my body rest. My bed was calling and I could not wait to lay my head on my pillow that night.

~Part Two~

Life After Loss

Chapter 20

What Do I Do Now?

Coming home after burying your child ranks high up there as one of the most awful feelings in the whole grief process. Your body is completely depleted and has no energy left to give to anything. You come home to where your child once lived but is no longer there. The realization that the dynamic of your family has changed, that you will no longer see your child running through your home or making messes to clean up, nor see them sleeping in their bed ever again is heartrending. The aching in your body pierces so deep that you wonder how you will ever be able to endure this level of pain. Suddenly you can hear every tick of the clock as you sit and stare in silence. The quietness of the home is haunting.

The devastating effects of cancer were visible around our home. Kendall's bedsheets were blood-stained, IV poles were still in place, hospital bags still needed to be unpacked, and medical supplies were everywhere. Her tiny shoes were left behind, her clothes, and her favorite toys too. The reality is that things really don't matter because you can't take them with you to Heaven. Relationships and people are what matter, so love others well.

Trying to describe what it was like in those first few days and weeks after Kendall went to Heaven is not easy. But I do remember the pain that was consuming my body from the grief. My leg pain would still not let up. My pain in my side was growing worse, my headaches were still there, and my body felt so heavy. Even my eyes hurt from crying and sleep deprivation. Alexa was my saving grace because without her I may have drowned in my sorrow. She gave me a reason to get out of bed each day. She still needed me.

I rested as much as I could while still trying to care for Alexa. We had the weekend together and then on Monday, Alexa wanted to return to school. She had been off school the entire time Kendall was home on hospice so she was anxious to go back. I imagine that was a comfort to her to return to her normal routine and take her mind off of our tragic life.

My wonderful friend had already made a special visit to Alexa's classroom to help her classmates understand what had happened and why Alexa may be sad. She was previously a teacher and was so good with kids. She brought in some books to help explain the situation, and when Alexa returned, she had no problem adjusting and was supported by her teacher and classmates. School had been her safe place all through Kendall's journey and I was so glad that she had that. The school even played one of Kendall's favorite songs on the loudspeaker in her memory on the day Alexa returned to school.

***

Meanwhile, Wes was still off work so it was nice to have him at home with me while Alexa was at school. Our house was a train wreck and hadn't been cleaned properly in quite some time. Gifts were stacked into corners around the house and flower arrangements from the funeral were in every room on the first floor. The neat freak inside of me wanted to tidy up so badly and organize the clutter, but my body said no. We spent several days just resting and enjoying meals that were brought to us when we felt like eating.

During the day while Alexa was at school, Wes and I would spend some of that time reading through all the cards we received and also started on some of the books people gave us on grief. We had quite the stack of books about Heaven, healing from grief, and stories of people who have had near-death experiences and what they saw on the other side. The first book I decided to read was called, *Safe in the Arms of God*, by John F. MacArthur. The book drew me in and began answering a lot of questions that I had about suffering and Heaven. It is one that I recommend today to anyone who has lost a child. The comfort found on those pages was what helped me to start to rise out of the deep pit of grief I had fallen into.

Once I finished one book, I would move on to another. I looked up books from parents who had lost a child and ordered them. Hearing how they had survived and held onto their faith through their great loss gave me hope that I too would be able to write to tell about it someday. That I too could make it out of this darkness and find the light again. I loved seeing the redemption in their stories and how God made beauty from their ashes. It made me hopeful that God would do the same in our story. Knowing I wasn't alone and there were so many parents like us out there in the world was a great comfort. I couldn't get enough of reading their stories.

Still, the days were long to endure, and I had no idea what I was going to do now. I was a caregiver for so long running on overdrive and then it was all so suddenly halted, which attributed to what my body was going through. What would I do with my time now? Sitting in my house day after day was starting to suffocate me, but I feared leaving my home and seeing people. How would they react to us? Would they see us in the grocery store, but pretend they didn't and run the other way? How was I going to react to people? What would I say? I didn't know how to do this. I dreaded the awkwardness.

After weeks of sitting at home, Wes had decided it was best for him to go back to work. It would give him something to do and would help him get back to his routine. Life had to go on. I didn't want him to leave me, but I understood. I was the only one of the three of us who didn't have a normal routine to go back to. Taking care of Kendall had been my job and now I was left to figure out what my purpose was and how I would use my time.

Thankfully, there are many gifted people in the world who help you to do this very thing. In my grief journey, they were my counselors. I was offered free counseling through hospice and I took them up on it. They would counsel me for a year after Kendall's passing. I also went to counseling at the cancer support center where Alexa went because that also was free to me the first year. My thought was that I was going to learn as much about grief as I could and get the tools and resources needed to help me survive. I started going to counseling weekly and Wes and I met occasionally with our congregational care pastor for his Godly wisdom and guidance in our grief.

I can't say enough good things about counseling. If you are finding yourself struggling with anything in life, you don't have to figure it out on your own. Counselors are there to help you navigate life. They help you make choices that are beneficial to you and give you tools to cope. Spending time in counseling early on helped me to process my thoughts and feelings and validated that what I was experiencing was all normal in my grief.

Before I could face the grocery store again though, or head back to church, I made a Facebook post letting friends and family know where we were at. I let them know that they might start seeing us out and about again. That we were still Krista and Wes, yet forever changed. I told them it was okay to say Kendall's name around us and that we wanted to talk about her. I explained that if they didn't know what to say to us, to just give us a hug. I said that I knew that most of them had never experienced a loss so tragic, but that we would all learn to navigate it together.

I decided that I would still be open and vulnerable in this next chapter so that people would know how best to help us. More than anything I just wanted to still be accepted socially and not feel like an outcast. I felt that being honest about what this grief journey was like and inviting people into our brokenness was the most beneficial approach.

I decided to start a new blog to share my grief journey. Writing was always therapeutic for me and my counselor highly recommended it to process my grief. It gave me a space to share what I was feeling and learning in my grief. Writing helped me to not feel alone because I knew people were reading my words and some would leave comments, which I enjoyed reading. I was hopeful that my writing would help others in my shoes to not feel so alone as well. I was proud that I had taken a tiny step toward figuring out what to do with my time.

***

In the months following Kendall's death, I focused on self-care. Aside from the counseling and trying to catch up on sleep, I was getting weekly massages for the pain in my legs. I had also scheduled an appointment with my physician to get checked out which led me to get a mammogram for the pain on my side under my arm. The only office that they could see me at quickly was downtown at the main Cleveland Clinic campus, the absolute last place I wanted to be. Luckily it was in another building that I didn't pass through often, but still being back on campus felt unsettling. My results came back normal and in time that pain resided. My doctor attributed it to grief pains.

My headaches also finally improved with time, but I was lacking in energy. The hour-long Zumba class that I used to be able to rock was no longer attainable. I could barely make it one lap around our block. I wasn't used to feeling this way. I had never felt extreme exhaustion like this before where it makes you feel like you have the flu. It was a tired that sleep couldn't fix.

I ended up making monthly appointments with my doctor for the whole first year after I lost Kendall. There were too many different things going wrong in my body and I wanted to make sure I could get in to see her to address them. My thyroid was out of whack, and I had so many strange pains which always were chalked up to grief pains after ruling out anything serious. I seemed to catch a cold every month and anything else that was going around due to my immune system being weakened from the grief.

The pain in my legs though would not budge. Nothing seemed to alleviate the pain. At a grief recovery course Wes and I took at our church a few months after Kendall's death, I learned that it was common to carry grief in your legs. It was comforting to know that I may have found a reason since the tests that were run were not giving me any answers. I was diagnosed eventually though with fibromyalgia and was told that could be what was causing the pain. So, I started anxiety meds which is one way fibromyalgia is treated, which also helped with my mood. Double win!

I was told that fibromyalgia can turn on in your body after you experience trauma so I was hopeful I had my answer and relief was on the way. While it did offer relief for a while, the pain still seems to come and go today even after going through a vein surgery to try to help. I don't think I will ever be the same. I carry the pain of losing her in my legs.

***

Another way I cared for myself was by going to Bible studies at church that were related to what I was going through. It created other safe places for me to share and learn truths from the Bible that I could apply to my grief. The grief recovery course Wes and I took at church was monumental for us in starting to process our grief and heal from our loss. We even had homework to complete each week and then shared our assignment with our group. The great thing about this course, versus the counseling I was receiving, was that God was included. I was not seeing Christian counselors so having a Christian perspective on grief in this class was so helpful. The class was called "Grieving with Hope," because like the Bible says, we can grieve with hope.

"Brothers and sisters, we do not want you to be uninformed about those who sleep in death, so that you do not grieve like the rest of mankind who have no hope. For we believe that Jesus died and rose again, and so we believe that God will bring with Jesus those who have fallen asleep in him" (1 Thessalonians 4:13-14, NIV).

As I was staying in the Word and learning so much about God, Heaven, and suffering, I decided to share what I was learning in my Facebook group called Faith Seekers. I started this group when Kendall was in treatment to teach the many people who were asking me questions about my faith. It was the best way I could help them grow their faith while I was stuck in the hospital with Kendall. I was excited to continue to process what I was feeling in another safe place, as well as to share what God was teaching me in my grief.

Just a few months after Kendall passed, Wes and I also joined a local support group for bereaved cancer parents. This was extremely healing for us to find friends in our area who knew our pain, and whom we could talk about death with. It was comforting to have other parents we could walk with on this journey and offer support to one another. We were not alone. It was an instant bond we had with these parents. We have met for many lunches and dinners and still keep in touch today.

I also started meeting up with friends again for lunch dates. It was nice to catch up with so many friends that I hadn't been able to see in so long. The impenetrable sadness was relieved a little more each time I was able to be with them. The hard part was when someone wanted to take a photo because in those early days of grief, smiling felt so wrong. It was even hard to form a smile some days and then I wondered what people would think of me on Facebook if they saw me out having fun and smiling.

Over time I came to realize that Kendall would want me to smile and that I didn't have to live my life sad. My counselor once told me that no one can live sad 24/7. It is not sustainable. You must find ways to cope. Of course, I will always carry the sadness in my heart daily, but I still have to live in this world. The world didn't stop when Kendall died so I had to learn to live in it without her. Withdrawing from the world was not going to be good for me or my family.

I knew the pain was never going to fully go away, but I had to find ways to feel happiness again so that the pain and sadness did not consume my entire life. Only I knew what I was going through and what was needed for me to survive each day and avoid falling into depression. Being around my friends, laughing and smiling, was good for my soul. They were great at getting me out of the house and helping me to feel comfortable out in the world again. I was thankful that my friendships remained through everything I had been through. I had to do what was going to be healing for me and try hard not to care what people thought of me.

So, as you can see, there are many resources out there available to help you if you are willing to find them. Sometimes we have to leave our comfort zones in order to grow and begin the healing process in grief. Day by day, little by little, I was finding my place in the world again.

Chapter 21

Making Sense of Suffering

Even though I was taking steps early on in my grief to help me begin the healing process, I was still struggling with my faith and had so many questions. Grief can test your faith like no other. I remember when Kendall's cancer kept progressing, and I feared what would happen to my faith if God didn't answer our prayers to heal her on Earth. My faith was publicly on display through her journey, which felt uncomfortable, but necessary, to explain how we were getting through each day. I feared that I wouldn't know what to say about my faith, or how to justify God's love and goodness to my friends, family, and followers in the event that she died.

I spent a lot of time the first year after Kendall's passing studying the Word of God, desperately searching for answers. I spent time with God, trying to make sense of why there is suffering in the world and why he allows it. I could easily have just given up on God and blamed him for everything but I had to at least try to find the answers so I could have peace. So often people turn their backs on God when he doesn't do what they want him to do. And in the case of tragedy and trauma, people doubt God's goodness and wonder why he couldn't prevent the suffering in their lives if he is all-powerful. That was me at times, struggling with doubts and wondering why God chose to answer some people's prayers, but he didn't answer mine. I was left perplexed and confused.

Though some days I doubted and questioned God, I had to make a choice. One morning not long after Kendall's passing, I was in my pastor's office sharing with him all of the hard questions I had about God and my faith that were going through my mind. He said something to me that day that helped steer me back on the right path. He said, "You are going to have to make a choice. Are you going to choose to trust and believe Jesus and what he promises to you? If you choose Jesus, then every day you keep saying to him, 'I trust you, Lord. I believe,' even through the doubts."

Through my tears, I decided to choose Jesus that day. I didn't have the answers, but I knew that I didn't want a life without him. I didn't want a life without hope. How could I turn my back on God when now was when I needed him most? I had followed him since I was a little girl, and I didn't want to walk away from my faith. I had seen his faithfulness in my life and experienced his goodness too many times to not believe. He was the only way to true comfort, peace, and joy and I chose to continue to trust him.

After that day, I still had moments of wrestling with God. It was necessary to take all of my pain, doubts, and frustration to him so I could work through it with him. He could handle it. He would rather us express our feelings to him than shut him out or not talk to him at all. Then, on other days I would read something in my Bible or devotion book that led me to feelings of comfort and understanding and I wouldn't be so confused anymore. This was a back-and-forth battle in my mind for months after her passing. But even through my disappointments and doubts, my faith was growing because I was spending so much time with him. Faith is a journey, and I am always learning something new.

***

We returned to church about a month after Kendall passed. I didn't want to be away too long because I feared that would allow a chance for the enemy to get in my head even more.

Being back in our worship center where Kendall's little body lay was triggering. I could see her coffin in the front of our worship center in my mind and it was distracting as I tried to worship. Then came the songs. Songs I once belted out in praise now seemed too hard to sing. How could I sing songs about God being a good Father or that he has never failed me when I hadn't been able to get to a place to confidently sing those words? I also felt funny singing those words in front of other church members. Like singing them somehow would make less of the pain our family had been through. So instead of singing those particular songs, I prayed and told God this was really hard and asked him to help me get back to a place where I could sing those songs again and be able to say that he was still good.

The first time we sang "Amazing Grace" in church after her funeral was very tough also. It still is today since we chose that song for her service. Every time I hear it, it brings me right back to that day, and tears pour out. There were many songs and sermons that brought out a ton of emotion for me as we attended church in those early months after Kendall's death. Sometimes it would take everything I had to not completely break down in a church service. There were times I did have to step out. Usually, though, I could control my emotions and only have a few teardrops leave my eyes. It seemed that every sermon and song was directed right at me and what I was going through. Like God was speaking right to me. Isn't God amazing like that?

So as hard as it was to attend church, I was learning so much and being loved on by our church family. They truly were the hands and feet of Jesus and they helped love us back to life by speaking truths over us, as well as by their steadfast prayers.

***

Aside from church to help guide me to finding answers to some of my tough questions, I continued doing a lot of work on my own at home. I've mentioned how much reading I did in the beginning and that continued on and still does today. I have gained so much wisdom learning from people who have written about grief, and from pastors and other Christian authors who have written books on pain and suffering.

One book that has become a handbook for me in answering some of life's hardest questions is the book *If God is Good: Faith in the Midst of Evil and Suffering*, by Randy Alcorn. It's one of those books that you highlight and take notes throughout. So much good content and truths are contained in the pages of that book. Truths that finally helped me to see that God is truly good and answered many of the questions I was wrestling with. It is a thick book, but if you struggle with understanding why there is suffering in our world, I highly recommend that you read it.

As I did my research and studies over months and months, I was experiencing God's love deeper than I ever had before. I had come to have a better understanding of Jesus' heart and his character. He was teaching me so much and walking hand in hand with me in my grief. I learned that he had warned us long ago that our lives here on Earth would not be free of suffering. Jesus says, "I have told you all this so that you may have peace in me. Here on earth, you will have many trials and sorrows. But take heart, because I have overcome the world" (John 16:33, NLT). God never promised us a life free of pain.

Because of man's first sin, the world God had created for us was altered (This is referred to as "The Fall"). Adam and Eve chose to do what they wanted and ate the forbidden fruit instead of obeying God. That is the day that sin entered our world and

God's heart broke, just like it did when cancer took my daughter from me. He wept with me. He never intended for his children to endure so much anguish on this Earth. It wasn't supposed to be this way.

People can be quick to place blame on God when disappointments and tragedy strike. But it was Satan in the garden that tempted Adam and Eve to disobey God, and it is Satan today that brings evil and suffering into our world. Evil and suffering do not come from God. In fact, God promises that one day there will be justice for the evil in this world (See 2 Thessalonians 1:6-8 NIV). He did not give Kendall cancer. Yes, he knew that was going to be part of her story and yes, he allowed it to happen and didn't stop it.

So why would a good God allow a four-year-old to die of cancer? That's a tough question, isn't it? One that I wrestled with God on for so long. A question that I may never have a completely satisfying answer to this side of Heaven. But I will share with you my thoughts and what I have come to know from my studies on suffering.

Let's first look at Hebrews 2:17-18, "Therefore, it was necessary for him to be made in every respect like us, his brothers and sisters, so that he could be our merciful and faithful High Priest before God. Then he could offer a sacrifice that would take away the sins of the people. Since he himself has gone through suffering and testing, he is able to help us when we are being tested" (NLT).

Jesus came to Earth and lived like us so that he could understand us. He was fully human and experienced the same things that we do in life, even suffering. He suffered through an excruciatingly painful death. He was tortured, beaten, whipped, mocked, and nailed to a cross to die. He knows what it feels like to cry out to God asking for there to be another way, just as I did so many times. Jesus prays to God before his arrest, "My Father! If it is possible, let this cup of suffering be taken away from me. Yet I want your will to be done, not mine" (Matthew 26:39, NLT). He knew he had to endure the cross for a greater purpose.

He ultimately surrenders to God's will so that one day we can live in Heaven with him in a world free of suffering. It is marvelous that he could love and care for us that much to willingly take on all that pain and not save himself from the cross when he certainly had the power to do so. It's the greatest love story of all.

God allowed his son to die a painful death even though it hurt him deeply because he knew greater things were to come. Jesus had to die on the cross so that we could be forgiven of our sins and have everlasting life in Heaven with him.

I came to the realization that God watched his son suffer and die, just as I had watched my daughter. If anyone knew my pain, it was him. He could relate to what I was going through. Realizing this helped me to draw closer to him and have complete trust that he would redeem my pain someday just as he did in his own son's story.

We may never get to see the redemption God has for us in our own stories during our time on Earth. But we can look at the story of Jesus and hold onto hope that God is working all things together for good. Romans 8:28 says, "And we know that God causes everything to work together for the good of those who love God and are called according to his purpose" (NLT). This verse doesn't imply that all things are good, but it is saying that for the believer, God will redeem all things in his timing.

We can't see the whole picture. Only God can. He works in and through all circumstances to create something beautiful and good for his children. Not an ounce of our pain will be wasted. There are so many different moving parts and pieces that we may know nothing about until we are in Heaven, but we can trust that God is weaving our story together to make beauty in the end.

Remembering Jesus' story helps me to have a better understanding of suffering. Keeping an eternal perspective is key. There are so many other stories you can read in the Bible about people whose suffering was redeemed and beauty was made from the ashes. Job is a great book of the Bible to read to see this play out.

***

Another reason that God sometimes allows us to suffer is to draw us to him. Sometimes people don't find Jesus until he is all they have left. Sometimes we have to go through hard things in order for him to mold us into his image and to grow our faith. And sometimes, it is in our pain that God teaches us things we otherwise never would have learned. Remember earlier I said I thought I was being punished for my sins? Well, actually God was shaping me and helping me to be a better reflection of him through my suffering. He wasn't trying to harm me.

Giving your life to Christ will not exempt you from suffering. I know there were times in my life when I felt so blessed and thought it must be because I follow and serve Christ and read my Bible. I was doing all the right things so he wouldn't let anything bad happen to me. But I was clearly wrong. That is not how it works. Following Jesus does not equal a life free of suffering. Let me say that again…

Following Jesus DOES NOT equal a life free of suffering.

Suffering is part of our world, and no one can escape it. Jesus who was sinless still suffered. But because of the suffering Jesus endured on the cross, those who believe in him have an eternity free of suffering that awaits them.

Romans 8:18 says, "Yet what we suffer now is nothing compared to the glory he will reveal to us later" (NLT).

Yes, God may allow suffering in our lives, but he does not allow it for all of eternity. What we experience and endure here is just a tiny dot in the grand scheme of our existence. We have an entire eternity to look forward to where our lives will be truly perfect and without pain. I have eternity to spend with my daughter where I will live with her longer there than in my time on Earth and I cannot wait!

***

The time I have invested trying to make sense of the loss of my precious daughter has not been easy. It has been hours upon hours of studying God's word and meditating on it, yet I still don't fully know the reason why she had to go home so soon. I most likely will never fully know why this side of Heaven, but the Bible gives me hope that one day I will. Paul says, "Now we see things imperfectly, like puzzling reflections in a mirror, but then we will see everything with perfect clarity. All that I know now is partial and incomplete, but then I will know everything completely, just as God now knows me completely" (1 Corinthians 13:12, NLT).

I have read a few books on near-death experiences and some who have had them and went to Heaven say that when they saw Jesus face to face, they had all their answers. Everything they wanted to know was revealed to them at that moment. I have to say I am looking forward to that day of fully knowing why.

For now, shifting my focus off of the "why" and instead choosing to trust, believe, and move forward with God keeps me in his perfect peace. Isaiah 26:3 has become my life verse through Kendall's story and it says, "You will keep in perfect peace all who trust in you, all whose thoughts are fixed on you" (NLT). Being able to truly experience the peace of God in this grief journey has been so beautiful. The verse is true! I have kept my eyes and my thoughts on the Lord and he has provided a peace like no other. A peace that has helped me heal. A peace that runs through me and has unfolded in me as I have spent time with him. It is a beautiful gift from God to be able to feel His peace.

One verse that I found that covered me in peace and freed me of my "what ifs" that haunted me was Psalm 139:16: "You saw me before I was born. Every day of my life was recorded in your book. Every moment was laid out before a single day had passed" (NLT). God knew Kendall would only be here for four years. We all have different assignments and purposes on Earth. There was nothing Wes or I could have done differently to change that.

I had been haunted by thoughts of wondering if we had done enough with her care and treatments. I had been haunted by wondering if my sins had anything to do with her suffering. I had been haunted by thoughts of wondering if we had prayed wrong or didn't have enough followers on Facebook praying for her.

Finding Psalm 139:16 a couple of years after Kendall's passing finally broke those chains that were holding my mind captive. I could finally release those "what ifs" and have peace in knowing that what I was worried about did not have any effect on her death. We made the best decisions for her care that we could with the information we had. Yes, our children suffer because of sin in our world (going back to The Fall), but they do not pay for the sins of their parents. Let's look at this passage from the Bible:

"As Jesus was walking along, he saw a man who had been blind from birth. "Rabbi," his disciples asked him, "why was this man born blind? Was it because of his own sins or his parents' sins?" "It was not because of his sins or his parents' sins," Jesus answered. "This happened so the power of God could be seen in him" (John 9:1-3, NLT).

I do think that when I see Jesus face to face he will tell me this very thing. Because you can't hear Kendall's story without seeing God's power in it. The light of Christ shines so brightly in her story. Ezekiel 18:20 also says, "The child will not be punished for the parent's sins, and the parent will not be punished for the child's sin" (NLT). These verses gave me the peace I needed.

When addressing my thoughts about our prayers, I realized with the help of Psalm 139:16 that we didn't need to have 20,000 followers praying for her on Facebook. We weren't praying wrong. We had prayed truly believing in her miracle and that God could make it happen. It was always God's plan for Kendall to leave us at four years old, just as it was the plan from the beginning for Jesus to die on the cross.

This then led me to a new question…Why then do we pray? I found that prayer is showing your dependence on God and your trust in Him. It is when you have a conversation with him, just like a friend, which then draws you closer to him and helps you to understand him more and what his will for your life is.

The apostle Paul says, "Do not be anxious about anything, but in every situation, by prayer and petition, with thanksgiving, present your requests to God. And the peace of God, which transcends all understanding, will guard your hearts and your minds in Christ Jesus" (Philippians 4:6-7, NIV). Prayer changes us and may alter our circumstances through it. Prayer transforms our hearts. He may not resolve every situation as you want or in the time frame you desire but continuing to bring your requests to him will make your relationship with him stronger and cover you in his peace.

When it comes to prayer, God answers with a "yes," "no," or "not now." It's important to remember Jesus' prayer to God asking to spare him from the cross. Even Jesus received a "no" from God. If God answered "yes" to every prayer we would never long for Heaven. We would take so much for granted and we would never get that chance to be fully dependent on him or come to know him in a deep, personal way.

While my greatest prayer was not answered how I wanted, God still did answer many prayers throughout Kendall's journey and sent us many blessings. There has been so much evidence of his kindness and goodness to us through the years. And ultimately, God did answer my prayer to heal Kendall. He just chose for her to receive her healing in Heaven instead of on Earth. He rescued her from any more pain.

With God's help, I have been able to get back to a place to be able to confidently sing those songs in church again and declare that he is indeed a good Father.

Chapter 22
Finding My New Purpose

A common theme I was finding through reading my Bible and grief books was that you could turn your pain into purpose even without an answer to the "why". Sometimes we can stay fixated on trying to figure out why something bad happens to us when we may never know the reason. This can leave you stuck and unable to move forward.

When you lose a part of yourself, it is hard to find that purpose and meaning in your life again and it can take time. As you have read, it is a process. As I was nearing the first anniversary of Kendall's death, I was proud of myself for how far I had come and all the wisdom I had gained. I was learning to shift my focus off the "whys" and instead focus on "how" I could use my pain to help others.

Some days trying to find my purpose took more energy from me than I cared to give. On other days I had to just tell myself it was okay if my only purpose for the day was to tell people about my amazing daughter Kendall, my hero. But when I did have the energy, my mind raced with ideas on how I might turn my pain into purpose.

So many bereaved parents around me and in these books found purpose in starting up foundations and gave back in incredible ways. I did feel a little pressure that we too should do something big, but I also wanted to be gentle with ourselves and only allow what we could handle into our lives. I knew that was not going to be a foundation. It just was not for us.

Throughout the first year after Kendall passed, we dabbled in a few different projects to start giving back to all of those who so kindly gave to us. I had a whole list of the people and organizations that I wanted to thank, volunteer with, and donate to. Before I share some of these projects, I just want to say that if you are a bereaved parent reading this book, please don't feel like you have to do anything like this. Remember that your grief journey will look different than mine. What is healing for me might not be healing for you. I share to give ideas in case anyone needs them and to show how I found my purpose and happiness again.

***

One of the first things we did as a way to support children with cancer was to sign up under the umbrella of the Beat Childhood Cancer Foundation (Beat CC), previously Beat Nb. This meant that we could have our own fundraising page and name through this foundation but didn't have to do all the paperwork and legal aspects of running our own foundation.

A month after Kendall passed, we had our site ready to go. It was named "Because of Kendall," and we were ready to start raising money for Beat Childhood Cancer. This foundation had meant a lot to us as they were working hard to raise funds for better treatment for kids with cancer. They were the other founders who worked with Dr. Scholler to develop the DFMO drug that we had always intended for Kendall to receive had she made it through frontline treatment. At the time, the drug was only given to children once they were finished with treatment and in remission. The DFMO drug stopped cancer cells from growing which prevented relapse in so many children and we fully supported it.

We had so many great ideas and intentions for having our own fundraisers to bring in money for Beat CC. We thought it would be so fun to have a family Halloween costume fundraiser around the one-year anniversary of Kendall's passing, and I had the idea of hosting a running event. These ideas fell flat though as we learned quickly how much work it takes to host events like these, and we just didn't have the energy early on in our grief.

As time has gone on, we have gone with much simpler avenues for raising money on Kendall's Beat CC page such as Facebook fundraisers and asking for donations on her birthday and Heaven day. My dad even sold his handmade soaps which brought in $1000 in one Christmas season!! We also sold memorial car magnets and decals and donated the profits. Others who had their own direct sales business would also donate a portion of their earnings and over time we could see the money adding up, all in Kendall's name.

***

One of the first big hospital projects we did to give back was a holiday toy drive during the first Christmas without Kendall. I had found myself grieving hospital life so much. I lived there with Kendall for so many days that our team felt like family to me. I had missed having their support and sense of comfort surrounding me. They helped me care for my daughter and saw us at our lowest of lows. They walked with us through incredible pain. I was thinking of ways I could give back to the hospital and be able to see our care team again…enter toy drive!!

You may be wondering how I would be able to go back to the hospital as I mentioned earlier how much I didn't want to go there for my appointment. One good thing was that right as we were going home on hospice, the new children's outpatient hospital was opening. I didn't have memories there with Kendall as I did in the old wing. So, I would be going to a new place and avoiding where we stayed for inpatient treatments, though I would still have to drive by there.

Knowing there were children up on that floor suffering gave me all the incentive I needed to press forward with the toy drive for pediatric cancer patients. Kendall loved to get new toys brought to her at the hospital. It brightened her days and mine too as it gave us something new to do. All it required of me was to make some flyers to post on social media and before we knew it our porch was full of toys that people dropped off daily. My family took the opportunity to buy toys for the children that we knew Kendall would have liked for Christmas. It was a wonderful way to honor her on our first Christmas without her.

We ended up with so many toys that we had to take multiple carloads to the hospital. We had enough to donate to not only Cleveland Clinic Children's, but also to UH Rainbow Babies and Children's, and A Special Wish Northeast Ohio. It was truly an incredible sight to see all the toys that were donated in Kendall's name. I loved that our community realized the importance of a toy for a child fighting cancer and showed their love for Kendall and our family by helping us give back.

***

One of the organizations that did so much for our family all throughout Kendall's journey was the Radiate Gold Foundation. They dropped off hospital care kits and toys to us, helped me plan some gatherings like Alexa's birthday party, and decorated Kendall's room for her on more than one occasion. The founder reached out to me after Kendall had passed to see if she could start a new program in memory of Kendall that would provide room decorations for pediatric cancer patients at the hospital. She was inspired by all the room decorations I put up for Kendall during her stays. I was so excited for another way to keep

Kendall's memory alive at the hospital and she allowed me to work with her on this new project as my time allowed.

It was so fun to piece it all together and work on a name and logo. I came up with the name, "Room for Joy" and we got to work creating room kits full of themed room decorations. We made them for every holiday and created custom room decoration kits upon request. We mainly sent the kits to Cleveland Clinic Children's, but also sometimes had enough to drop some off at UH Rainbow Babies and Children's. Every kit included a small postcard with a photo of Kendall on it and shared how she inspired Radiate Gold to start the Room for Joy program. My family, friends, and community once again jumped right in to purchase items for our room kits so that other kids fighting cancer could decorate their rooms too.

***

On Kendall's first heavenly birthday in July 2019, we took a two-hour trip to the American Girl doll store to purchase Kendall Wellie Wisher dolls. A year earlier was when Kendall received this very doll on her fourth birthday, so we thought it was a great way to give back on her special day. We had asked if anyone wanted to make a donation towards this project and we raised enough money to buy 12 dolls! They were $60 each so we were very happy we could purchase so many. Shoppers in the store were looking at us like we were either crazy or loaded with money as we brought stacks of dolls to the counter.

Once the store manager heard why we were buying so many dolls, she was quick to throw in many more donations. We left there with an additional 20 American Girl dogs, doll headbands, and boxes of books! We could barely fit it all in our car. Wes, Alexa, and I were so happy that we were able to do this for Kendall's birthday and knew she would approve. We were able to split the donations between Cleveland Clinic Children's and UH Rainbow Babies and Children's.

As the one-year anniversary of Kendall's death grew closer, I felt like I had taken a lot of steps toward healing and self-care. I had done the grief work and was finding my way in the world again. Helping others was helping me and gave me great purpose. I could feel happiness again.

***

It was around this time that an administrative assistant job became available at my church. After much thought and prayer, I decided to apply. Without going into too many details, I ended up not getting the job I applied for at my church but instead was hired as an administrative assistant at a sister church of ours. That church then merged with our church, creating one church with multiple campuses. I was hesitant to leave our church with all our history there, but there were too many signs to deny that God wanted us at the new campus.

For one, the new campus was just a couple minutes from Kendall's resting place. I would pass the cemetery every day on the way to work/church which allowed me to stop often. The new campus was closer to our home and just one city away. Also, I didn't have to leave my church family because we now were one big family across campuses. And lastly, the head pastor at the new campus had lost his son suddenly several years ago so he knew what I was going through. I felt that God had orchestrated all of this. I had always wanted to work at my church and I felt that God couldn't have given me a better place to ease back into the workplace. A loving, compassionate environment was what I was seeking and my church provided just that.

I started working at my new church campus 10 months after Kendall passed. Being able to work with pastors was an honor and I was eager to learn from the head pastor who had lost his son. I knew he would be a great example to me in my grief and would be able to answer any hard questions I may have needed help with.

I was still so broken when I started. Some days were very hard for me and the littlest things would make me upset. I would think of Kendall and cry at my desk or share about her in a meeting and tears would pour out. One day, I said that I was sorry while I was crying. The head pastor said, "Don't apologize for your tears. Your tears are healing and they are welcome here." His words confirmed I was in the right place and that my team there would be gentle with me as my grief ebbed and flowed.

I was excited to be working again and getting out of the house. A reason to shower, get dressed, and learn something new. I was looking forward to being able to share my story and all that God had done in my life with my church family. I was eager to see how God would use me to help others who were grieving and in need of hope. He had placed me right where he wanted me so that he could help me continue to turn my pain into purpose.

Chapter 23

Honoring Kendall in Everything We Do

What bereaved parents want more than anything is for their child to be remembered. We wake up every day and have to relive their death all over again. Every morning Kendall is the first thought on my mind and that I lost her, so when people remember her with me, it means so much. When people shed tears when they hear my story, I thank them for their empathy. Because of my great love for her, I will grieve for the rest of my life so know that saying her name or bringing her up isn't going to remind me that she is gone. I want her life to be honored and remembered so we strive to keep Kendall's memory alive by speaking her name and including her in all that we do. So, what does that look like?

There are so many ways to honor your child and I already mentioned many in the previous chapter. One simple way I honored Kendall and continue to do so was by sharing photos with a memory of her on my Facebook page. Or sometimes I would share a photo and a grief quote with it that spoke to me.

Many friends and family would comment, and I loved reading each one. Shortly after Kendall passed, we started a thread on her Facebook page where people could leave their favorite memory of her. Reading what they remembered about her was so special. Some memories people had I didn't even know about. A friend later turned that thread into a beautiful book for me so I'll always have those memories.

In our home, pictures of Kendall remain on our walls and tables. After checking to make sure Alexa and Wes were okay with it, I dedicated a space in our home to Kendall. It is in our upstairs hallway, and it is a console table with shelving where I can display some of the beautiful memorial gifts made for us, some of her favorite toys, angel figurines, and little signs with inspirational words. I also put some photos of her on the walls above it too. Every morning we walk past her table as we head downstairs and tell her good morning, and then we do the same in the evening and tell her goodnight. Sometimes I will even kiss her portrait on the wall and pretend I am really kissing her, though the canvas material on my lips feels nothing like her soft, smooth skin.

When Kendall was brought to the funeral home, there was an option for them to take her fingerprint and turn it into jewelry for us. I knew I had to have a necklace so a piece of her could stay close to my heart. I would wear that heart-shaped necklace every day in hopes of someone asking me about it so I could talk about her. I went on to make other necklaces with her picture on them and bracelets that had her name. I even found a bracelet that someone had made for Kendall that she wore from time to time. It had her name on it and I discovered one day that it fit me. I loved that I could wear something that was hers.

We went on to make many keepsakes of her. Not immediately, but a couple of years after her death, we took her t-shirts and had a lady make a quilt out of them. It is so nice to be able to cover up with her clothing and have a piece of her close to us. For Christmas one year I took some of her pajamas and then found a picture of her wearing the exact pair. I then took a photo frame and made the background a piece of her pajamas and glued the photo of her wearing them to the fabric. They were gifts to our immediate family members so they all could have something of hers.

We also made Shutterfly blankets with her photos on them, button pins with her photo to put on our bags, stuffed animals made from her clothing, photo books of her cancer journey, remembrance t-shirts (which we sold, and donated proceeds to A Special Wish Northeast Ohio), and recordable bears with clips of recordings I had with Kendall's voice. I made many others and felt like I just couldn't get enough. I needed to have keepsakes of her everywhere.

The recordable bears were special because Alexa's recording was Kendall saying, "I love you, Lexa" (what Kendall called her) and on mine, she says, "Goodnight, Momma." On nights when I can handle it, I will press the button and hear her tell me goodnight, then I will say it back. Sometimes, though, I find I can't press it because tears will start flowing and then I can't get to sleep. I just have to see how I feel that particular day.

The remembrance t-shirts are very special and a great way to keep Kendall with us and share her story. Her shirt says "Choose Joy" in the middle of it and the "O" in "JOY" is a cancer ribbon. Then there is a circle of words around it that says "In Loving Memory of Kendall Stump" with the dates of her life. Many of our family and friends have one and wear it proudly. I love when I see them wearing their shirts to keep memories of Kendall with them, as well as her legacy of choosing joy.

The cancer support center where Alexa and I went to counseling had the option to buy a brick paver in memory of your loved one. We had wanted to give back for all the free services we had received and thought that was a nice way to do so. Kendall has a brick paver now in their beautiful memorial garden. My grandma (G.G.) also bought her one at her church so when we would go visit, we could stop and see her paver in the beautiful church gardens, and Grandma had a place to visit with Kendall too.

***

A couple of months after Kendall's passing, our church was hosting a remembrance service for Christmas called "Blue Christmas." I signed us up and sent Kendall's photo in. Many of our friends and family attended with us and we were so touched by the moving, beautiful service. Every song was chosen so carefully and the lyrics were my heart's cry. They lit a candle on the stage for every loved one being remembered in the service as their photo came across the big screen. It was a beautiful sight to see all the light shining from the candles in the dimly lit room. You couldn't help but be moved and shed some tears for all the beautiful souls that had passed.

I knew I had to be a part of this ministry and the next year; I joined their team. (As you can see, staying busy has been a huge way I have coped with my grief.) I was so excited to be able to help with the planning of this service and to come alongside others who were grieving. Three years after Kendall's death, I shared my testimony and Kendall's story at the remembrance service. I had spoken a few times before at my church and at a fundraiser so I had some practice, but this was the big time. I was on our Livestream and YouTube channel, and spoke in front of a couple hundred people in the worship center, but probably hundreds more when factoring in the internet! It was incredible to see how far my story reached as emails came pouring in from people who were moved, even some from different states.

That was one of the most incredible days of my life. I got to see God work in the hearts of others. I got to share truths from the Bible to help a room full of grievers find hope and peace in Christ. So many people wanted to meet me after and they shared how my story had impacted them. This day showed me that I had to move forward with writing this very book you are reading to be able to spread the gospel hope and how God has loved me through my pain. 2 Corinthians 1:4 (NLT) says, "He comforts us in all our troubles so that we can comfort others. When they are troubled, we will be able to give them the same comfort God has given us." I've seen and learned too much to not share it with the world and try to comfort others in their grief. I never would have imagined that God would use my pain to launch me into grief ministry.

***

At the beginning of the new year of 2019, Wes, Alexa, and I decided to take the wish trip Kendall didn't get to take. We had promised Alexa and Kendall both that we would be going to Disney World once Kendall was done with treatment. Well, she was now done with treatment and graduated to Heaven and we didn't want to go back on our promise to Alexa. Plus, we felt like going to the most magical place in the world filled with many of Kendall's favorite things would help us to feel close to her and we could fulfill her wishes.

I had a large-sized metal photo made of Kendall in her Cinderella dress to take with us. It was light and could fit easily in my backpack that we carried with us each day at the park. We took the photo out every time we met a princess and shared her story with them. We took family photos around the park while holding her photo, including one in front of the Cinderella Castle. Her name was being spoken inside that park and her beautiful smile was shared through the photo. As sad and disappointing as it was to not have her there with us physically, she was there with us in spirit.

We also had special Disney shirts made with a tribute to her on the back of them. We all three had worn our Nike shoes that Kendall had designed with Project Outrun just weeks before she passed. Kendall had wanted them all red because of her superhero obsession at the time so they matched the red bows on our Minnie ears well!

We had a wonderful time watching Alexa be transformed into a Princess at the Bibbidi Bobbidi Boutique. She wore her Cinderella dress that matched the one Kendall had on in the photo to honor her sister. We enjoyed watching the parades, magical fireworks, and just being in a place that Kendall truly would have loved.

Kendall had also wanted to swim with dolphins as part of her wish trip. Since we were at Disney in January, it wasn't quite warm enough for us to fulfill this wish for her. What we were able to do though was feed and pet dolphins at Sea World. We had the best time doing so, and it brought many smiles to our faces. We felt we had honored Kendall's wishes the best we could and one day we will swim with dolphins for her.

***

The first spring after losing Kendall, I decided I wanted a space in our yard dedicated to her. We had a perfect empty area in one of our backyard mulch beds that I decided to turn into a flower garden for her. We had already received so many garden stones at her funeral as gifts, as well as wind chimes. The first year it wasn't much and I pieced it together the best I could. But every year I have added a little more and made it more colorful and vibrant. Some friends and family also purchased flowers and stones to add to it and the school that Kendall would have attended had a large rock engraved with her name and dates of her life on it, as well as our motto, "Choose Joy." The school also made a smaller duplicate rock that sits in a tiny garden by the entrance of the school today among a few other memorial rocks of children who were taken too soon from our community.

Tending to her garden helps me to still feel like I am taking care of her. When I purchase things for her garden, it gives me a chance to still buy something for her. I pick out things that represent her or that I know she would like, such as pink dragonfly solar lights to wrap around the tree in her garden. I also added a bird bath and solar fountain for more tranquility. I talk to Kendall while I weed and plant flowers in her garden, or while lounging in the nearby hammock.

We also planted a tree for her in our front yard. When we went shopping for a tree, the sales attendant showed us a lollipop crabapple tree. It was meant to look like a Dum-Dums sucker, or a lollipop. We thought that was just perfect for her and would represent her well. It has the most beautiful pink and white flowers on it in the spring and red berries in the fall. We made a special memorial plaque to sit at the bottom of the tree and hope that when neighbors walk by and see it, they pause to remember the beautiful little girl that once lived at our address.

Another memorial spot for Kendall has been provided for us by Prayers From Maria, the beautiful sunflower field where Kendall's prayer service was held. I am so grateful to Maria's parents for giving us bereaved cancer parents a place to share our children and keep their memory alive. They have beautiful signs with the children's photos and dates of their life on them. I love seeing Kendall's photo amongst the beautiful golden sunflowers. The sunflowers' short blooming season represents the short lives of the children who have passed.

***

On Kendall's first heavenly birthday, I wanted to do something special. I had some ideas gathered from seeing what other bereaved parents in my community had done. I knew I didn't want to be alone that day, and that I didn't want to be sad. I wanted to celebrate her, so I pulled together some of my favorite ideas and decided to have friends and family join us at her grave.

Kendall had many friends, so I split up the day by having her friends come out in the morning, and my family in the evening. I brought a folding table to set food on, some decorations, her favorite strawberry frosted sprinkled donuts, bubbles for her friends, and butterflies and balloons to release. On the butterfly envelopes, it read "Happy First Heavenly Birthday" and I had enough to pass out one butterfly in an envelope to each family there that morning.

I said a few words about Kendall, read a poem, and we just hung out at her grave. We blew bubbles, ate donuts, and wrote messages on biodegradable balloons to send up to Kendall in Heaven. We took a lot of photos of Kendall's friends around her grave and when we released the butterflies, a few of them stuck around and hung out with us too for a while. It was so beautiful and symbolic.

Then, in the evening when my family members came out, we had pizza and cupcakes, more of Kendall's favorites. We brought our lawn chairs and sat around her grave sharing memories and enjoying our time together. I also had butterflies and balloons for my family members. Kendall was one of the first buried in her area so there was a lot of open grass around her which was nice. It was very peaceful and we had a large space to gather. Some of the people who work at the cemetery drove by in a golf cart when we had our morning party. I was hoping I wouldn't get in trouble. Luckily, they were so happy we were doing this for Kendall and said this is what they like to see and wished more people did.

For the first anniversary of Kendall's death, Wes, Alexa, and I all took the day off work and school. It was also our niece's first birthday so we met up with her and her family at the zoo, one of Kendall's favorite places. On the way to the zoo, we stopped at Krispy Kreme per my husband's request. We would often take the girls out for donuts after church and Kendall loved the day we went to Krispy Kreme because she could look through the window and see them making the donuts.

At the zoo, we made sure to feed the giraffes in Kendall's memory since she loved to tell the story about how the giraffe licked her when she fed him. We also had pizza for dinner that day and visited her at the cemetery. It was a beautiful fall day and it put a smile on our faces to feel the sun and do some of Kendall's favorite things. It was also nice to hold and snuggle my niece, our bundle of joy in our sorrow.

Alexa's counselor had suggested to us that we should pick a yearly tradition as a way to honor Kendall on her Heaven day. We knew the zoo would be one way, and then she suggested the best idea for us. She explained how Alexa talked a lot about the early Christmas we had in their sessions. She felt that Alexa associated that with Kendall's death. She thought we could put up Kendall's tree and have an early Christmas, which would give

Alexa something to look forward to. Something that would make a hard day more bearable and would be a way for her to remember her sister.

So, we had arranged for us to have an early Christmas that day too. Family and friends helped us to find ornaments for Kendall's tree that were her favorite things like princesses, pizza, giraffes, and poop emojis (of course!) We placed the tree in her bedroom and decorated it together with the special ornaments. We had purchased a couple of small gifts for each other to open and I played Jingle Bells while we exchanged them, one of Kendall's favorite Christmas songs. It was a full day fitting in many of the things Kendall loved and a day of celebrating her life.

Since then, we do not do as much as we had done on that first anniversary. I found that I was a little stressed and worn down trying to fit everything in. I didn't want her special days to be like that. So, in the years that have followed, we typically spend her Heaven day with just the three of us. We always give back to the hospital or help a family who has a child with cancer on that day. We have kept the tradition of going to the zoo on her Heaven day, as well as having a small early Christmas. We try to take it easy on these days and leave time to reflect and remember instead of trying to cram so much into one day.

For her birthday we have changed it up each year. In 2020, when we were isolated during the Covid pandemic and supposed to stay six ft apart, we asked everyone on Kendall's Facebook page to have a dance party for her. We listed what her favorite songs were and asked them to post a video on her page of their family or children dancing in Kendall's memory. The videos warmed our hearts and made us smile on a difficult day.

Our neighborhood went an extra step and asked our neighbors to gather outside in front of our home for a socially distant dance party. One neighbor brought the boom box with all of Kendall's songs downloaded and ready to go. There were cupcakes, snacks, and kids in their Kendall shirts dancing in the street while remembering her (don't worry we live in a quiet circle with minimal traffic). It brought us so much joy to see everyone having fun on her birthday and we felt so loved by our neighborhood.

***

There are other things we do to honor Kendall like lighting a candle at her place setting at the table on holidays, including her in our Christmas cards, and asking Jesus to tell her we said hi and to give her a hug from us during prayer time. We also have sent out many thank you cards for the support over the years with Kendall's photo on them so we walk into many homes today to find our little girl's face on people's refrigerators. Even some of the hospital staff keep photos of her at their desk or keepsakes that Kendall made for them, like bracelets and drawings. Knowing she is remembered, missed, and talked about in people's homes is the best gift.

One of the most recent ways we honored Kendall was by attending CureFest for Childhood Cancer in Washington D.C. It is a multiple-day event that raises awareness for childhood cancer. The festival took place the first night in Freedom Plaza, which wasn't too far away from the White House. The CureFest team created an Angel Wall and Survivor Wall where the children could be honored. Kendall's photo was up on the Angel Wall where many people could walk by and see her beautiful face. That evening there was a candlelight vigil for all the children lost, and we sang "Amazing Grace." We also were able to go on stage and say our child's name and then the crowd repeated their name back. It was a beautiful sentiment to hear her name spoken.

On the next day of the event, it was held right by the Washington Monument. Laid out on the hill next to the monument were 1800 pairs of shoes to represent the number of children who pass each year to cancer in the U.S. We were able to send in a pair of Kendall's shoes to represent her. It was sobering to see her shoes displayed there among all the others. It really put into perspective how many children are affected by this disease and helped us to see that we were not alone in our loss.

They held a shoe memorial ceremony for the bereaved parents around the shoes and also had the bereaved parents lead the CureFest Walk on the path around the monument. Both days on the stage were childhood cancer survivors and fighters, siblings of cancer patients, doctors and researchers, and bereaved parents who spoke, sang, or danced. It was such an incredible event where we felt loved and seen. It was a beautiful way for us to take time out as a family to remember and reflect on Kendall's life together.

***

I hope this chapter has helped you to see not only how you can honor your loved ones, but that you can still have a relationship with them. It's just different. These are all ways that I still get to mother Kendall while she is in Heaven. She will always be part of our family. Honoring her and telling her story is my job now. When people look at me, I hope they see Kendall.

I would never choose for it to be this way, but I am embracing the mother that God has called me to be. This is the story he has given me and with his help, I have learned how to walk in it.

Chapter 24

Signs and Dreams of Kendall

There is so much beauty around us. So much to take in. From the trees and flowers, gorgeous sunsets, mountains, oceans and birds, there is much to admire and be thankful for. Once I had a daughter in Heaven, I became more mindful of the world around me, wondering where exactly in that beauty she was now. I felt more connected to the spiritual world than I ever had, mostly because I was now in tune to it. I had an open mind and was keeping my eyes peeled for any signs from Kendall. I was desperate for them. Desperate to know she was okay.

I would spend time outside in nature searching the skies for a connection to the other side. I would quiet my mind and be still, trying to connect. I would ask Kendall to please send me a sign. I was skeptical at first when I would see things happen, but there were some signs when I couldn't deny that Kendall was around communicating with us. There was no way they were just coincidences.

There are common signs our loved ones in the spiritual realm use to get our attention that I am sure you are familiar with. Things such as cardinals, butterflies, coins, rainbows, numbers, flickering lights, license plates, songs, and feathers to name a few. Our loved ones use these things to put in our path to reassure us that they are okay. Not every penny or feather you find is a sign though. There are feathers on the ground from birds all the time. To distinguish between a true sign or just a coincidence, it's important to pay attention to the timing and if you continue to see the same item. Also, if the item has a significant meaning between you and your loved one it could very well be them trying to connect to you.

I hope you will enjoy reading about these signs we have received. I have documented every one of them in a journal. I won't be sharing all of them, as some are very special and just for our family. But these meaningful signs that I share here show that there is a way to connect with our loved ones in Heaven. I'm not sure how it all works but I am fascinated by it.

***

The first sign that I ever received was at the cemetery. It had been just a couple of days after Kendall's burial and my sister and I had gone out to check on her grave. We were sitting on chairs surrounding her grave when I asked my sister if she thought God would allow Kendall to see us sitting there. Within the next minute, I saw something forming over the sun. "Oh my goodness!" I exclaimed with much excitement. I asked my sister if she could see it too and she could! It was becoming brighter and brighter, with more and more color. Before our very eyes was something we both had never seen before. It was a rainbow arch over the sun. It wasn't completely around the sun; it was just an arch above. My sister got her camera out to take a photo for me and we were in awe over this beautiful sight. It was one of those moments where I got goosebumps and could feel the connection in my soul.

This was the sign I had been waiting for since her death. I just knew it, and my sister did too. I was so glad that she was there to experience it with me, and that I had someone else witness this incredible sign. It faded away just as quickly as it had appeared. The timing of it forming seemed to us that it was clearly God and Kendall letting me know she was okay. God had answered my prayer in his timing and sent my rainbow. My sister-in-law enlarged and printed the photo for us, and it sits on Kendall's table in her special area of our home. It is our reminder that Kendall is safe in Heaven.

***

There have been many occurrences where we have felt Kendall's presence through songs. The first time was for Alexa's birthday, which was just a few weeks after Kendall's passing. A Special Wish Northeast Ohio had set up a special day for Alexa and her cousin at the American Girl doll store which was two hours away from our home.

We made it a weekend trip with our family and brought Kendall's American Girl doll with us too. The manager of the store had gifted Alexa and her cousin (as well as Kendall's doll) a free lunch in their café along with a hairstyle, ear piercing, nail painting for the dolls, and a free outfit they could pick out. Alexa was in her glory and I knew Kendall would be too. I was so sad that she couldn't be with us. We were still so incredibly broken at this point but trying our best to make Alexa's birthday special for her.

Alexa and her cousin's doll were up first in the salon. It was as cute as it sounds and they got to pick out a hairstyle for their doll, as well as nail color and earrings from the catalog. Once their dolls were done, Kendall's doll was placed in the chair next. Alexa picked out everything for Kendall and the lady began braiding the doll's hair. Then, the "Let it Go" song from *Frozen* came on over the radio. We all got chills, and tears formed in my eyes. Alexa even noticed the song and turned her eyes toward me. It stopped us in our tracks. It was one of

Kendall's most favorite songs and I just knew she sent it to us to let us know she was with us.

The next song that came on while her doll was still in the chair confirmed even further that she was there. It was the "Fight Song" by Rachel Platten. A song we listened to often throughout her journey. I think Kendall was happy we took her doll for her, and she was letting us know. I was so glad we were receiving signs from her so early in our grief.

Songs have continued to be a common sign we receive. One night Wes and I were having dinner at our kitchen table while music played in the background. We were both missing her extra that day and we were talking about her over dinner and tearing up a little. We made a toast to her and then the next song that came on a random channel on our Amazon Echo (had to rename ours since our daughter's name is Alexa) was "Somewhere Over the Rainbow," the same version we had in her slideshow for her service. We just knew that she was once again telling us she was around and she was okay.

Another day while I was home alone, I had the Christian station playing on my Amazon Echo. I was cleaning my home while listening and all of a sudden, I heard the song "The Wheels on the Bus" playing. A song I sang often to Kendall when she was younger. I found it so odd that that song would interrupt the praise songs that were previously playing. I realized that I had been thinking about Kendall while I was cleaning so it must have been her again! These signs were like little hugs from her, comforting me in my pain.

The last music sign I'll share is the day I went in for a brain MRI. I was having dizziness and headaches so my doctor wanted to have my head scanned. I was put into a tight tube with a fitting over my head. It felt claustrophobic and gave me a bit of anxiety. I had worn my Kendall bracelet and told myself to be strong like her as I always do now with any difficult medical procedures. I had been stuck twice while they were trying to insert my IV and all I could think of was Kendall and all the pain she had to endure. I had always wanted to take the pain for her so I didn't care how bad they hurt me. I would be brave like Kendall.

The tech asked me if I wanted a local radio station on while they did the scans. I said sure and asked her to tune it to 104.1, an FM station I listen to often. She asked if it was loud enough for me and I said I still couldn't hear it. She turned it up some more and it was all static. The lady said, "Well that's weird that it isn't coming through." She said she was going to change the station to 102.1.

Wouldn't you know it, the song that came through loud and clear was "Party in the USA," by Miley Cyrus, a song that Kendall enjoyed bobbing her head to. I felt her presence so much in that room at that moment. It was like she was holding my hand through the scan. Tears were falling from my eyes, which I couldn't catch because I had to stay still. Again, it is all in the timing. Our loved ones are always trying to find ways to connect to us if we are open to it. What were the chances that 104.1 was all static, and then one of her favorite songs came on when the station was changed? I could feel her energy in that room. This could not have been a coincidence. It just couldn't. My MRI came back with good results in case you were wondering.

***

Another sign we have also received is cardinals and butterflies. Wes and I had never seen cardinals before in our yard, or maybe we just weren't open to seeing them. The common saying is that "When a cardinal appears, a loved one is near." We were so desperate for a connection to Kendall on the other side that when we started seeing them, we believed that it was a sign.

As time has gone on, I do have a little trouble believing that every cardinal I see is a sign as I see them so often now, and the timing doesn't seem right. But in those early days of grief when a cardinal would hang out with us in our yard or hang out above

Kendall's swing on the swing set, it would make us smile and think she was around. And when we had a cardinal hang out with us by the pool on vacation in Florida, that seemed like a sure sign she was showing us her spirit was with us on our trip.

There have also been numerous times when a beautiful butterfly would flutter by at just the right moment, or even come and hang out with us for a while. One time on a family trip to Michigan, Alexa was playing at the beach. This beautiful butterfly came and hung out with her by the water. It didn't fly away. It just sat on the sand next to her, would flutter around her occasionally but land right back next to her. This butterfly stayed with her for at least 30 minutes! We really felt that too was Kendall saying she was on vacation with us. It was a beautiful moment and Alexa was so tickled by it!

Another sign I receive that I believe is not only from Kendall, but God as well are crosses in the sky. The first time I saw them was within a few months after Kendall passed. It was a day that I was really sad and driving in my car talking to God. I pulled off at my exit and what appeared before me in the sky were multiple crosses in the clouds. It was like God was saying, "I'm here. I'm listening."

I have seen crosses many times since while I was out on a walk with God or talking to him about Kendall. I have even seen them at the cemetery. Every time I get one it puts a smile on my face and gives me more hope. Sometimes it appears that they are cloud lines that form a cross, but other times they are airplane smoke trails.

One time, I was having a down day and decided to head out for a walk. I was talking to God on my walk and since I had received crosses before, I asked him if he and Kendall could please send me a cross because I really needed one. I was praying to God while walking through a wooded trail and when I came out of the woods, right before my very eyes in the sky was a big cross. My mouth dropped open and I was in awe that I received my cross. I smiled and looked up at the sky and said, "Thank you, God and Kendall. I know that was you!"

It is not only my family that receives signs, but other friends and extended family have too. One of my sisters has found beautiful white feathers in the most random places. A good friend of mine was out on a run one day thinking of Kendall during her birthday week. She looked up and saw a message written in the sky. It said, "Love U" and it looked like it was all clouds that formed the letters. I am guessing an airplane wrote it, but it certainly seemed like a sign that my friend was to give to me during a difficult week.

One of my favorite signs that we also received on a vacation was sent to us while we were driving to our destination. We always have Kendall on our minds but we were talking about her a lot and we were sad that she couldn't be with us on our trip. As we were driving along, a billboard popped out at us. In giant letters that took up most of the billboard, the name "Kendall" was spelled out. It just so happened to be an ad for a septic service company. We had to chuckle since Kendall had her love for potty humor. We felt it had to be more than just a coincidence seeing our daughter's name in big, bright letters across a billboard along the highway we were traveling.

***

Dreams are another way our loved ones can connect with us. Again, I don't understand how it all works, but there have been some dreams I have had where it felt like I spent time with Kendall again, and that she was sending me a message. One example is when I saw her in my dreams a couple of months after she passed. I was surprised to dream of her so soon, as I know many bereaved parents long to see their child in their dreams and are still waiting.

In this dream, I saw her wearing her Sheriff Callie costume (what she wore for Halloween the year before she got sick) and she was illuminated. There was a bright light surrounding her and she was beaming. She looked so happy and had a huge smile on her face. She had her beautiful, blonde locks back and some of her hair was pulled into a tiny ponytail on the top of her head, which was how I would often do her hair. She didn't say anything, she just radiated love and happiness. She was restored and full of joy. I still have that image of her in my dreams engrained in my head. I never want to forget it.

I have been blessed to dream of Kendall multiple times, though not every time makes me wake up with peace and joy. There have been some dreams I would describe as disturbing and left me wondering what they meant. There were a couple of dreams where Kendall was back in the fight. She had gone home on hospice but then she was able to get treatments again and continue on. In one dream, her doctors were telling me they had missed something on her scans and they knew how they could cure her now. I guess maybe I dreamt of these scenarios because I wished we could have had her here with us a little longer.

Most of the dreams I have had though are reflective of the memories I have with her, such as the time I saw her and Alexa with me at the mall shopping, or when I saw the girls running and laughing together. I've held Kendall in my dreams and then when I woke up, it felt like I really did hold her. I document every dream as well which is how I was able to jog my memory to write this chapter. If I wake up from a dream of her in the middle of the night, I will get out of bed and write it down so I don't forget it by morning.

My favorite dream was the one I received on Mother's Day in 2021. She was a toddler in the dream with her blonde, wispy hair in her face. She was making a puffing sound with her mouth while carrying a broom up our stairs. I said to her, "Kendall what are you doing?" and then she started laughing. It was a short dream, but it was one that affected me deeply. I woke up and felt like I had really spent time with her. It even made me cry because it felt like I had her back but awoke to the reality that she was still gone. Nonetheless, I was so grateful for her gift of visiting me in my dreams on Mother's Day. It was a wonderful gift from her from the other side.

It isn't just me that dreams of Kendall, just like it isn't just me that receives signs. Many friends and family have seen Kendall in their dreams and have shared them with me. There have been some amazing, beautiful dreams people have had. I am so grateful for all the ways that Kendall continues to communicate with us. The signs and dreams help me to keep going. They are my hugs from Heaven. I am so glad that I have been able to open my eyes and my heart to accept these gifts from God and Kendall. She will always be with me.

Chapter 25

The Difficulties of Being a Bereaved Mother

I knew that life as a bereaved mother would not be an easy road. Unfortunately, I have no choice but to face each day without my daughter and navigate what may come at me the best that I can.

In addition to living with a broken heart each day, there are multiple scenarios that have come up where I found myself rehearsing in my head what to do in advance. One of the very first questions I had was, "What do I tell people when they ask me how many children I have?" This was a question that brought me much worry and fear over how people would respond if they knew the truth. I found myself asking many bereaved mothers and fathers what they say when they are asked this question. It seemed that no one had a simple answer and it was dependent on the situation and environment you were in at the time asked. It was complicated and I have experienced the struggle myself over the years.

I remember the first time being asked how many kids I have a few months after Kendall had passed. I had thought about what I would say when faced with this question so I responded by saying that I had one daughter at home with me and one daughter in Heaven. My answer came as a shock to this person and they struggled to find the words. Then I found myself trying to comfort them and help them not to feel bad for asking such a simple question.

Well, still to this day that question is so difficult to answer. I find that every scenario is different, and my husband does too, which makes us have to rehearse how we will respond beforehand if we can. One time I was getting a pedicure and strangers were all around me. Suddenly I was supposed to talk about my life with the nail technician when he asked that very hard question. I knew that wasn't the place to share that I had a daughter in Heaven. I just said I had two daughters and went along with all the questions that followed, acting as if Kendall was still here with us. The questions usually are, "How old are they?" "Are they in any sports?" "What school do they go to?" "What grade are they in?" So, you can see how complicated it gets if we don't share that our daughter is in Heaven.

A perfect example of this is like the time Wes and I went on a vacation alone. We decided that if we met any other couples at our resort, we would just say we have two daughters and share their ages like Kendall was still here. We didn't want to make anyone sad on their trip or feel bad for asking, and we wanted to just feel normal and not talk about cancer on our relaxing vacation.

We did end up meeting a couple and went through with our plan. We ended up seeing this couple multiple times throughout the week and so many questions about our girls kept being asked. Talking about Kendall like she was still here ended up not feeling so good either. Then on the last day of our trip, the wife of the couple we met gave us some face masks that were handmade (during Covid times) and she said that there were some that maybe my girls would like. I didn't look through them then, but later back in our hotel room I pulled them out of my coat and sure enough, there was a mask she made with *Frozen* fabric. It just so happened to be the same pattern that Kendall had a headwrap in. I called out to Wes and said "Oh my gosh look at this! This has to be a sign," and he agreed. It was like Kendall was saying, "It's okay Mommy I understand why you pretended I was alive. I'm here with you."

You may have never thought about how asking someone about their family can be tough for some people to answer, or just how frequently that question is asked in everyday life. I am faced with it often. I still dread going to the doctor's and making small talk with the nurses and other staff. I dread going to parties and meeting someone new and then having to drop our sad story in the middle of the fun. Again, every scenario is different but if there are people around that know our story, it is kind of impossible to not come out and say what happened when we are asked if Alexa is our only child.

Wes and I both have tried saying we only had Alexa and that does not feel good at all, nor is it true. That made us feel guilty and we both agree that we would rather deal with the awkwardness than not mention Kendall. This has been very difficult to navigate and hinders me from being my friendly self when I am in a situation where there are new people to meet. I am generally an outgoing person so to see myself hide and avoid new people has been a change for me. Some days I am confident and want to share her story, but some days I just can't handle all that comes with sharing it with someone.

It is not just Wes and me who have to navigate this difficult question, but Alexa will as well for the remainder of her life. A few months after Kendall's death, I overheard a teacher in Alexa's classroom at church ask her if she had any siblings. I myself had been so worried and consumed with the question about my family that I hadn't even thought about Alexa having to navigate that question too. Alexa responded with the truth and came straight out and said that her sister died. It turned out that her teacher's sister had died too so she could relate to her and it was a sweet bonding moment for them. I stood in awe of how easily Alexa answered that question with the truth. I wonder often how many times she is asked if she has a sibling and how she will respond. She was more open about it when she was younger but now that she is older, she is careful about who she shares with.

Remember those "All About Me" sheets elementary kids are often asked to complete at the beginning of the school year? Well, those can be challenging for a child in Alexa's shoes. She too must make the decision on how much she wants to share with her classmates.

Then this past year she had to take it a step further and present a slideshow about herself to the class. There was a template to follow which included a slide about your family. She was torn on what to do and really thought hard about it. She decided to include her sister but she said that she would move on to the next slide quickly. There was a chance for students to ask questions at the end of her presentation which is why she was hesitant to share she had a sister. I can't blame her as that would be incredibly awkward to share her sad reality while standing in front of all her classmates. There hasn't been a year yet though where she hasn't included Kendall as one of our family members. Her counselor had once said that was a good sign that she was processing her grief.

***

There have been other difficult scenarios in my grief journey that I was not prepared for. Like the time I went to return a bottle of CBD oil after Kendall had passed. Because it was a high-ticket item, the clerk had to call the manager over. He threw me for a loop with his question, "Can I ask why you are returning this?" There was no rehearsing for that moment so the words that came out of my mouth in response were, "Well, it didn't heal my daughter of her cancer and she died so I won't be needing it now." Oh, that poor manager. I am sure he never expected me to say that in a million years. It was awful for us both as I shared that personal information while strangers were in line behind me. I just wanted to melt into the floor.

Another time that left me struggling to muster up the words was when I was at the dentist with Alexa for a routine cleaning. She was about finished when the receptionist came over to ask if I wanted to keep the girls on the same cleaning schedule and make an appointment for Kendall at the same time as Alexa. There was another patient and their parent nearby to hear our whole conversation and my anxiety rose within me. My heart began to race and my body temperature elevated. "Actually, Kendall passed away so you can remove her from your records," I responded. Awful. Just awful. That poor receptionist never saw that coming.

Then there were all the things that we had to do after her death such as removing her from our health insurance plan, picking out her headstone, and receiving her death certificate in the mail, which made it so final, so real, so painfully sad.

After the funeral was over, we returned home to her clothes hanging in the closet, her shoes by the door, and toys on the shelves. I couldn't bear to do anything with her items for a long time. But eventually, I started to sort through them. I purchased a large storage bin with pretty fabric covering it. I bought gold letters to affix across the top of it and spelled out her name. I then put all the items that were extra special and that I never wanted to lose in the bin. Things such as her locks of hair, the blanket we wrapped her in when she died, her artwork, her favorite hats and costumes, her favorite dolls, hospital bracelets, news articles that featured her, and the voice recorder with our sweet conversations.

I sort through her things every so often and have given some items to her cousins and friends to take care of for her, such as her stuffed animals, Barbies, and costumes. There are still some things that I just can't part with that have many memories attached to them, like her Little Tikes food truck that was gifted to her from the hospital during her transplant. I also have kept every piece of clothing that I have a memory of her wearing or that was for a special occasion. Seeing all of her things left behind continues to keep it in perspective for me how much our things really don't matter. We buy so many things and waste money but we don't get to take them with us when we die. One of Kendall's little friends once asked me why Kendall didn't take her things with her to Heaven. It was the sweetest, most innocent question coming from a four-year-old.

Kendall's room is the same as it was when she was here but has some memorial items added to it. I don't know how we could ever change her room. I feel like it would be like she never existed if we did. Having her room and all her things contained in there is proof that she lived. That she was here in our home and took up that space. I enjoy going into her room to talk to her, look through her things, and remember her. It is a beautiful memorial for a beautiful girl.

***

It is also hard as a bereaved parent to think about all the firsts your child will never get to have. Kendall never had her first day of Pre-K or kindergarten. She will never have her first choir concert, first school dance, first school trip, or first sleepover with a friend. She never learned how to swim or ride a bike. She will never get to graduate from high school, visit colleges, or get married. These are things cancer stole from her that we will always grieve over.

I often look out my front door to see Alexa playing with all the neighbor kids on our street and think of how much Kendall would have loved growing up with them. I wonder which child she may have been closest to. I think of what sport she would have liked playing, or what she might be into now. Would she look like Alexa still? Would she be tall like Alexa? Would her hair be brown or blonde? Would she be shy or outgoing? So many questions fill my mind.

***

It has been hard worrying about what people think of me. As I said in an earlier chapter, I felt like I would be judged if I was smiling and happy, as if that meant that I wasn't grieving. But I came to learn through other bereaved parents that you can be both happy and sad at the same time. The sorrow I have over losing Kendall is forever a part of me now. It doesn't go away. But that doesn't mean that I can't be happy and still experience joy in life too.

I have now come to a point where I don't care as much about what people think of me and have gained more confidence in my bereaved mother role. What others think of me is their thoughts and perception of me. That doesn't mean that it is true. There is no way anyone can possibly understand what this is like unless they are in my shoes. I try my best though to explain it to those who aren't in my shoes so they understand that just because I am enjoying life does not mean that I miss Kendall any less. I ache for her every day and memories of her fill my mind.

The stark reality is that life goes on after loss and there are responsibilities you must tend to. You still have to work, pay the bills, and make dinner for your family. I still have a child here on Earth to take care of. I have to do what I need to so I can survive each day here without Kendall. So that means putting fun things on my calendar to look forward to and doing things that bring me joy. I have always said that smiling is the best medicine. Smiling makes me feel good. I lost my smile at times and it was depressing. I know that smiling and enjoying all that God has put on this Earth for us helps me to heal. I don't have to feel guilty for smiling and having fun. I am free to be me.

***

Photo Credit: AzkaLynn Photography, LLC

The last hard thing I will share is how we handle holidays, her birthday, and her Heaven day. I have found that the days leading up to these significant days are always harder than the actual day. I guess because I begin bracing myself and reflecting days in advance. Sometimes the sadness hits me after the significant day has passed. It is dependent on what all we have going on in the days leading up to and surrounding these difficult days.

Days like Christmas are filled with so much joy in being with family and remembering Jesus' birth that it is a distraction from the sadness of Kendall not being there. And on her birthday and Heaven day, we are so busy doing all of the traditions we have put in place to remember her that again, we are distracted. But after the busy rush, when it is quiet and I am by myself, that is when the grief hits me hard. It's when I wake up in the middle of the night and she is the first thing that comes to my mind. Or when I'm packing up her Christmas tree and I am in her room surrounded by all the memories. That is when the tears come and the ache in my heart grows stronger.

I am learning as I go in this bereaved mom life. What helps at times doesn't help at others. The sad reality is that every day I wake up I lose her all over again, so the grief will never go away. While this is a hard road, I am finding my way through one step at a time. I have learned that I can do hard things.

Chapter 26

Continuing on in Life

At the time of writing this book, I am almost five years into my grief journey. They say that "time heals all wounds" and while I don't fully agree with that, I can say that every year since Kendall has passed, I have healed a little more, and wait with great expectation for my full healing in Heaven.

The thing about death is that while you grieve the loss of someone, the world continues to go on around you. Eventually, you must rejoin society and learn how to live in this world with a broken heart. Many have said to me that I am so strong, that they don't know how I do it, or that they couldn't be like me if they were in this situation. But think about it - what other choice would you have? I know it's unimaginable and you never think you could live through something like this. I never thought I could live through the loss of my daughter, but I am doing it with God's help, just like so many other parents out there are too. I'm not sure I would be where I am today without my faith and the hope that Jesus provides.

I continue on because I know what a gift each day is and my assignment on Earth is not done. You only get one life to live and I know now more than ever just how precious life is and how quickly my time here could be up. So, I choose to make the most of what time I have left here. There are still so many blessings and beauty to be found, even in grief. There is still so much goodness in my life and plenty to be thankful for. Perspective is everything.

I also still have a family here on Earth to love and care for and that gives me great purpose. I enjoy caring for them and spending time with them. If I focused on all that I have lost, I would miss out on the beautiful life that is right in front of me. Alexa has seen and been through more than any child her age should go through. It's my job as her mother to make sure she has what she needs to handle her grief and infuse joy into her life. Her counseling and art therapy over the years has been very beneficial for her and having so many kids on our street to play with has helped fill the void of missing her sister.

The siblings are often the forgotten ones, but grief affects them too. Alexa has had many ups and downs in her grief through the years and she experienced some PTSD, along with anxiety. She feared hospitals and doctors' offices (and had good reason to). I could barely get her to her appointments as she cried and tried to run the other way. She covered her ears and ran for cover at the sound of any siren or beeping noise. We had a hard time leaving our home at times as she battled these fears. Thankfully, with some intense counseling, she was able to overcome her fear and anxiety and she is truly in a good place today.

As for Wes, he stays busy with work and the occasional sport, such as softball. He takes a lot of walks to think and clear his mind. Playing his guitar has also been therapeutic for him, as well as family time and outings. We love to travel together and make each other laugh. I am so blessed to walk in this grief journey with him by my side. We have been through the unimaginable yet have come out the other side with our marriage intact and stronger than ever.

Staying busy has been key for me in my grief. Aside from coffee and lunch dates with friends and family, my calendar stays full taking Alexa to her activities, serving at and attending church activities, as well as indulging in various other hobbies of mine such as decorating, reading, writing, exercising, and gardening. These things have brought happiness back into my life.

**

Over the last few years, I have been spending a lot of time redecorating our home. I had the urge to update some things in our home while Kendall was in treatment, but time and her care simply would not allow it. After her passing, I couldn't stand the dark wall colors and décor any longer. It felt so sad and gloomy in our home with all the browns, reds, and oranges. Whites and grays were the latest trends, so I jumped on board and started painting over the dark colors one room at a time. It felt good to have a project and something else to focus on other than my grief and sadness.

I started on the darkest rooms first and what a difference it made changing burnt orange wall paint to a light, calming gray. I also chose other serene colors like a light sage and a light blue to add some pops of color. After a couple of years of painting projects, my first floor was so much brighter, calmer, and happier with fresh coats of paint. I felt like I could breathe so much better in our home and my mood was lifted. It's amazing what a can of paint can do!

Decorating made me happy, and I found great joy in it. I took many trips to Hobby Lobby and other home décor stores to change out pretty much every piece of wall décor I had previously hung. I even started painting my darker furniture to whites and grays to give it that updated farmhouse look that was in style, thanks to Chip and Joanna Gaines. My decorating projects have given me something to work on through the years while I was trying to find myself again.

* * *

Speaking at events and getting to share Kendall's story has also helped me to be able to heal and continue on in life. It is a vulnerable position that I put myself in, but if I don't share her story then I wouldn't be able to help others find hope and peace in their own story. Sharing is healing.

I continue to speak because I see the fruit that grows not only in me but in others who are touched by Kendall's story and by the message God has given me to share. The positive feedback and notes I have received after a speaking engagement give me encouragement to continue to share. I love any chance to get to talk about Kendall and to give other grievers hope that they too can survive a tragic loss. Getting the privilege to see how Kendall's story still impacts the lives of others to this day makes me so proud to be her mother.

Speaking didn't come easy for me at first and I was very nervous, but we all must start somewhere. The more I speak, the less nervous I get, though I do usually feel butterflies the day of the event. Leading up to it though I feel more excited than nervous and I do feel that I improve a little more each time. There are so many powerful and engaging speakers I look up to and I watch and listen to them so intently to try to mimic them in my own speaking.

At the time of writing this book, I have spoken at seven different events sharing Kendall's story and what God has done in my life through it. I most recently had the honor of speaking to a room full of parents who had lost their child at the Cleveland Clinic Children's Remembrance Ceremony. It was a wonderful experience for me to get to share how I have survived my loss with other bereaved parents and talk with many of them one on one after my speech.

After speaking at a few church and childhood cancer events, and serving on the Blue Christmas team, I began to find my new purpose. A calling, perhaps. I felt strongly pulled toward helping people in their grief. I had thought to work in ministry that I needed to be on church staff, but then I realized that I could work in ministry right from my home through my writing, or out in my community by speaking and continuing to serve those grieving in our church. So, after two and a half years of working in my church office, I decided to step down to pursue what I felt God calling me toward.

After leaving my church position, I was able to focus more on writing this book, which has become my ministry and has been so healing and therapeutic for me. I also started volunteering with a childhood cancer organization and I continue to serve on the Blue Christmas team at my church. I hope to volunteer in the future at a local grief center and can't wait to see where else God leads me.

I have found in my grief that I just want to help people. Life can be so very difficult at times and being able to help someone through their storms and find joy again helps me to heal and feel better too. I think this is what I was made for all along. I love when someone comes to me and wants to know more about my faith, needs resources on grief, or needs advice on how to move toward healing. I never want anyone to feel alone in their grief, so I am more than happy to help them find their way, just like so many did for me. Life was never meant to walk in it alone.

One thing is for sure - Kendall's life has opened up a world of possibility for me which I never would have found without her. I never knew what to do with my life, but now there are so many things I want to achieve and new goals I have for myself. I am thankful that I can move forward in life with a great sense of purpose.

Before I end this chapter, I want to leave you with this. The reality is that we will all die someday. It's 100% fact. It could be today, tomorrow, or years from now. We just don't know when our time will be up. What if you lived every day as if it were your last day here? Would that change your perspective on life? Would the dirty dishes in the sink or the never-ending to-do list really matter if today is your last day here? What might you need to change in your life if today is your last day to live?

Every day you live you get another opportunity to make a difference in this world. You have the choice of how you will spend your remaining days on Earth. Remember, you only get one chance.

Chapter 27
Kendall's Legacy

Have you ever wondered what people will remember about you after you are gone or what they might say about you at your funeral? Have you ever thought about what mark you have left on the world, or if you made it a better place while you were here? Have you maintained integrity? Have you loved people well? Have you touched many hearts in a positive way during your time here that will leave a lasting legacy of yourself behind?

Though Kendall was only four years old, her life has left an imprint on many. She taught people so much in her short four years. As everyone watched my little girl fight cancer, there were many life lessons we all were learning from her.

She taught us all how to fight big battles with bravery and courage. She taught us how to find light in the darkness, joy in the journey, and beauty in the pain. She showed us what it looks like to have fun and stay positive in the hardest of times. She taught us about perseverance and never giving up. She taught us how to keep things in perspective and that our problems weren't so big in the grand scheme of things.

She taught us to enjoy the little things. She taught us how to always find something to be thankful for. She showed us the love of Jesus and taught us to be bold in our faith, as her child-like faith touched us all. She taught me to not care what other people think and to just be myself.

One little girl has forever changed the lives of many.

I am so honored that God chose Wes and me to be Kendall's parents. He knew she would only be here for four years and he entrusted us to love and care for her during that time. We were hand-picked and chosen by God to give her life and walk her to the gates of Heaven. It was a great joy and privilege that God gave her to us to raise, treasure, and teach her the righteous way of living.

Even if God would have told me that this was the plan he had for her life, I would have signed up anyway. I would have never wanted him to choose someone else to be Kendall's mom. Without her, I wouldn't be who I am today. Even though it was four short years, I got four years with her! It was the best four years of my life. It was the years I had my whole family together under one roof. It was the most monumental, life-altering, impactful years of my life. As painful as it has been to lose her, I would surely take the four years I had with her over none at all. I am a better person and mother today for knowing and loving her. I have never been more beautifully broken.

***

Kendall's journey and death made me love people harder. I feel so much love for other people that it's hard to contain it (beware, I'm a hugger)! I know how much relationships matter since that is all that you have left in the end. Our relationships will carry over into Heaven so it is so important to love others well. My friends and I don't hold back when it comes to love. When we have something nice to say to each other we say it. We build up, encourage, and bless each other with words of affirmation. Before Kendall, this would feel cheesy to me and I would be afraid to show love to my friends. But now, knowing how short life is, we just want each other to know how much we mean to each other. And the same goes for my family. We know how quickly we could lose one of us so we love harder than ever. Tomorrow could look a whole lot different so do what you can for others right now and hug your loved ones tight!

I will always think of Kendall whenever I face hard things in life or tough medical procedures. Whenever I have to get my blood drawn or times when I need an IV, I wear my Kendall bracelet and think of her and all she went through. If she could endure so much, I can surely withstand a little needle prick. I'm no longer scared of giving blood. I now know the importance of donating to help others and save lives. Did you know you can save up to three lives with your one blood donation? Though it's a little uncomfortable, I will gladly take on any pain after seeing what Kendall has gone through. It is nothing in comparison.

I get notes often from others who feel the same way when they are facing difficult medical diagnoses. They share how they think of Kendall and remember her "Choose Joy" message. They will text me photos of them in the hospital with their Kendall shirts or bracelets on to let me know they are being "Kendall Strong."

Her little friends and cousins still have memories of her and wear their Kendall memorial shirts proudly. Kids that never even met her have called her their best friend or they come over to look through her room and learn about who she was. My favorite ever was when one little girl down the street asked me if Kendall had a phone in Heaven so she could call her. Oh, the sweet innocence of children. If only it were that easy and we could call and check on our loved ones in Heaven. I am so glad that Kendall still makes friends here even while she resides in Heaven.

You know your daughter left an impact on people when they get a tattoo that says Choose Joy (multiple people have) so they can remember to look for joy in every day, even the hard days.

Or you walk into someone's home and there is a picture of her on their refrigerator so they can remember her story and live a better life because of her. Or they grow their hair out and cut and donate it to make a wig for someone with cancer. Or they start volunteering for a childhood cancer organization to make a difference in the lives of children with cancer. It truly has been amazing to see how Kendall has inspired so many people. I am one proud mother.

***

We had given back in many ways since Kendall's passing, but we came to a point where we felt we needed something more permanent. Something we could focus on. Because she spent so much time at the hospital, Wes and I knew we wanted her memory to live on there. We wanted to continue giving back to the hospital for taking such good care of Kendall and providing entertainment and toys for us during our stays. We thought about it for a while and tried to figure out what was going to be best for Kendall's legacy and what could bring joy to the pediatric cancer patients.

We knew that we wanted it to be something with costumes. Kendall loved to dress up and be fancy. She often wore costumes to her appointments or while inpatient in her hospital bed as I mentioned before. She looked forward to showing off her costumes and fancy dresses to her nurses. She loved the attention. She was always dressed to the nines, complete with headbands and fancy shoes.

We worked with Kendall's favorite child life specialist to come up with a way that we could bring costumes to the hospital. She suggested a rolling cart that we could purchase and stock and that was all it took to get this idea off the ground running. Before long we had a name. We would call it "Kendall's Kloset." The cart would be stocked with items you might find in Kendall's closet. This included costumes, hats, slippers, pajamas, dresses, etc. We also included accessories and trinkets such as bracelets, necklaces, watches, headbands, purses, makeup, and nail polish. Kendall loved to put makeup on and do her nails when she was inpatient so that is the reason why we decided to include those items on the cart too.

The thought was that this cart would be mobile and able to reach the kids in both the inpatient and outpatient pediatric cancer wings. We created an Amazon wish list and reached out to our community with our idea and ways that they could help. The boxes began piling up at the door and Alexa and I had so much fun seeing what came every day and stocking the cart together.

My brother-in-law did all the graphics for us for her cart. He came up with a beautiful design for a sign to hang on the cart that said "Kendall's Kloset," as well as business cards and postcards with a photo of Kendall wearing her Cinderella costume, and a synopsis about the cart. We attached a business card to every costume and on the back, we shared our email address so that parents could share a photo of their child in a costume with us if they wished. We have loved receiving many photos over the years of children enjoying costumes from Kendall's Kloset. It puts a smile on our faces every time and brings us joy!

We were so happy to have found a way to spread Kendall's joy throughout the hospital. When I look at the cart, all I see is Kendall. It represents her so well. We are so grateful that the hospital and staff allow her cart to have a home there.

It was the second anniversary of her death when we delivered Kendall's Kloset to Cleveland Clinic Children's so that her memory could live on, and a part of her would still be with those she loved at the hospital. Kendall's Kloset remains our main focus today as a way of giving back.

It was also around this time that I wanted to write a song for Kendall. I thought about having someone help me write it, but one day while driving in my car, the words started to pour out of me. I had been in conversation with God about it, so I know he helped me to write this, just like he has helped me write so many other things. What was crazy is that I also had a melody. I was completely shocked that this was coming out of me. I quickly pulled off the road and reached for my phone to record the words so I didn't forget them by the time I got home. And that is how I came to write Kendall's song, "Someday."

It took some time to find someone that could help me write the chords to it, but once I did and had Wes try it out on his guitar, I was in love. It sounded beautiful and perfect, just as I had imagined. It was so special that Wes and I could work on the song together, him learning the chords and me perfecting the vocals.

The Chorus goes like this:
"You're forever in our hearts
We'll forever miss your face
We'll hold onto our hope
That we have in our true King
The One who rescued you
The One who set you free
We'll hold onto our hope
That we'll see you again someday
Someday"

I am not a songwriter by any means so it isn't the fanciest, but it's for Kendall and the verses show the deep aching in my soul for her and the love in my heart. We hope to record it someday to have another way to honor and remember her.

JOY IN THE BROKEN

Kendall has left a beautiful, lasting legacy. As I continue on in life, I will choose joy instead of bitterness or anger in honor of my daughter. I know that is what she would want and what is best for my soul. I will continue to hold firmly to the hope I have in Jesus and trust that she is living her best life in Heaven. I will keep my thoughts fixed on him so I can continue to be covered in his peace. If you wish to experience this Living Hope in your own life, read the following pages at the end of this book to see how you can begin your own faith journey with Jesus.

Kendall received the ultimate healing in Heaven and never has to feel an ounce of pain again. I can rejoice in that! Knowing how our story ends helps me to continue surviving and thriving on this grief journey. One day I will get my happy ending and be reunited with my daughter in Heaven. I think of that reunion often and what it will be like to see and hold her again. I cannot wait to experience the joy I will feel at that moment. You see without Christ, this would just be a very sad story I wrote about. But with Christ, there is so much beauty and redemption on the pages of this book. With Christ, it is so much more than a sad story. Death does not get the final say!

One of the greatest gifts Kendall's life has given me is the joy I have found in Jesus. The joy that can never be stolen from me and that sustains me through the unimaginable. It is the joy that has nothing to do with happiness, but everything to do with Jesus. It is the joy of his promises, his love and grace poured out for me, his kindness to me, and the hope of Heaven where I will live forever with my sweet Kendall. That is the reason for the smile on my face. Because I can still say that God is good after all I have lost, and at one point I wasn't sure I would be able to.

Because of Christ, he will one day wipe away all my tears and the pain will be gone forever (Revelation 21:4). Because of Christ, I have hope in the depths of my soul. Because of Christ, I have found peace. Because of Christ, I have the strength to go on. Because of Christ, there is victory over death!

Because of Christ…I have JOY in the broken.

Accepting the Gift of Christ

Because of all that I have experienced through Christ in my life, I can't end this book without giving you an opportunity to respond to God's call. The gift of salvation is available to anyone who wishes to receive it. It is a gift that you freely can walk into. You must come to your own decision about what you believe and who Jesus is to you.

I have no idea of the depths of your pain or the struggles and trials you are facing in your life today, but God knows. Psalm 46:1 says, "God is our refuge and strength, an ever-present help in trouble" (NIV). He is reaching his hand out to meet yours. You can choose whether or not to reach back. You don't have to walk alone in your pain and difficulties. You too can receive help and strength from the Lord.

You can receive his peace, hope, and unshakeable joy into your heart. He wants that for you! The Lord rescued me from a life of darkness and despair. He continues to help heal my heart and bind up my wounds. He has saved me. He can save you too!

"For God so loved the world that He gave His one and only son, that whoever believes in him shall not perish but have eternal life" (John 3:16, NIV).

GOD LOVES YOU SO MUCH! So much so that he sent his only Son to Earth to pay the penalty for your sins. "For all have sinned and fall short of the glory of God" (Romans 3:23, NIV). Our sins result in separation from God. But Jesus provided a way for us to reach God when he died on the cross. When you put your faith and trust in Jesus and receive him into your life your sins will be forgiven, you will have eternal life in Heaven, you will be filled with his Holy Spirit, and you will no longer be separated from God.

Jesus says, "I have come that they may have life, and have it to the full" (John 10:10, NIV).

Do you wish to experience the abundant life in Christ? Do you believe that God loves you so much that he sent his son Jesus to die on the cross for you and that he rose from the grave so you can live forever with him in Heaven? If you believe this and want to follow Christ for the rest of your days, pray this prayer below.

Dear Lord Jesus,
I believe that you are the Son of God. I believe that you died on the cross for my sins, rose from the grave, and reign in Heaven today. I receive your forgiveness from my sins and open my heart and life to you. I choose to trust you as my Savior and will follow you from this point forward.
I pray this in Jesus' name, Amen.

If you prayed this prayer to accept Christ, I am so happy for you! Your life will forever be changed from this point on. I would love to hear about your decision to follow Jesus so I can pray for you in your new faith journey. Find me on my Facebook page at, "Krista Stump, Author." Your next steps will be learning how to have a relationship with Jesus Christ and growing your faith.

Next Steps:
- Find a church home so that you have other believers to encourage you and guide you in your faith.
- Make a public declaration of your commitment to Jesus Christ through water baptism.
- Start reading the Bible daily and find a good devotional book. The Bible is God-breathed. It is alive and active. It is his Word or voice and our roadmap for life. Download the YouVersion Bible App so that you can have access to the Bible 24/7, along with access to many daily devotionals specific to your needs.
- Pray to God. Prayer is just a conversation daily like you would have with a friend. You can talk to him about anything. Prayer keeps you in touch with God and draws you closer. You can praise him for his creations and for what he has done in your life, confess your sins and ask for forgiveness, tell him what you are thankful for, ask him for what you need, and pray for others in your life who need prayer.
- Find an Alpha class at a nearby church to learn more about the Christian faith and who God is (alphausa.org).
- Strive to reflect Christ. You become like the people that you spend the most time with so the more time that you spend with Jesus, the more you will be like him. People will see Jesus in you! How cool is that!?
- Listen to sermon podcasts from various pastors/ministers across the country and in your area to grow your faith.
- Resist the temptation to sin and obey his Word. I promise your life won't be boring! It will be so abundantly full!

Without the hope and redemption that Christ offers, I don't know how I would go on in life. How can you survive without hope? You see, we do not have to live hopeless, meaningless lives. The gift of Christ is the way to a hope-filled life and a bright future ahead. Hope is powerful. Hope motivates you to continue on when life gets tough. Hope empowers you to truly LIVE!

We are all broken people, but we can live a better life and have joy in our brokenness because of Christ.

I will leave you with one of my favorite verses that I will be praying over you:

"May the God of hope fill you with all joy and peace as you trust in him, so that you may overflow with hope by the power of the Holy Spirit" (Romans 15:13, NIV).

God Bless,
Krista

How to Help a Family That Has Lost a Child

When someone is grieving, it is often hard for them to tell people about their wants and needs. Grievers are often in a fog, numb, and can't even tell you what day it is. So many people want to be a helping hand but don't know what to do. I appreciated it when people saw a need and just took it upon themselves to fulfill it. I loved for example when I would see my neighbor out mowing our lawn, or even the day Kendall died, my friends started cleaning out my pantry and making sure our fridge was stocked with meals. Hopefully, these suggestions I have will help you in the future to come alongside someone grieving in a helpful way. Some of these are also useful for any family walking through a challenging time.

How to Help a Family That Has Lost a Child

- *Bring flowers for their yard.* Flowers always made me happy and were a nice surprise when I pulled into the driveway.
- *Clean their home.* Grief leaves you exhausted and often in bed. My aunt came and gave my home a full cleaning

the week after Kendall passed and it was the best gift. Offer to vacuum, do dishes, or clean bathrooms.
- *Cover them in prayer.* I know I barely could find the strength to say more than "God please help me" in those early days of grief. I knew so many people were praying for my comfort, peace, and strength and over time I could feel the prayers working and holding me up.
- *Donate to their cause.* Many times, parents start foundations or memorial funds in their child's honor. I love the support we have received in all our hospital projects and how involved my family and friends are in the childhood cancer community today. We couldn't do what we do without them.
- *Don't compare grief.* Don't say you know how they feel or compare their loss to one of yours. No two losses are the same.
- *Give gift cards for food.* Sometimes we just craved some of our favorite restaurant food and would get takeout to avoid being in public.
- *Help them write thank you notes.* It was important to me to make sure we thanked all who sent flowers, made donations, and dropped off gifts at the funeral. Having a helping hand with writing those out would have been great.
- *Listen.* Don't try to fix their pain. Acknowledge it and sit with them in it, as uncomfortable as it may be. You don't always need to have the words. Your presence is enough.
- *Make meals for the family.* Meal trains are still useful after a child with cancer passes so the family is fed. It's helpful to not have to think about making dinner. Even if the parents don't feel like eating, chances are there will be guests in their home who will.
- *Make memorial gifts for them.* I loved all the gifts dropped off in the weeks and months after Kendall

passed. So many keepsakes were made that I will treasure forever. Some examples are bracelets/necklaces with their child's name or photo, wind chimes, garden stones, ornaments, drawings of their child, photo blankets and pillows, photo mugs, etc.

- *Mow their lawn.* Grieving parents likely don't want to see anybody in those first few weeks and often don't have the energy to do the usual chores.
- *Offer to babysit the parents other children.* Kids do not grieve as adults do and still need to be entertained. Taking them out to a mall or jump park for an afternoon so their parents can rest would be a welcome gift.
- *Offer to do their grocery shopping.* Again, leaving the home early on in grief is difficult. When someone asked if they could pick something up for me while they were out, there almost always was something I needed.
- *Offer to do their laundry.* I had a friend that would come pick up our laundry and take it to her home, wash it, fold it, and then deliver the clean clothes in a basket. It was the best!
- *Offer to run any other errands they may need.* Dry cleaning, pharmacy, take kids to activities, etc.
- *Remember important dates with them.* Such as diagnosis date, birthday, and day their loved one passed. These are perfect days for "thinking of you" texts or mailing a card. I have a couple of people who still write cards to us on Kendall's Heaven day. They are filled with beautiful words and I look forward to them every year. It means so much to me that they remember and take the time out of their day to write us a card.
- *Remember their pets.* Offer to walk their dog or care for any pets they have. Bring a new treat or toy for their dog as they could be sad too.

- *Stay involved.* Keep checking in occasionally. Offer to take them out for coffee or ice cream when they're ready. Don't leave them alone in their grief.
- *Wash and/or detail their cars.* This is the last thing you care about cleaning when you are a caregiver or grieving, but a clean car is needed and much appreciated.

In Memory of
Kendall Rae Stump

7/19/2014 – 10/13/2018

Acknowledgments

This book took over two years to complete. When I set out to write it, I had no idea it would take that long. It has been a journey in itself. There were many late nights, frustrating days, and tears cried through this process. There were so many times I wanted to give up, but I kept going because I knew it would be so worth it in the end. I want to thank some very important people below who helped to make this book a reality.

~ Thank you to Wes and Alexa for being patient with me and allowing me the time to work on completing this book.
~ Thank you to Pastor Dennis Barta for his Biblical wisdom and guidance.
~ Thank you to Betsy Bradshaw for her thorough copyediting.
~ Thank you to Brigid Danziger for guiding me through the self-publishing process.
~ Thank you to my brother-in-law Ed Thomas for creating the beautiful cover design.
~ Thank you to AzkaLynn Photography, LLC for taking such treasured photos of Kendall during the years she was with us and for allowing me to use your beautiful work for the book cover.

~ Thank you to my dear friend Stacie at Kimberly Lane Photography for taking my author photo.
~ Thank you to my friends and family who believed in me and encouraged me to write our story.

Made in the USA
Monee, IL
17 December 2023